PERSPECTIVES OF COMMUNICATION AND COMMUNICATIVE COMPETENCE

By the Same Author

Effective Business Communication, 1992

About the author

Dr. Marayan Rodriques is the Head of the Department of English and Communication in a post-graduate management and social work education and research institute—SIBER at Kolhapur. He has triple Master's degrees— one in Linguistics in English, the another in American Literature and the third in Industrial Sociology. His doctoral research is accomplished in the area of 'Communicative Competence in Management'. His teaching career of two decades and active research in 'Communication' has earned for him an immense popularity among the students and the academic world. He is known for his book *Effective Business Communication*, all over the country. He has presented a number of research papers in workshops/symposium/conferences. He teaches 'Managerial Communication' to the MBA Classes and 'Social Communication' to the MSW Classes.

PERSPECTIVES OF COMMUNICATION AND COMMUNICATIVE COMPETENCE

M.V. RODRIQUES

Chh. Shahu Central Institute of Business Education
on Research, Kolhapur

CONCEPT PUBLISHING COMPANY, NEW DELHI - 10059

ISBN-81-7022-778-X (HB)

First Published 2000

Published and Printed by

Ashok Kumar Mittal
Concept Publishing Company
A/15-16, Commercial Block, Mohan Garden
NEW DELHI-110 059

Phones : 5648039, 5649024
Fax : 091-11-5648053

PREFACE

If there is one thing that most professional courses like MBA, MSW, Journalism etc. have in common as an applied branch, it is Communication. The knowledge and practical communicative competence is an essential personal asset for the Managers, Social workers, Teachers, Politicians, Businessmen and for the people in all walks of life. It is a proven prerequisite of success for everybody in this increasingly hectic and competitive world. Keeping this in view, the present book has been written to provide essential knowledge of the fundamentals of communication. And secondly, as the professionals have to enhance their communicative competence, the various aspects of it are described in detail.

Regarding the organization, the book is arranged in a coherent manner in four parts and consists of sixteen chapters. The first part, Fundamentals of Communication, consists of seven chapters. Chapter One presents an overview of the significance of communication in various areas of human interactions. Chapter Two explains the meaning and process of communication and presents a comprehensive model of communication process. Chapter Three dwells on the formal and informal channels of communication in organizations. The Fourth Chapter describes the various aspects of the oral and written media of communication. The nature, significance and the types of non-verbal media are described in Chapter Five. Chapter Six presents twenty-two obstructions in human communication. These obstructions are classified in four broad categories. Chapter Seven is the last chapter in the First Part of the book which presents all the essentials of effective communication.

The second part of the book deals with the various aspects of communicative competence. The Eighth

Chapter describes the multiple dimensions of communicative competence. The Ninth Chapter deals with the evaluation techniques of communicative competence. Chapter Nine is about the evaluation of communicative competence in general English.

The third part consists of the two chapters which deal with the nature and evaluation of communicative syllabuses. Chapter Ten deals with the notion and types of communicative syllabuses. Chapter Eleven deliberates upon the syllabus evaluation. The fourth part of the book deals with the practical aspects of evaluation and testing of the communicative competence. Chapter Twelve describes the plan of preparing a comprehensive testing design. Chapter Thirteen deals with the syllabus analysis and specification of objectives. Chapter Fourteen elaborately explains the evaluation and development of the communicative competence test. Chapter Fifteen presents analysis of the communicative competence test results; and finally, the Sixteenth Chapter gives the summary of conclusions and pedagogical implications.

The book is primarily intended to serve as a text-book of 'Communication' for the students of the professional courses like MBA, MSW, Journalism, Language Teaching etc. However, as communication is becoming an applied branch of many other subjects like Linguistics, Library Science, Sociology of Communication, Anthropology, Marketing Communication, Organizational Communication etc. This book will be immensely useful for the students and teachers alike in their subjects.

I am indebted to my students and learned collegues in my Institute who provided necessary stimulus for writing this book.

I shall feel highly rewarded if the book proves helpful in the development of the communicative competence and enhancement of communication skills of the readers.

M.V. RODRIQUES

CONTENTS

PART - I

FUNDAMENTALS OF COMMUNICATION

1

SIGNIFICANCE OF COMMUNICATION IN HUMAN INTERACTIONS

"In the beginning was the Word,
and the Word was with the God,
and the Word was God."

—St. John 1:1

In any organization, the people come to know what their co-workers are doing by communication. The managers give orders, instructions, warnings and advices to the subordinates and receive information and suggestions from the departmental heads, supervisors, and workers. Communication is always instrumental in the management of an organization because the orders are issued, the advice is sought and given, the decisions are conveyed by the functional authorities to the concerned people, the instructions are given by the supervisors to the operators and a number of other activities such as planning, directing, coordinating, organizing controlling, etc., are carried out by means of communication. According to Wofford, *et al.* (1977), communication is a skill required at every level of organizational functioning for organizations of all types. The efficiency of a person in almost any organization, whether social, governmental or commercial, depends in large measure upon his ability to communicate effectively.

The lack of communication invariably results in the collapse of an organization. When people do not communicate their needs, thoughts and feelings to each other, the cooperation and mutual understanding becomes impossible. Thus, the hardening of the information arteries results in the impaired efficiency of the organization.

An effective communication is the key of sure success in the modern world of scientific and technological advances, global politics, social work, trade and commerce and the other areas of human interaction. The increasing specialization and the expansion and complexity of today's tradefare have also brought about a revolution in the systems of communication. A businessman or a politician who wants to survive in the competition has to develop his communication skills. He must know how to communicate with the help of the new and speedy technical devices of communication. The efficient management executives spend more than ninety percent of their time in communication. Their efficiency depends on their skills and effectiveness of communicating with others. 'To decide and to achieve are management purposes. Planning, organizing, activating and controlling are management functions. Communication implements those purposes and functions' (Wolf, *et al.* 1979: 7).

The fact that all people are different is supported by science too. When they form a group or an organization, they manage to do it by communication. The organizations are the social systems formed on the basis of mutual interest. The mutual interests are safeguarded by various activities of planning by the management. They need to skillfully apply the communication systems to keep the healthy organizational environment. It must be remembered that the activities of the management and the employees in any business organization are governed by social as well as psychological laws. If the management has to keep the healthy organizational environment and healthy relations with the individuals from outside, other business houses, the government authorities, etc., they must use the communication channels and media effectively. Sociologically, organizations are social systems in which people have their individual as well as social roles and status.

A genuine interest in other people, their groups and organizations is required for strong and stable personal relations and for the success of business activities of a businessman who is genuinely interested in others, shares their hopes, aspirations, successes and even disappointments. The following questions asked by Wolf, *et al.* (1979) throw light on the importance of effective communication in achieving business goal: "Unless you admit the importance of others to yourself and of yourself to others, how can you succeed as a human being or as a business person? And unless you use words and actions to establish and sustain beneficial human relations, how can you reap the profits of goodwill ?". — (Wolf, *et al.* 1977: 16). As organizations need people and people also need organizations, people can use organizations and organizations can use people to reach their objectives by communicating properly with one and other. When the objectives of the organization are made clear to the employees, the workers are motivated to work in that direction. It should be made clear that the organization can not survive if its objectives are not reached; and, if the organization does not survive, there would be no chances of employment opportunities in it. The employees and the management should develop the link of communication for better mutual understanding and encourage each other to achieve their self-interests.

An executive of any organisation finds it necessary to maintain both the internal and external communication. Communication between the management and workers is an internal communication. The management needs to be well-informed about the internal activities of the organization. They require the information about the efficiency, qualifications, capabilities and the training of the workers and also about the production, marketing and sales capacity of the organization itself. The progress and profitability of the organization depends upon how well the management and the employees are informed about these matters and what steps are taken by them in order to improve the situation. When the management is informed about the faults related to job assignments, exact designation of the officers and their decision-making power, their responsibilities, etc., the management can make necessary changes and the business can thrive after the relevant changes are made. "The dynamics of the internal system influences the activities of the external system. Communication about the product studies and market analyses flow smoothly between persons of equal status, between friends and between persons who support and encourage one another, conflicts growing out of the internal system of the group can hinder the communication regarding external activities. The manager must give attention to both the internal and the external group systems." — (Wofford, *et al.* 1977: 34).

The effective internal network of communication is essential today because of the large size of organisations, especially the multinational and the national organisations in the areas of sports, politics, health, law, economics, trade and commerce, etc. They have their branches and sub-branches which are further divided into functional departments. Some organizations are spread over the different places in the country. These divisions and branches maintain a link with the management of the central organization. The appointments, designations, relationships, responsibilities, functionalization, objectives and all the activities and duties determined by the division of work are communicated and assigned to the branches by the central management of the organization. A branch manager who is appointed by the board of directors accepts the responsibilities and assignments which are assigned by the parent body. Through branch manager, the centre gets reports about various activities of the branch. He has to accept the directives of centre which are given by centre after receiving reports from the branch. He acts as the delegate of the board of directors and has to clarify the objectives and directives of the organization to his subordinates. In some of the multinational corporations, the directors and the managers spend above ninety percent of their time in maintaining communication links.

The division of work into different kinds of duties can be called functionalisation. For example, the difference between an office supervisor and a machine shop supervisor is a functional one. This idea of functionalisation naturally leads to specialization. The most salient feature of this age is specialization (Pal, *et al;* 1979). There are specialists who acquire a vast knowledge and experience in their limited subject. This specialized knowledge, training and experience is useless if it is not communicated. The accountants, engineers, scientists and the experts of many kinds must be able to communicate their knowledge to the management and the employees. The organization may be benefited by the advise, suggestions and information provided by these experts.

Though specialization has brought great benefits to the business organizations, it has rendered modern business activities into an extremely complex phenomenon (Doctor and Doctor, 1977; Pal & Korlahalli, 1979). As the specialization is most fundamental to the modern civilization, the industrial society cannot exist without it. In an organization, planning, finance, accounts, purchase, production, advertising, marketing, stores, sales, labour-welfare, cultural activities, adjustments of complaints and claims and a number of other activities are handled by the people who have developed unique skills and knowledge in their fields. As these functions are assigned to different departments, they have to coordinate among themselves by communicating with one another horizontally. They have to communicate with the management to which they are responsible for carrying out their duties. The functionalized group within the organization is more complex and difficult to co-ordinate than the original group of workers which is not divided into different kinds of duties. The managers and the supervisors must be well versed in communication skills in order to bring co-ordination among the functionalized groups. The productivity gains of the specialization can be achieved only if the harmonious human relationship and co-ordination of departmental activities are well maintained.

The businessmen are mostly after productivity gains and other economic and technical benefits. Sometimes, this tendency of the businessmen comes in conflict with the problems which are primarily human. The employees are now more conscious of their rights than ever before. They are organized into trade unions which continuously demand for rights of the employees, better working conditions and dignity of the labour (Doctor, *et al*, 1977). The progressive employers are convinced that there ought to be some ways of effective communication between the management and the workers to develop better employees satisfaction and a sense of security. If the insecurity and frustration of employees is successfully dispelled by the management, the employees feel motivated for better working. In order to satisfy the security needs of employee, a number of companies have started welfare programmes based on custodial model of organization which is popularly known as paternalism by which employees depend on the organization for their security and welfare. As the success of custodial approach depends on the economic resources of the organization, the management must be able to communicate with the employees regarding financial state of the organization and should motivate them for better work in order to make the organization financially strong enough to support its employees.

Modern business relationships have spread worldwide and the communication links play a significant role in establishing and strengthening such relationships (Pal, *et al*, 1979). Multinational business can help the economic as well as social development, therefore it can also be regarded as a social institution. When a business expands beyond the national boundaries, it is also a step into different legal, political, social, economic and educational environments. With the expansion of business, the communication links are also lengthened because of which the control of the multiple business activities becomes more difficult. It is hard enough to run a multinational business in one language. When there are number of other languages in a country and the overall languages are used as the media of communication, the management faces the compounded difficulties. The complexity of the business has increased to the maximum. Under these circumstances, the management has to put its communication skills to their limits.

Businessmen seek to obtain profit from the sale of their goods and services and the consumers seek the satisfaction of their wants by buying them in the market. In a free market economy, production is for profit and consumption is for the satisfaction of wants. Both the producers and the consumers naturally try to promote their own interests. This system works fairly when free competition is present in the market place. The products of common consumption are available in the market in many brands and the buyers are free to buy any of them. As the decision to buy depends on their own initiative, they cannot be forced to buy a particular product or service. The similar products with different branding from different companies cannot enjoy equal demand from the buyers. A businessman who wants to survive in this world of free competition, should know his competitors, the quality and the prices of their products, the discounts, terms and conditions of sale, the policies of advertising, government laws, etc. (Pal, *et al,* 1979). If they are not able to communicate better in this respect, their sale will not be satisfactory. A good salesman is efficient communicator who can attract the customer, induce him to buy his goods and services. The demand for an absolutely perfect and fair competition, production and marketing, is an idealistic concept. We can approach closer to perfection but can never reach it. When people are very much aware of the products available in the market, their brands, qualities and prices, there can be keen competition. A businessman who knows the market situation properly by keeping communication links alive, can bring about certain changes in his advertising policies, or he might find some way to minimize the cost of the product or he might just change the wrapper, and give some discount, or he might offer some attractive terms to the buyers. All these and other measures at his disposal can be effective if he has the qualities of a good salesman; and, salesmanship depends on his art and skills of communication.

Participation, co-operation and team-work of the management and employees can yield best results because of their common commitment to goals that encourage better performance. Participative managers communicate with their employees. They ask for the opinions, views, suggestions and recommendations of the employees in the decision-making process so that they work together as a team. But the benefits of participation in decision-making process may not be substantial if the superiors neglect the delegation of authority. "The term 'delegation' is generally used to mean the granting of rights and approval to others to function within the prescribed limits." (Davar, 1980: 196-7). The delegation of authority trains and develops the efficiency of the subordinates and reduces the manager's burden of performing the duties of routine nature. The delegation of authority can be communicated in oral or written form, but it is always better to use the written form in order to avoid the conflict and confusion.

In participatory management, the manager retains the ultimate responsibility of his unit, but he shares the operating responsibility with the employees who actually per form the work. This gives a sense of involvement and satisfaction to the employees who work with high morals to achieve the objectives of the organization as the manager seeks participation of the employees in policy matters and decision-making.

References

Davar, R.S., 1980: *Principles of Management*, Bombay: Progressive Corporation Pvt. Ltd.

Doctor, R. and Doctor, A., 1977: *Principles and Practice of Business Communication.* Bombay: Sheth Publishers.

Pal, R. and J.S. Korlahalli, 1979: *Essentials of Business Communication.* New Delhi: Sultan Chand & Sons.

Wofford, J. Gerloff, E. and R. Cummins, 1977: *Organizational Communication*, Tokyo: McGraw-Hill Kogakusha Ltd.

Wolf, M.P., Keyser, D.F. and R.A. Aurner, 1979, *Effective Communication in Business*, Cincinnati, Ohio South-Western Publishing Company.

2

THE MEANING AND PROCESS OF COMMUNICATION

"Let your speech always be with grace seasoned with salt."
— Colossians 4:6

INTRODUCTION

The civilisation is reflected in three priceless possessions of mankind, the first is the human ability to think, the other is his innate capacity to communicate and the third is his specie's specific competence to acquire and use the arbitrary symbol systems of language. The manifold gifts of civilisation and all the branches of human knowledge have their origin from this ability to think in abstract and to communicate the abstract thoughts through arbitrary symbols of the language.

The process of communication permits us to use and reuse the experiences of others in present as well as in future. We can draw the experience and knowledge from the past into the present and make it ready for reuse in future with the help of the symbols of communication which stand for some abstract idea.

Communication is the means by which people relate to one another. The society in general or an organization of any type cannot exist without the relations that are built and strengthened by communication. Throughout our lives, we are involved in communication situations. When we talk and work with our colleagues, friends, subordinates, superiors, experts, teachers, students, family members and with the people in all walks of life; when we read and/or write the books, pamphlets, periodicals, special journals, reports, letters, memos, newspapers, etc.; when we listen to or deliver speeches; when we listen to the radio or watch the television and films; when we buy or sell the products or services; when we manage our businesses and when we are involved in any other activity, we are invariably involved in communication situation.

THE DEFINITIONS OF COMMUNICATION

The scholars who define communication give stress on the transmission and reception of information. The concept of communication is broad enough to mean almost anything to almost anybody. As it is the binding agent of all social systems and sub-systems, it is understood and used in different ways by the people in different walks of life. Therefore, it was essential to study how this concept is understood by them and later to arrive at a comprehensive definition in precise terms. Let us consider some definitions of communication.

i. "Communication is the process of transmitting feelings, attitudes, facts, beliefs and ideas between living beings". — Birvenu (1987)

ii. "Communication is any means by which thought is transferred from one person to another". — Chappell and Read (1979)

iii. "Communication is an exchange of facts, ideas, opinions or emotions by two or more persons". — Newman and Summer (1977)

iv. "Communication is process for conducting the attention of another person for the purpose of replicating memories." — Cartier and Harwood (1977)

v. "Communication is a process which involves the transmission and accurate replication of ideas ensured by feedback for the purpose of eliciting actions which will accomplish organizational goals". — William Scott (1977)

vi. "Communication is the process by which

information is transmitted between individuals and/or organizations so that an understanding response results". — Peter Little (1977)

vii. "Communication is a continuing and thinking process dealing with the transmission and interchange with understanding of ideas, facts and courses of action". — Terry and Franklin (1984)

viii. "Communication is the broad field of human interchanges of facts and not the technologies of telephone, telegraph, radio and the like". — Charles Redfield (1954)

ix. "Communication is the sum of all the things one person does when he wants to create understanding in the mind of another. It is a bridge of meaning. It involves a systematic and continuous process of telling, listening and understanding". — Louis Allen (1958)

x. "Communication is composite of information given and received, of a learning experience in which certain attitudes, knowledge and skills change, carrying with them alterations of behaviour; of a listening effort by all involved; of systematic fresh examination of issues by the communicator himself; and of a sensitive interaction of points of view leading to a higher level of shared understanding and common intention". — Ordway Tead (1959)

xi. "Communication is the exchange of meanings between individuals through a common system of symbols". — I.A. Richards (1928)

xii. "Communication is the process of passing information and understanding from one person to another." — Keith Davis (1981)

xiii. "Communication is the process of meaningful interactions among persons in an organization resulting in meanings being perceived and understanding effected among such persons." — Rustom Davar (1980)

xiv. "Communication means that information is passed

from one place to another." — Miller (1951)

xv. "It is a word that describes the process of transferring meaning from one individual to another". — Catchcart (1966)

xvi. "It is the intentional transmission of information by means of some established signalling-system". — Lyons (1977)

Appraisal of the Definitions

Most of the above definitions have dwelt on some common characteristics of communication. Birvenu's (1987) definition appears to be simple and straightforward but it does not mention anything about feedback which is a part and parcel of the communication cycle. He has given more emphasis on the transmission of ideas, feelings, attitudes, facts and beliefs, but he is not clear about the reception, understanding and response. On the other hand, Louis Allen (1958) and Ordway Tead (1959) have given more stress on listening and understanding of the message by the receiver. Chappell and Read (1979) think that the message transmitted by the communicator consists of only 'thoughts', but on the other hand, Birvenu (1987), Charles Redfield (1954), William Newman and Charles Summer (1977) have stated that the feelings of a person, his attitude towards different persons, objects and things, his beliefs and ideas are also transmitted along with the facts and figures. Peter Little (1977), William Scott (1977), George R. Terry and Franklin (1984), and Louis Allen (1958) have given weightage to the communicator, the message and the transmission; but unlike Birvenu (1987), they have also given equal importance to the receiver, his understanding of the message and his response to the communicator's message. Peter Little (1977) has pointed out that the aim of communication between individuals and/or organizations is to get the response indicating that the receiver has understood the message. His emphasis on 'transmission of information' means the transmission of news, knowledge, attitudes or 'the frame of mind' of the communicator. Chappel and Read (1979) have neither accounted for the transmission of feelings and attitudes of the communicator nor for the feedback from the receiver but William Newman and Charles Summer (1977) have said that communication is an 'exchange' of facts, ideas, opinions or emotions by two or more persons. The word 'exchange' in this definition denotes that there is a feedback to the massage transmitted by the communicator.

The definition given by F.A. Cartier and K.A. Harwood (1977) differ from the definitions given by Birvenu (1987), Peter Little (1977), Chappell and Read (1979), and Newman and Summer (1977). Cartier and Harwood (1977) have used the concept of 'replicating memories'. They say that the purpose of communication is to replicate memories. When the message is received by the receiver, he perceives and interprets it in the light of his past experience. Therefore, the same message can be interpreted differently by the two receivers. In order to fulfill the purpose of replicating memories, the communicator has to direct or influence the attention of the receiver to refer to his past experience. He has to bear in his mind the fact that the message is perceived and understood by the receiver in his own way. The words that carry the meaning are important but the sense in which they are perceived and understood is of real significance in communication. For example, when the word 'childhood' is uttered, it may bring pleasant memories to one receiver whose childhood days were happy but may depress another person whose childhood was passed in misery and hardships. This definition does not explain the nature and transmission of message, the role of the communicator and the need of feedback. Cartier and Harwood (1977) have given dominance to the receiver and have underestimated the role of the communicator. The term 'replication' also appears in the definition given by William Scott (1977). He states that the process of communication involves 'the transmission and accurate replication of ideas'. According to Cartier and Harwood (1977), the purpose of communication is to 'replicate memories' whereas William Scott (1977) has said that the purpose of communication is to elicit the 'actions'. To him, all the actions elicited by the accurate replication of ideas are directed towards the accomplishment of the organizational goals. Rustom S. Daver (1980) and Keith Davis (1981) have defined communication in the context of the interactions that take place among the persons in the organizations. Charles Redfield (1954), in his definition, points out that a good deal of misunderstanding prevails about the nature and function of communication. In our everyday life, we use the word 'communication' for a variety of meanings. We generally use it for a letter, newspaper, radio broadcast, TV programmes, periodicals, telephone, telegrams, etc. Redfield (1954) says that communication is the broad field of human interchange of facts and opinions and not the technologies of telephone, telegraph, radio and the like. He gives more importance to the purpose, spirit, objectives and the substance of communication than to the technology, which is as a means to carry out the act of communication. No other definition of communication, except the one given by I.A. Richards (1928) refers to the 'common system of symbols', which is used for encoding the message. I.A. Richard's (1928) definition of communication is very broad and general in nature. It includes almost all kinds of human and animal communication systems.

According to Miller (1951) and Lyons (1977) communications is 'transmission' of information. They do not give importance to the reception, interpretation and understanding of the message. Secondly, though feedback or the response of the receiver is crucial in any communication, they do not seem to be aware of its role. To Miller (1951), communication is the information passed from 'one place to another'. Yet, it is necessary to mention that in communication messages are passed and received between the 'participants' - the communicator and the receiver and not between the 'places'. However, it is possible for the communicator and the receiver to communicate from distant places. Like Miller (1951) and Lyons (1977), Catcheart (1966) too has not paid any attention to feedback. According to Miller (1951) and Lyons (1977), communicator transmits 'information' whereas according to Catchcart (1966) 'meaning', is transmitted from one individual to another. Miller

(1951) and Lyons (1977) do not include feelings, attitude etc. in communicable messages. Lyons (1977) 'intentional transmission of information' signifies that communication is a goal oriented activity.

Having considered the merits and demerits of the above definitions, we are now in a position to define the concept of communication in the following words :

Definition of Communication

> "Communication can be defined as an exchange and exact replication of thoughts, feelings, facts, beliefs and ideas between and among the individuals through a common system of symbols to cause some actions or changes in behaviour." (Rodriques, 1992: 28)

THE PROCESS OF COMMUNICATION

Introduction

In order to deal elaborately with the process of communication, it is essential to see some models of communication process, explain the components of communication situation and then to arrive at a comprehensive Model of communication process. The elaborate description of the communication process is given in 'The Process of Communication' after evolving the comprehensive model of communication process.

Some Models of Communication Process

Let us scrutinize some existing models of communication process before undertaking to evolve a comprehensive one.

APPRAISAL OF THE MODELS OF COMMUNICATION PROCESS

Sharma and Mohan (1986) have included four factors - the sender, the channel, the receiver and the response in their model. Yet the model does not include the media (verbal

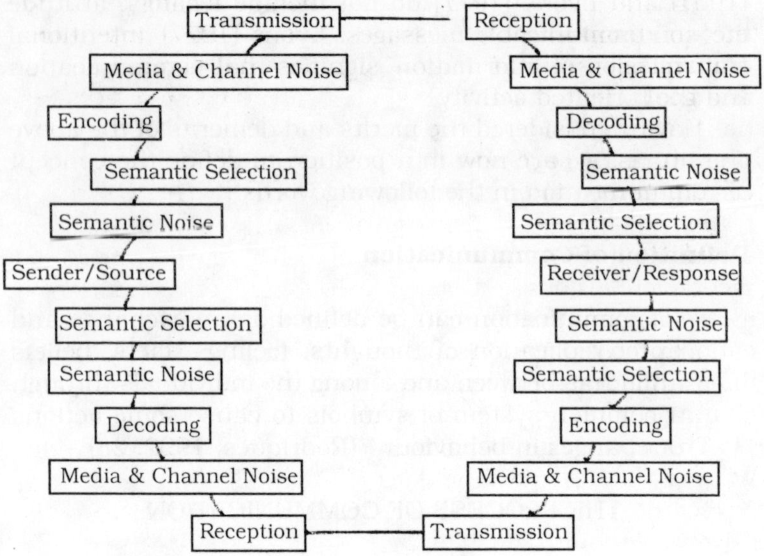

FIG. 2.1 Rodriques' (1992) Model of Communication Process

and non-verbal) without which the message cannot be carried to the receiver. Semantic gap is shown between the message sent by the communicator and the message received by the receiver. But nothing is said about the various interferences that cause the semantic gap between the feedback sent by the receiver and the feedback received by the original sender. The model does not consist of all the essential factors of the communication process. Especially, the absence of certain factors like encoding, decoding, semantic noise (before encoding the message), semantic selection, media and channel noise, signal transmission, signal reception etc. shows that the model is incomplete.

The communication process model presented by Hicks and Gullet (1974) include the factors — idea in the sender's mind, selection of a communication medium, selection of a communication channel, meaning given to the message by the receiver, and feedback to the sender. An advantage of this model is the presence of two additional factors 'idea in the senders mind' and 'selection of communication medium'. The former leading to the source of communication and the later to the distinction between medium and channel. The model of Sharma and Mohan (1986) lacks in presenting these two vital factors. However, the absence of certain important factors like encoding, decoding, signal transmission, signal reception, semantic noise, semantic selection, media and channel noise etc. makes the model incomplete. Hicks and Gullet (1974) do not seem to be aware of communication barriers or noise in the communication process. Yet this model is prominently notable for differentiating communication media and communication channels.

The model of communication process presented by Wofford, *et al.* (1977) includes communication source, encoder, message channel, decoder and communication receiver. They introduce two factors namely, encoder and decoder. They differentiate between the source and encoder as well as between the decoder and the receiver. The encoder is treated separate from the communication source. The encoder is an agency involved in the process of encoding the message. This process takes place in the brain of the sender. The encoder as an agency for encoding is the brain of the sender. Similarly, the decoder is an agency responsible for the process of decoding the message. The decoder is the receiver's brain. The procedures of encoding and decoding take place instantaneously. The sender and the receiver are not aware of this process. Wofford, *et al.* (1977) have added the factors of sender's and receiver's brains which are responsible for encoding or decoding. However, this model is not comprehensive as it does not consist of all the essential factors of the communication process. Especially, the absence of certain factors like encoding, decoding, medium, semantic noise, semantic selection, medium and channel noise, signal transmission, signal reception, feedback etc. shows that the model is incomplete.

Lasswell's (1948) model of communication process includes communicator, receiver, message, medium and effect. Though Lasswell is aware of the importance of feedback in communication process, he does not show the transmission of effect (feedback) to the communicator. It is incomplete because it does not include the important factors like encoding, decoding, signal transmission, signal reception, semantic noise, semantic selection etc. Lasswell (1948) has not differentiated between channel and medium. He seems to have equated channel with the medium.

Vogel and Brooks (1977) model of communication process is remarkable in showing 'noise' in the message sent by the source, in the channel used by the source, and also in the source itself. Similarly, noise is shown in the channel used by the receiver, in the message sent by the receiver, and in the receiver himself. However, this model is incomplete because of the absence of some important factors of communication process like encoding, decoding, media, signal transmission, signal reception, semantic noise, semantic selection etc.

Though the factors included in the model presented by Thomas and Fryer (1988) like signal, attending, interpreting, evaluating, responding, and remembering are seldom seen in the other models of communication process, it lacks several important factors of communication process. It does not mention the signal, transmission, encoding, decoding, semantic noise, semantic selection, communication media, media and channel noise etc.

Rai and Rai's (1989) model includes the factors transmitter, encoding, channel, medium, decoding, and receiver. In this model feedback is absent. The process of communication is never complete without feedback. Beside feedback, the other important factors like semantic noise, semantic selection, media and channel noise, signal transmission, signal reception etc. are not included in the model. This model is incomplete.

Doctor and Doctor's (1977) model includes the factors like the sender, the receiver, encoding, decoding and publics. This model is incomplete because it does not include the important factors like semantic noise, semantic selection, channels, media, channel and media noise, signal transmission, signal reception etc.

Pal and Korlahalli's (1979) model of communication process includes source, encoding, dispatch, reception, decoding, and response. It appears that Pal and Korlahalli have replaced receiver with 'response' for which no explanation is given. The receiver of the message encodes the response and dispatches it to the original sender for reception. At this level again the decoding of response takes place. This model in more comprehensive than the previous ones.

Finally, though (Rodriques, 1992) model of communication process includes most of the important factors of communication process, it requires a few more factors to make it comprehensive. The factors are given below :

i. Need to communicate
ii. Emergence of idea or impulse
iii. Need to comprehend
iv. Comprehension of idea or experience
v. Media and channel selection
vi. Media and channel interpretation

However, the comprehensive model of communication process can only be the evolved if we have a clear idea of communication situation or speech situation and also of all the essential factors of communication process.

Communication Situation

All communication is possible only in a speech situation. A speech situation is communication situation. This speech situation requires certain factors for its existence. The factors are (1) Participants, (2) Contact, (3) Context, (4) Common Code, (5) Form of Message, (6) Goal of Communication.

1. Participants

There are always two parties in a communication situation: the sender and the receiver. The sender sends the message to the receiver and the receiver interprets the message and acts accordingly. The communication is a goal oriented activity. The sender has some goal or intention towards the receiver: persuading the receiver, making him to do something or believe something etc. The receiver must respond to make it clear that he has received the message. There arc different ways of doing this. What the receiver does to indicate that he has received the message is called 'feedback'. This feedback may be verbal or non-verbal. Unless the sender receives the feedback in some form, the communication process remains incomplete.

The sender is both the sender of the message and the receiver of the feedback. And the receiver is both the receiver of the message and the sender of the feedback.

The sender and the receiver are not necessarily present at the same time and place. If the communication is through written media, generally the sender and the receiver are distanced, that is, they are not present at the same time and place.

2. Contact

For successful communication contact must be established between the participants. The sender must make the receiver to give attention to his message. In order to attract attention he uses short calls (Vocatives etc.) like 'dear', 'hey', 'John', 'Sir' etc. The contact is later maintained by physical testing of the channel. The sender asks the receiver 'Can you hear me?' 'Do you follow me?' etc. The sender must also establish rapport with the receiver. The sender sometimes does it by talking about the weather, health, praise, encouragement etc. These are the small talks, but they matter in communication. The contact is established not only physically but also psychologically by asking questions like 'Do you get me?' The sender also uses many linguistic techniques to maintain the contact and for helping the receiver by using the linguistic expressions like 'My next point is....', 'First of all ...', 'Secondly ....', 'Thirdly....'. These are explanatory techniques. Establishing and maintaining contact between the sender and the receiver is very crucial as it accelerates the process of communication.

3. Context

Communication cannot take place in a vacuum. It requires a physical and temporal setting. In other words, it takes place at a particular place and time. However, the topic of communication is more important in communication situation. It is the background knowledge which is shared between the sender and the receiver. It helps the receiver to interpret the message. It helps the receiver to predict what the sender is going to say. This prediction is very important in understanding the message. Besides, it is also important in planning the message that the sender sends to the receiver. Thus the setting and the topic form the context of communication.

4. Common Code

A code is a set of conventions used for communication. Both the sender and the receiver must be in possession of some common code. The code must be shared by both the participants. This common code may be linguistic, paralinguistic or non-verbal.

5. Form of Message

The message which is transmitted from the sender to the receiver must have the same form. This form depends upon the situation. If the setting of the situation is noisy the form is loud. If the setting is short-timed, the form is brief. The form may also be formal or informal, polite or impolite. The form depends upon the roles of the participants and the goal of communication. There are a number of ways to send the same message.

6. Goal of Communication

Communication is a goal-oriented activity. Communication

must have some goal. In fact, the goals are not the same everywhere. The goal changes according to the focus of communication. It is in fact the function of the language used in communication. The goal may be speaker-oriented. It is the personal function of language. Here, the language is used to express the speaker's attitudes, personality and emotions. It is used to indicate whether the speaker is sad, happy, angry, upset, dissatisfied etc. The goal may be receiver-oriented. It is the directive function of the language. It is aimed at controlling the behaviour of the hearer by influencing, persuading etc. Commands, requests, warnings and other functions like these are hearer-oriented. The goal may be contact oriented. Here, the language carries out the function of establishing contact. This is also called phatic function of language. The language is used to establish and maintain relations and to promote the feelings of goodwill. There are also set formuliac or ritualistic linguistic expressions to carry out this function like 'bye bye', 'hello'. In order to establish contact, there are certain formuliac or ritual activities like greeting, leave-taking, talking about weather and health or making inquiries. This phatic function is also carried out by using gestures and facial expressions.

The goal may be topic-oriented. This is referential function of language. Here, the language is used for expressing thought-content by making statements for putting forth propositions.

The goal may be code-oriented. This is metalinguistic function of language. Hence, the reference is to some set of rules and conventions. Its aim is to test mutual understanding of the rules and conventions.

Finally, the goal may be message-oriented. This is the imaginative function of language. The sound, rythem and tune are used in such a way as to give pleasure to the hearer and help comprehension. Even in written communication, this goal may be achieved by using different graphics. This is also called aesthetic function of language.

The process of communication takes place in the communication situation. All the essential factors of communication process are given below.

THE ESSENTIAL FACTORS OF COMMUNICATION PROCESS

In addition to the factors accounted for in the ten models of communication process discussed earlier, there should be some more factors which are essential to explain the process. All the essential factors needed for completing the process of communication are enlisted below:

1. There is a communicator who is a part of the communication event.
2. There is a receiver who is a part of the communication event.
3. There is a suitable medium for transmission and reception of the message. The medium is a verbal or nonverbal means of communication (see 'Media of Communication' in chapter 4 for further details). The participants must select suitable medium. A medium which is suitable for transmitting the message may not be suitable for the receiver for reception. For example, a written medium may be suitable for a literate communicator, but an illiterate receiver finds the written medium difficult to comprehend.
4. There is a suitable channel for transmission and reception of the message. The channels are the formal and informal ways of communication. (See channels of communication in chapter 3 for further details). It is essential for the participants to select the suitable channels. For example, certain messages are suitable for downward communication only. A supervisor can order an operator to do a piece of job. An order cannot be issued by the subordinate to the superior. It cannot go through upward channel. Orders, warnings, instructions flow in downward channel. Similarly, upward channel and horizontal channel are suitable for certain other types of messages.
5. There is a common symbol system. The symbol system must be common to both the participants.

Language is an arbitrary symbol system. If communicator uses a language which is not known to the receiver, there cannot be any communication.

6. Both the parties cooperate by attending to each others message. The communicator has to understand the receiver's nature and needs. He has to understand the communication event in which he has to deal with the receiver. He has to think of the suitability of the means and materials (Gerbner, 1956) of communication. He has to select the media and channel which is suitable for himself and for the receiver. The receiver too has to cooperate with the communicator by attending carefully to the message received, and further, by interpreting and responding (Thomas and Fryer, 1988) to the message. The receivers response plays a vital role in the communication process.
7. Both the parties are conversant and skilled in the art of communication and know how to use the communication media and channel effectively. They ought to know the essentials of effective communication like clarity, correctness, completeness, courtesy, 'You' attitude, attentiveness, adaptability, positive and pleasant approach, appropriate tone, adequate knowledge of the subject, proper organization of message, appropriate formality, patience in listening etc.
8. The communicator has an idea or experience to share with the receiver. In the beginning this idea or experience is in the essence (abstract) form. This idea or experience is transmitted by the communicator if he feels the need of doing so.
9. The communicator has some need or purpose to communicate the message. The needs motivate the communicator to communicate and the receiver to respond.
10. The communicator faces some interference (Semantic noise) with the identification of the intended meaning which is to be transmitted to

the receiver. This noise is invariably present in the process of communication and neither the communicator nor the receiver can avoid it.

11. The communicator overcomes the semantic noise through definite realization (semantic selection) of a particular idea and its meaning clearly, completely and correctly.
12. The communicator encodes the message. Having realized the idea properly he translates the idea or experience into arbitrary symbol system or code which is common to both the participants. This arbitrary symbol system is also called 'signal' (Thomas and Fryer, 1988; Doctor and Doctor, 1977). This symbol system can be either verbal or non-verbal. It acts as an agent or means for the transmission of the message. The receiver must be conversant with the code system which the communicator uses for encoding.
13. The communicator faces and overcomes the media interference while sending the message. When the communicator selects some verbal media like oral media or written media, or the non-verbal media like facial expression, hand gestures, postures etc. for encoding the message, certain limitations of these media act as interfering agents in transmitting and receiving the message. The lack of knowledge and skill of using the media can also act as interfering factor. Unless the communicator overcomes these media interferences, the communication process cannot be complete.
14. The communicator faces and overcomes the channel interferences while sending the message. These are formal channels of communication like upward channel, the downward channel and the horizontal or later channel. An informal channel like Grapevine is also used for transmitting the messages. (See 'channels of communication' in Chapter 3 for further details.) The disadvantages and limitations of these channels act as the

interfering factors when the messages pass through these channels, for example status barriers, age, allness and closed-mindedness, halo effect etc. Sometimes the lack of the knowledge and skills of using these channels for communicative purposes is in itself an interference or noise.

15. The encoded message is transmitted by the communicator.
16. The communicator expects feedback from the receiver. To expect feedback from the receiver is to expect cooperation from the receiver to complete the process of communication. If the communicator does not expect feedback, he may demotivate the receiver from giving the response. And, if the respons is not given, the communication cycle remains incomplete. Therefore, the communicator must expect feedback from the receiver. He must expect some kind of reaction to the message that he sends to the receiver. In fact, to seek some response is the purpose of the message transmitted to the receiver.
17. The message encoded by the communicator is received by the receiver. Sometimes, it may also happen that the message is transmitted to the receiver but it does not reach its destination.
18. The receiver has a need to comprehend and react to the message received.
19. The receiver faces and overcomes the media interference while receiving the message.
20. The receiver faces and overcomes the channel interference while receiving the message.
21. The receiver decodes the message received from the communicator. In decoding the message, the receiver has to translate the arbitrary symbols received from the communicator. In decoding the message, the receiver has to translate the arbitrary symbols received from the communicator into the meaning for which those symbols stand. An arbitrary symbol does not have the meaning in

itself. It simply stands for or represents the meaning. The meaning attributed to a symbol by the communicator and the receiver can be different, and this may lead to misunderstanding between the participants. Different meanings can be attributed by the participants to the same word or signal. It may also happen that the different words or signals may stand for the same meaning. Such words or signals may lead to misunderstanding between the participants. In decoding the receiver has to translate the arbitrary symbol into its exact meaning.

22. The receiver faces some interference (Semantic noise) with the identification of the intended meaning of the message received from the communicator.
23. The receiver overcomes the semantic noise and identifies the intended meaning (semantic selections) of the message received.
24. The receiver comprehends the idea or experience which is received from the communicator.
25. The receiver reacts to the communicator's message.
26. In reaction to the communicator's message, the receiver has some idea or experience which is to be communicated to the communicator.
27. The receiver has a need or purpose to communicate the response.
28. The receiver faces some interference (semantic noise) with the identification of the intended meaning of the feedback which is to be transmitted to the original sender.
29. The receiver overcomes the semantic noise and identifies the intended meaning (semantic selection) which is to be transmitted to the original sender.
30. The receiver encodes the feedback. He translates the meaning into arbitrary symbol system or some non-verbal signal.
31. The receiver faces and overcomes the media interferences while transmitting the feedback.

32. The receiver faces and overcomes the channel noise while transmitting feedback to the communicator.
33. The receiver transmits the feedback.
34. The original sender becomes the receiver of the feedback and receives the message.
35. The original sender faces and overcomes the media interference while receiving the feedback.
36. The original sender faces and overcomes the channel interference while receiving the feedback.
37. The original sender decodes the feedback.
38. The original sender faces some interference (semantic noise) with the identification of the intended meaning of the feedback.
39. The original sender overcomes the semantic noise and identifies the intended meaning (semantic selection) of the feedback.
40. The original sender comprehends the idea or a experience in the feedback and, if necessary, reacts to it. If he reacts to the feedback the communication cycle starts again.

The comprehensive model of communication process is evolved with the help of all the essential factors described above.

THE COMPREHENSIVE MODEL OF COMMUNICATION PROCESS

In the process of communication, the observable factors are — communicator, signal-1, receiver, and signal-2. The signal-1 is produced by the communicator, and the signal-2 is produced by the receiver. Though communicator is an observable factor, his mental reaction to the event, his need to communicate, the emergence of idea or impulse, facing and overcoming of the semantic noise, selection of the meaning which is appropriate in the given context, encoding, selecting appropriate medium and channel, facing and overcoming media and channel noise etc. are the factors of the 'process' which are unobservable because these go on in the communicator's mind. Similarly, though receiver is an observable factor, his need to comprehend the message, his facing and overcoming of media and channel noise, his attention, evaluation and interpretation of the message that comes through a particular medium and channel, decoding, facing and overcoming of the semantic noise, selection of the contextually appropriate meaning, and his comprehension of the idea or experience etc. are the factors of the 'process' which are unobservable because these go on in the mind of the receiver.

When the communicator and the receiver encode the meaning into some conventional signal system (language), the two more observable factors are realized — signal-1 and signal-2. Signal-1 is produced by the communicator and received by the receiver. Signal-2 is the feedback produced by the receiver and received by the original communicator. Both the signals have either verbal or non-verbal form, and they are produced in the context.

There are two processes of productive performance: signal-1 is produced by the communicator and signal-2 is produced by the receiver. There are two processes of receptive performance: signal-1 is received by the receiver and signal-2 is received by the communicator. Any model of communication process must interpret these four processes. The following diagram shows the outline of the communication process.

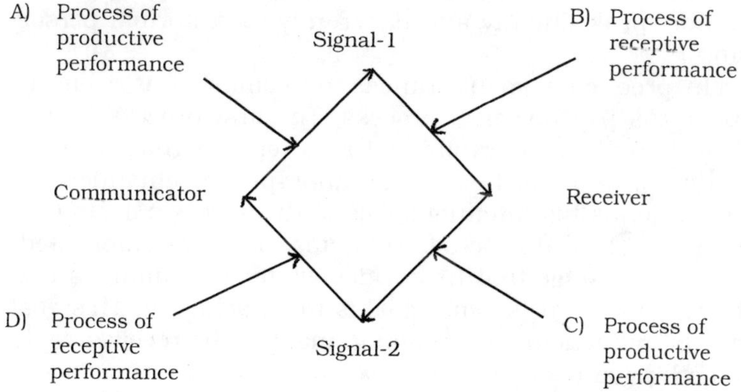

FIG. 2.2 : The outline of communication process

The communication process consists of two skills-productive skill and receptive skill. Traditionally, the productive skill is taken as an active skill and the receptive skill as a passive skill. Listening and reading are supposed to be the receptive skills, whereas speaking and writing as the productive skills. As both presuppose verbal behaviour, this distinction is deceptive. In other words, receptive skills include productive performances as productive skills include receptive performances.

Productive Performance

In productive performance, the speaker or the writer produces the utterances in order to communicate his intention which forms the message. In speaking the speaker produces the spoken utterances, and in writing, the writer produces the graphic representation of the message. Sometimes, he makes a gesture or some sign which conventionally expresses his message. This is non-verbal performance. Thus the speaker produces utterances for communicating his message. In communicating his message, the speaker must 'monitor' to control the parameters of sounds in speech or of graphics in writing. For this, he has to hear the sounds he produces or see the letters he writes. This is a sort of feedback that the speaker gets from his own production. If he doesn't get this feedback, his production lacks fluency and coherence. A deaf person cannot speak fluently and coherently as a normal person can.

In producing an utterance, the communicator has to undergo a psychological process. The first process is that of 'ideation'. In determining the utterance that he later produces, he must initiate the appropriate semantic content which is his intention. This is the 'ideational' stage of the psychological process. This stage is very complicated. It is at this stage that he decides what to communicate to the receiver, that is, what goal is to be achieved. This goal may be influencing, persuading, making the receiver to do something and so on.

The second stage of the psychological process of productive performance involves the linguistic competence of the communicator. He must encode his intention or the message in sentences. This stage involves the speaker's linguistic ability — the store of vocabulary and knowledge of grammar rules. This stage of the process is of 'planning'. At this stage the speaker plans an appropriate linguistic programme. He relates his intention to the context to make it appropriate.

The third stage in this process is the actual 'execution' of the programme. At this stage he selects the media — verbal or non-verbal, and actually produces the utterance through some media and channel. At this stage he has to face media and channel interferences and send the encoded message across to the receiver. It is at this stage that he needs the help of the feedback to monitor his performance which we have mentioned earlier.

Receptive Performance

The receptive performance apparently begins when the receiver hears the utterance, reads the letters or sees the signs. But in fact it begins when he listens to what he hears or actively attends to what he sees. The factor of 'attention' is crucial in this process. It is at this stage that the hearer distinguishes sound qualities and the reader distinguishes graphical signs. Thus, the first stage in this process is of 'recognition'. It is partly linguistic. At this stage the receiver's perceptive ability acts like a kind of intelligence. It involves problem-solving process. This ability either possesses a hypothesis or makes hypothesis against which the evidence of senses is tested. The senses comprise what he hears or sees. If he has hypothesis that a certain sign has certain meaning, he immediately solves the problem of recognition. If he doesn't have this hypothesis, he makes such hypothesis before he realizes the meaning of what he sees or hears. In other words, he hears what he wants to hear or sees what he wants to see. For example, when the receiver hears the cluster of sounds in the word 'come' and distinguishes sound qualities, he makes a hypothesis that these sounds make the word 'come'. The receiver has this perceptual schemata which helps him in the process of recognition of sounds or letters. The matching between the schemata and the sensation is the process of 'recognition'.

The media and the channel noise may create such disturbances that block the process of recognition. These have to be overcome by the receiver. For example, if the receiver hears the sounds of another language, he will fail to match between his schemata and perception.

The next stage is of 'identification'. This is linguistic process. At this stage, the receiver samples what he hears or sees and predicts the utterances. This factor of prediction is very important in his receptive performance. As language is essentially rule — governed, the receiver anticipates the sentences. For example, when he recognizes the sounds of the word 'come', he predicts that he is asked to come. He predicts that there is an instruction or order or request in the word 'come'. Here he understands the grammatical rule of forming an imperative sentence. This stage involves the linguistic competence of the receiver. The receiver has to overcome semantic noise in the 'identification' process. This noise may block his performance of sampling and predicting sentences.

The next stage is of 'understanding'. At this stage, the sentences identified are related to the context of the situation. This involves the communicative competence of the receiver. The receiver understands the appropriateness of the linguistic expression that he identifies in the earlier stage.

The various stages in the productive and receptive performances are simultaneous. For example, in productive performance planning presupposes ideation, and execution presupposes planning and ideation. Similarly, in receptive performance, understanding presupposes identification and recognition. Besides, the factor of 'monitoring' comes between execution and recognition, whereas 'anticipation' comes between ideation and understanding. The speaker monitors his utterances to help the receiver to recognize the utterances. Similarly, the receiver anticipates the utterances. That helps him to understand the speaker's intention.

Thus, the following figure will give the idea of the processes involved in productive and receptive performances.

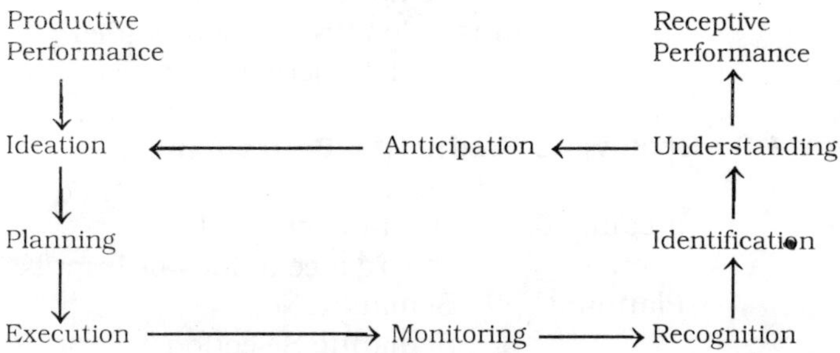

FIG 2.3 : The stages in productive and receptive performances.

This figure is based on S. Pit Corder's, (1973) model of productive and receptive performances.

The various factors in the comprehensive model of communication process are classified under the above given stages. The classification is given below:

Process - A: Communicators' Productive Performance:

Ideation : Need to communicate
Emergence of Idea or Impulse

Planning : Semantic Noise
Semantic Selection
Encoding

Execution: Media and Channel Selection
Media and Channel Noise
Signal-1 Transmission

Process - B : Receiver's Receptive Performance:

Recognition: Signal-1 Reception
Need to Comprehend
Media and Channel Noise
Media and Channel
Interpretation

Identification : Decoding
Semantic Noise
Semantic Selection
Understanding : Comprehension of Idea or Experience

Process - C : Receiver's Productive Performance:

Ideation : Need to Feedback
Emergence of Idea or Impulse
Planning : Semantic Noise
Semantic Selection
Encoding
Execution : Media and Channel Selection
Media and Channel Noise
Signal-2 Transmission

Process - D : Communicator's Receptive Performance:

Recognition : Signal-2 Reception
Need to comprehend
Media and Channel Noise
Media and Channel Interpretation
Identification : Decoding
Semantic Noise
Semantic Selection
Understanding : Comprehension of Idea or Experience

Thus the factors in the communication cycle are grouped under the four processes, i.e. Process-A, Process-B, Process-C and Process-D. The comprehensive model of communication process includes all these four processes. The model that accounts for all the essential observable and unobservable factors in the framework of communication process, is taken to be the comprehensive model and it is used for the further study. The comprehensive model of communication process is given in the Figure 2.4. The components of this model are given below.

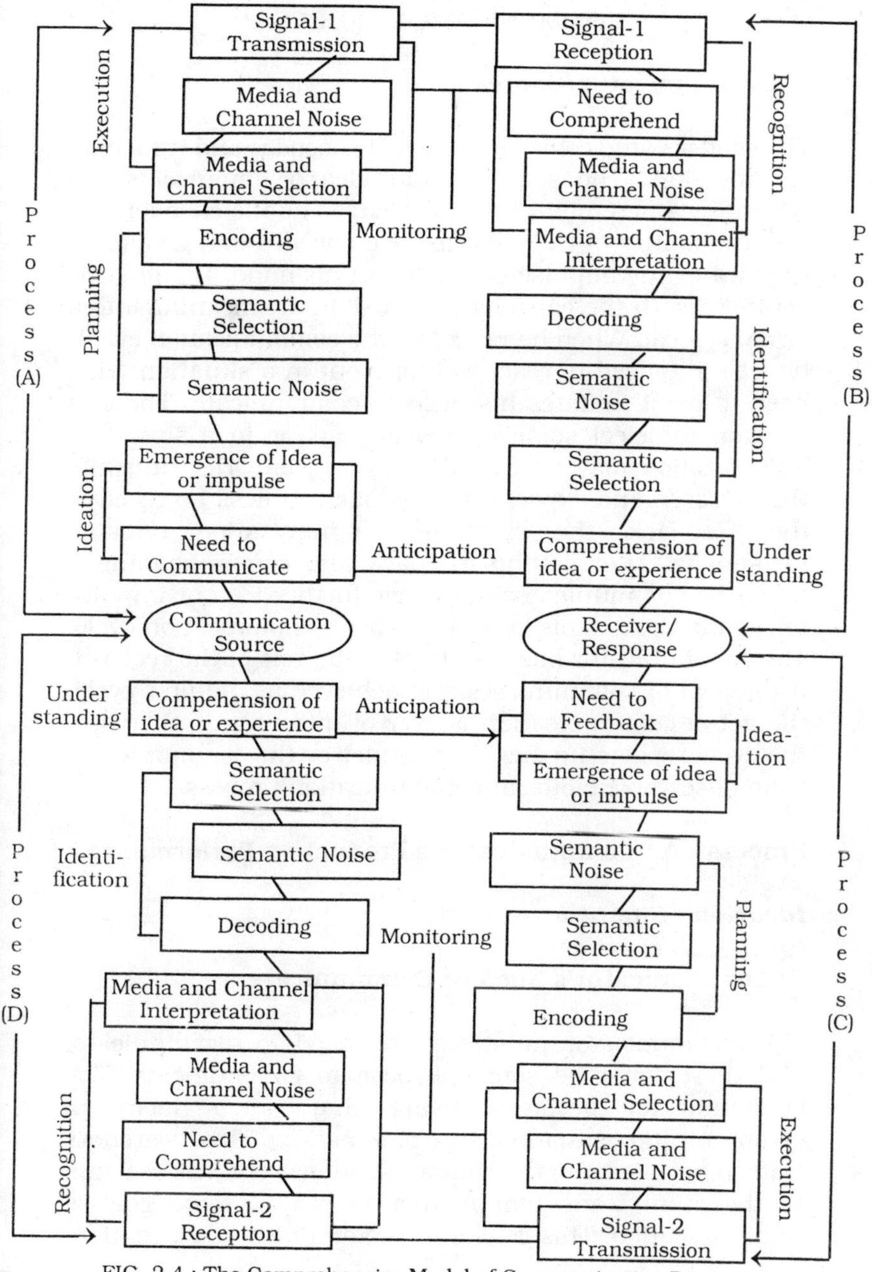

FIG. 2.4 : The Comprehensive Model of Communication Process

COMPONENTS OF THE COMPREHENSIVE MODEL OF COMMUNICATION PROCESS

1. Communicator/Source

The sender is the communicator who encodes and transmits the message. The source of an idea or impulse is the communicator's mind. He is also called as the encoder and the transmitter of the message. He encodes and transmits the idea or the impulse generated in his mind. He must be equipped with the capacity to translate the meaning into a signal system. When he perceives the communication event, he feels the need to react to this event in a situation. This need to react initiates his need to communicate. Then he goes on to select some means of reacting in a situation. This reaction may be verbal or non-verbal. He transmits the message and expects the feedback. Unless he receives the 'feedback' the cycle of communication remains incomplete. After getting feedback and comprehending it fully, the communicator may have further idea or impulse to communicate. This begins another communication cycle. The communicator has also to play the role of the receiver. If the goal of communication is achieved at the first cycle, the act of communication is over of this stage. Otherwise, the cycle repeats further. The sender or the communicator is an observable factor in communication process.

Process - A : Communicator's Productive Performance

Ideation : Signal-1

2. Communicator's Need to Communicate

The communicator must feel the need to communicate, and there must be some purpose to communicate. The communicator becomes aware that he is facing a communication situation (speech situation). This awareness leads him to react to the communication event. His reaction to the event leads him further to realize some goal of communication. This goal is the communicator's intention.

In order to achieve this goal he feels the need to communicate. He is under the pressure of this demand to communicate. Thus, the need to communicate is realized. The communicator's clear perception of the goal determines the need to communicate. The need to communicate motivates him to form the message and transmit it to the receiver.

3. Emergence of Idea or Impulse

This occurs in the mind of communicator. After the goal is realized and the need to communicate is felt, he must initiate the appropriate semantic content which is his intention. This is how the idea or impulse emerges in his mind. This idea or impulse is the source of communication. It is the result of the meaningful reaction to the communication event. This is very important part of the ideational process.

Planning : Signal-1

4. Semantic Noise

Semantic noise is the first stage in the 'planning' of the linguistic programme. It is an interference that the communicator has to face and overcome in determining the meaning of the utterance that he is going to produce. It is the interference which he faccs with the identification of the intended meaning. He has to communicate the idea to the receiver. In fact, the idea is to be replicated in the mind of the receiver. It is done through different types of code systems. Each code has its conventional meaning. To communicate the idea the communicator chooses the most appropriate code or sign. If it is verbal code, it has complexity inherent in its system. A particular sign of the code has a particular conventional meaning attached to it. Not only the communicator but also the receiver must have the adequate knowledge of this conventional meaning. The communicator has to confirm whether the receiver is conversant with this conventional aspect of code system.

This acts like a noise or an interference which the communicator has to overcome. Moreover, he has to take it for granted that the receiver is in possession of this knowledge of conventional meaning. However, if the communicator is doubtful about this, he has to face the semantic noise. Secondly, the communicator may also have doubt whether the receiver will understand the intended meaning of the code or may interpret it for some other meaning.

Thirdly, the communicator has to face other kinds of noises in selecting the ways to establish contact. There are various ways to establish contact as mentioned earlier in the section on 'communication situation'. In order to achieve the cooperation of the receiver by making him to respond, the communicator has to choose some means of contact which is not the part of content of the message. This may act as an interference or noise. The noises of this sort interfere the communicator's choice of codifiable meaning which he intends to express to the receiver through some code.

The efficiency of the communicator is directly proportional to his ability to overcome the semantic noise. He will lack confidence in semantic selection and also in encoding if he fails to face and overcome this noise.

The semantic noise is a part of the 'planning' process that takes place in the mind of the communicator. The next stage of planning is semantic selection.

5. Semantic Selection

The meaning in the communicator's mind is to be replicated in the receiver's mind (Cartier and Harwood, 1953; Scott, 1977). For this purpose, the idea in the communicator's mind must be clear, complete and correct. This is possible only when he overcomes the semantic noise.

The process of semantic selection involves the communicator's ability to exploit the resource of the common code. He has to select those aspects of the meaning of the message which can be encoded. He has to face several alternatives before he chooses the one of them. The test of the choice lies in the efficiency of the code in representing the meaning. The context imposes several restrictions on the selection of the aspects of meaning. The communicator has to take into account these constraints as he has to take into account the codifiability. These constraints have demands on the communicator for selecting the semantic fields to which the words belong and also for selecting the grammatical patterns imposed on the words. A word has conceptual meaning as well as grammatical meaning. The conceptual meaning of the word is conventional whereas the grammatical meaning is the function of a grammatical rule applied in a grammatical construction.

The communicator has many semantic alternatives. If he chooses one alternative in one form, he checks up whether this form will fit into the existing context. This phenomenon is unobservable and different communicators face it in varying degrees. An experienced communicator has to face it in such a low degree that it becomes almost automatic on his part. In other words, he faces very few alternatives, overcomes the semantic noise almost automatically or instantaneously and does the semantic selection. Semantic selection is context oriented. The communicator selects the meaning which is contextually appropriate. Semantic selection is a very important part of the 'planning' process.

6. Encoding

The communicator encodes the message. Having realized the idea properly, he translates the idea or experience into arbitrary symbol system which is common to both the participants. This arbitrary symbol system is also called 'Signal' (Thomas and Fryer, 1988; Doctor and Doctor, 1977). This symbol system can either be verbal or non-verbal. It acts as an agent or means for the transmission of the message.

Encoding is the last stage of the 'planning'. It involves encoding meaning in the common code. In verbal communication this is a very complex process. It takes place in the brain of the communicator. It is an unobservable part of the planning process. To express an aspect of the meaning the communicator has to select from different alternatives. He has to decide the exact utterances before they are produced orally or in written form. The communicator must have the stock of the words besides the knowledge of grammar rules. Encoding is a psychological process. The communicator has to choose not only well-formed constructions but also contextually appropriate utterances.

Execution : Signal-1

7. Media and Channel Selection

A medium of communication is a means of communication which may be verbal or non-verbal, for example, language is the verbal means which is the most dominant of all the media of communication. The facial expressions, gestures etc. are the non-verbal means of communication. All these means or media of communication are suitable for communicating at different times and for different purposes. Therefore the communicator has to consider their relative merits and limitations before selecting one of them. Sometimes he has to choose multimedia to communicate effectively. For example, while speaking he uses verbal medium, but to make his speech effective he uses certain gestures, facial expressional etc. which are non-verbal media. Moreover, he has to select a certain channel to communicate effectively. A channel is the tone of the media used in communication. It may be formal or informal, polite or impolite. In fact, the tenor is encoded along with the meaning of the message. It is the part of the contextual meaning which is already encoded. The media should transmit not only the message but also the tenor of the message— the channel of communication. The communicator must know the relative merits and limitations of both the formal and informal channels of communication before selecting one which is appropriate for the kind of message and the context of communication. Thus, the communicator has to select suitable media and channel of communication. (See 'Media of communication', and 'Channels of communication' in Chapter 3, for further details). Media and channel selection is the first part of the 'execution' process in productive performance.

8. Media and Channel Noise

Media and channel noise refer to the interference that may occur in the medium and channel of communication through which the message is transmitted.

Each medium and channel has its noise and the communicator has to face and overcome it. He has to choose a certain medium to communicator. If this medium is verbal, it is either oral or written. The oral medium has its own interferences. Speaker's inattention, outside noises effecting some loss of information, receiver's lack of attention and co-operation, distance between the communicator and the receiver, lack of redundancy in the message, improper articulation and pronunciation of sounds etc. If written medium is used, it has its own noises, for example — illegible handwriting, smudged typewritten copy, lack of proper visual sensation, lack of the knowledge and skills of following certain formalities of written communication, long sentences, absence of the addressee, delay, lack of redundancy in the message etc. The channel noise refers to the interferences in the formal and informal channels of communication. If socially and culturally person has a high status but he has a low status in a business hierarchy, he may find it difficult to keep up the channel in business communication. Status barriers, age, personal attitudes, values and opinions, allness and closed-mindedness, halo effect, awe of authority etc. are the examples of channel noise. (See 'Barriers to communication' in Chapter 3, for further details.) The communicator has to face and overcome the media and channel noise. This is an important part of the 'execution' process in productive performance.

9. Signal-1 Transmission

Signal-1 transmission is the transmission of the encoded

message by the communicator to the receiver. On the part of the communicator, it is not just enough to prepare the message. The message must be transmitted to the reccivcr. It is not enough just to select a particular medium and channel. The selected medium and channel must be used for transmission. The communicator has to send the signal to the receiver without impairing it. There are different devices of transmitting the messages, for example, telephone, television, letters, etc. This is the final part of the 'execution' process.

Process - B: Receiver's Receptive Performance

Recognition : Signal-1

10. Signal-1 Reception

The message encoded by the communicator is received by the receiver. Sometimes, it may also happen that the message is transmitted to the receiver but it may not reach its destination. Signal-1 reception is the initial part of the 'recognition' process. The receiver must have sensations of the signals received. It also involves receiver's attention. He must sense it with attention. The communication process remains incomplete if the message encoded by the communicator is not received by the receiver. The signal-1 is an observable factor.

11. The Receiver's Need to Comprehend

This is a part of the receiver's 'recognition' performance. The receiver receives the message and tries to comprehend it if he feels the need of doing so. A person may receive a letter but he may not go through its contents if he doesn't feel the need of it. Unless there is a need to comprehend, the receiver won't attend to the message, and further, the message will not be interpreted, evaluated and remembered.

12. Media and Channel Noise

As mentioned earlier, each medium and channel has its

noise. The receiver has to face and overcome it. When the message is received by the receiver through some verbal or nonverbal media, he has to face some noise present in the media. It must be noted that the medium is selected by the communicator and not by the receiver. On the part of the communicator, a 'noise' may be created by misuse or mishandling of the medium. On the receiver's side the noise may occur if the receiver is incapable of interpreting the message encoded in a particular medium. The receiver has to face and overcome the media noise.

The receiver has to face and overcome the channel interference while receiving the message. The receiver has to receive and interpret the message which comes to him through whatever channel. The receiver has to face the channel noises like status barriers, age, awe of authority, closed-mindedness, personal attitudes values and opinions, halo effect etc. Facing and overcoming of the media and channel noise is an important part of receiver's 'recognition' performance.

13. Media and Channel Interpretation

Having overcome the media and channel noise, the receiver has to interpret and evaluate the message received from the communicator. The act of interpretation is a communication skill. The receiver must be capable of interpreting the message in such a way that the idea in the communicator's mind must be replicated in the receiver's mind. Besides it should bring some effect in the receiver's behaviour. The message is interpreted in the context of the communication event. Messages received through different media and channels can be rightly interpreted if the receiver knows about the media and channels and also about how these are used in varying contexts. (See 'Channels of Communication' and 'Media of Communication' in Chapter 3, for further details.) This is the final part of the receiver's 'recognition' performance.

Identification : Signal-1

14. Decoding

Decoding is the first stage of receiver's 'identification' performance. The receiver decodes the message received from the communicator. It takes place in the brain of the receiver. In decoding the message, the receiver has to translate the arbitrary symbols received from the communicator into the meaning for which those symbols stand. An arbitrary symbol does not have the meaning of itself. It simply stands for or represents the meaning. Different meanings can be attributed by the participants to the same word or signal. It may also happen that the different words or signals may stand for the same meaning. This is an unobservable factor.

15. Semantic Noise

The receiver has to face and overcome some interference with the identification of the intended meaning of the message. The message received from the communicator is in the symbol system which is generally common to both the participants. But, the participants may attribute different meanings to the same symbols; and sometimes different symbols may stand for the same meaning thirdly. The denotative meaning of a word or symbol can be different from the connotative meaning. 'A word can have different meanings to different people at different occasions' (Rodriques, 1992, 120). Thus, the possibility of different perception and realization of the meaning of the code is the semantic noise. The possibility of the attribution of different meaning to the code by the other participant creates doubt in the mind of the receiver regarding intended meaning of the code. The receiver has to face and overcome this noise. This is a part of receiver's 'identification' performance.

16. Semantic Selection

The receiver's semantic selection indicates his ability of

overcoming the semantic noise. The receiver overcomes the semantic noise and identities the intended meaning of the message received. This is the last stage of receiver's 'identification' performance in reception process.

Understanding : Signal-1

17. Comprehension of Idea/Experience

This is a part of the 'understanding' performance of the receiver. 'Understanding' is the final stage of receiver's reception process. The receiver overcomes the semantic noise and makes the semantic selection. Having accomplished this semantic selection, he co-ordinates the meaning and comprehends the message.

18. Receiver/Response

The receiver is the decoder of the message. He receives the message, decodes it, interprets it, evaluates it and sends the response. Immediately after comprehending the idea or experience, the receiver feels the need of reacting to it. The process of response begins from this reaction in the receiver's mind.

The receiver is the part of the communication event. He gives the feedback of the message to the communicator. From this stage, the receiver becomes the communicator for response and the original sender becomes the receiver of the feedback. As mentioned earlier, this feedback has an important role of leading the communication cycle to completion. The communication cycle comes to completion when the original sender receives decodes, interprets, evaluates and remembers the feedback.

Process - C: The Receiver's Productive Performance

Ideation: Signal-2

19. Need to Feedback

When the receiver comprehends the message, he reacts to

it in the context of the situation. This reaction leads him to realize some goal or purpose of communication. In order to get the purpose fulfilled, he feels the need to feedback. The receiver's clear perception of the goal determines the need to feedback. This is a part of the receiver's 'ideational' performance in production process.

20. Emergence of Idea or Impulse

After the goal is realized and the need to respond is felt the receiver initiates the appropriate semantic content which is his intention. This is how the idea or impulse emerges in his mind. This is very important part of the receiver's 'ideational' performance in feedback production process.

Planning : Signal-2

21. Semantic Noise

Semantic noise is the first stage in the receiver's 'planning' of the linguistic programme. It is an interference that the receiver has to face and overcome in determining the codifiability of the meaning of utterance. It is the receivers doubt about whether the code will be understood for its intended meaning. Just as the communicator faces semantic noise in the production process of signal-1, the receiver too has to face it in the production of signal-2 (feedback).

22. Semantic Selection

This is an important stage in 'planning' the linguistic programme. In semantic selection, the receiver has to select those aspects of the meaning of the message which can be encoded. The receiver overcomes the semantic noise through definite realization of a particular idea and its meaning clearly, completely and correctly. He selects the meaning which is contextually appropriate.

23. Encoding of Feedback

Encoding of feedback is the last stage of receiver's 'planning' performance in signal-2 production process. To encode the feedback, the receiver translates the meaning into arbitrary symbol system. In the process of feedback encoding, the receiver who has definite realization of an idea or experience, translates the idea or experience into arbitrary symbol system which is common to both the parties. This symbol system acts as an agent or means for the transmission of feedback to the original communicator.

Execution : Signal-2

24. Media and Channel Selection

The receiver has to think about the relative merits and limitations of the available media and channels and select those which are more appropriate than the others for communicating response to the original sender. This is the first stage in the 'execution' process of signal-2.

25. Media and Channel Noise

As described earlier, the media and channel noise refer to the interferences that may occur in the medium or channel of communication. The receiver has to overcome the media and channel noise and transmit the feedback to the original communicator. This is a part of the 'execution' process.

26. Signal-2 (Feedback) Transmission

Signal-2 transmission is the transmission of the encoded feedback to the original communicator. The receiver has to use the selected medium and channel for transmitting the feedback. If the feedback is not transmitted to the original communicator, the cycle of communication remains incomplete. This is the final stage of the 'execution' process.

Process - D: Communicator's Receptive Performance

Recognition : Signal-2

27. Signal-2 (Feedback) Reception

The message encoded by the receiver is received by the original communicator. Signal-2 reception by the communicator is the initial part of his 'recognition' performance.

28. Need to Comprehend the Feedback

This is a part of communicator's performance of 'recognition'. The communicator receives the feedback and tries to comprehend it if he feels the need of doing so.

29. Media and Channel Noise in Feedback Reception

This noise occurs in the medium and channel through which signal-2 is received by the communicator. The communicator has to face and overcome the media and channel noise. Facing and overcoming of this noise is an, important part of the communicator's 'recognition' performance.

30. Media and Channel Interpretation

Having overcome the media and channel noise in feedback reception, the communicator has to interpret and evaluate the signal-2 (feedback) received from the original receiver. Feedback received through different media and channels can be rightly interpreted if the communicator knows about the media and channels and also about now these are used in varying contexts. This is the last stage of the communicator's 'recognition' performance in reception process.

Identification : Signal-2

31. Decoding of Feedback

This is the first stage of communicator's 'identification'

performance. The communicator decodes the signal-2 (feedback) received from the receiver. In decoding the feedback, the communicator has to translate the arbitrary symbols received from the original receiver into the meaning for which those symbols stand.

32. Semantic Noise

The communicator faces and overcomes some interference with the identification of the intended meaning of the feedback received from the receiver. The feedback received by the original communicator is in the symbol system which is generally common to both the participants. But as it is mentioned earlier, different meanings can be derived from those symbols; and, sometimes, different symbols may stand for the same meaning. A meaning attributed to a symbol or to the unit of symbols by the communicator and the receiver can be different and this can lead to misunderstanding between both the participants. Different perceptions and understanding of the meaning leads to semantic noise. The possibility of the attribution of different meaning to the code by the other participant creates doubt in the mind of the communicator regarding intended meaning of the code. The communicator has to face and overcome this noise. This is a part of the communicator's 'identification' performance in reception process.

33. Semantic Selection

The communicator's semantic selection indicates his ability of overcoming the semantic noise. He overcomes the semantic noise and identifies the intended meaning of the feedback received. This is the last stage of the communicator's 'identification' performance.

Understanding : Signal-2

34. Comprehension of Idea/Experience

This is a part of the 'understanding' performance of the

communicator. Understanding of feedback is the last stage of communicators reception process. The receiver overcomes the semantic noise and makes the semantic selection. Having accomplished this semantic selection, he coordinates the meaning in the context of the communication event and comprehends the feedback. This is an unobservable factor in communication process. If the original communicator feels the need of reacting to the feedback he can again start the communicator cycle.

THE PROCESS OF COMMUNICATION

The idea or impulse in the mind of the communicator is the source of communication process. The communicator transmits the message to the receiver in order to get the response. The idea of the message in the mind of a communicator must be clear. If the communicator himself is not clear or certain about the message he has to transmit, his message will lack clarity and completeness. This lack of clarity and completeness is a kind of semantic noise. The receiver is likely to receive a wrong message if the communicator does not overcome the semantic noise. The semantic noise in the process of communication can be defined as any interference with the transmission or reception of the intended meaning by the communicator. "Noise is perhaps best defined as anything present in the perceived signal which was not present in the original message" (Wofford, 1977: 32). While receiving the message, the semantic noise occurs when the receiver's interpretation of the message is likely to be at variance with the intended meaning in the mind of communicator.

The semantic selection for the communicator means selecting the exact meaning without any ambiguity for encoding the message. For the receiver, semantic selection means selecting the appropriate meaning of the encoded message. For the receiver, semantic selection is possible only after decoding the message whereas for the communicator, it takes place before encoding the message. The study of the receiver and planning of the message are helpful activities to the communicator in his semantic selection. In case of the receiver, the meaning derived from the symbol system depends on his knowledge of the communicator, clarity of the encoded message and adequate knowledge of the media. The semantic selection will become a difficult task for the receiver if the communicator uses improper vocabulary and writing style.

Encoding means to prepare the message by covering the ideas into the code signals which are mutually understood by both the parties. The code signals are composed of a systematic arrangement of arbitrary symbols. After semantic selection, the communicator encodes his ideas for transmitting meaning to the receiver. The communicator or the sender of the message is also called the encoder because he encodes his ideas and impulses for transmitting them to the receiver. The translation of the perceptions into code signals is a formal expression of the message. The code signals or the symbol systems stand for an object or idea perceived by the communicator. Language consists of systematic structures of arbitrary sound symbols. When we write something we use the letters which stand for the consonants, vowels and dipthongs. Different arrangements of systematic sound structures stand for different ideas and objects. For example, the letters *e-a-r* stand for the organ of hearing and a different arrangement of the same letters, like *e-r-a* stands for a period in history. All the language communities adopt such arbitrary and conventional symbol systems for the transmission of meaning. The encoded signals have their arbitrary prearranged meanings. The arbitrarily accepted meaning has conventional usage in that language community.

The set of symbols used by the encoder is a type of code or language which must be arranged in a systematic structure so that the message does not get distorted. "In the process of encoding and decoding the message, language could act as a barrier to effective communication. The sender of the message has to make sure that the appropriate symbols are chosen to communicate the intended message so that there is no room for misinterpretation or confusion as the receiver decodes the message" (Sekaran, 1989: 104-105). The morphemes or the words are the symbols of language. These symbols are organized into correct structural patterns to avoid defects in the encoding process. Sometimes, the correct composition of symbols with accepted structural patterns appear to convey more than one meaning due to the conventional attribution of the various shades of meanings to the symbols used in the encoded message. The symbols must be selected carefully and arranged properly to avoid the ambiguitics.

The encoded message has two sides, the message perceived by the encoder and the message perceived by the decoder. As the sources of information are of infinite variety, the form and content of the message is encoded with a variety of systems and sub-systems. This enables different people to understand different meanings of the same encoded message at different times and situations.

Before encoding the message, the encoder must consider the multiple meanings of a symbol. Then he can select a particular meaning which is conventionally attributed to the symbol. Proper semantic selection is essential for the accurate replication of the ideas on the mind of the receiver. Still there remains uncertainty about the exact perception of the message by the decoder because of the multiple denotative and connotative meanings of the symbols used for encoding the contents of information.

Human perceptual mechanism is responsible for drawing different meanings from the conventional symbols and their systems of organization. Every individual has his own 'personal' perceptual lens. The experience of the same situation by two individuals brings quite different reactions. Research concerning variability of human perceptual mechanism concludes that individual needs are important determinants of his perceptions. The experience, education, training, intellectual and emotional set of two individuals are responsible for the perception of entirely different meanings of the same message.

Any of the verbal or non-verbal media of communication like face-to-face conversation, hand-gestures, eye-contact, touch, postures, letters, newspapers, memos, telegrams, telephone, books, periodicals, films, radio, television, etc., are used for the transmission of signals. These and innumerable other media are used to establish the channels of contact between the encoder and the decoder. There is an infinite variety of communication media and the communicator has to select any one or more of them. He has to select the most suitable medium available to him for his set communicative purpose and may even change it and take over another medium which is more effective when the situation changes. The correct choice of the medium which is suitable for the related encoding and decoding system can help to enhance the effectiveness of the communication process. In the selected media, there can be several other barriers to effective communication like defects in the devices used for communication, variety of interfering sounds, smudged typewritten copies, illegible handwriting, etc. The channel noise refers to misunderstanding caused by the defects in the hierarchical pattern of the organization. When the lines of upward and downward communication are very long, the message which passes through many levels of authority is likely to be delayed and distorted. In the selected channel, there can be a number of other barriers to communication, like loss of information, exaggeration, making understatements or overstatements, undercommunication, or over-communication, awe of authority, emotional states of mind, personal attitudes and opinions, closed-mindedness, inattentiveness, bypassing the authority, etc.

Thus, in this chapter we have defined 'Communication', evolved a comprehensive and precise 'Communication Cycle Model' and explained elaborately the 'Process of Communication'. In the next chapter we shall deal with the various aspects of 'Business Communication'.

References

Allen, Louis, 1958 : *Management and Organization*, Tokyo: McGraw-Hill Kogakusha Ltd.

Birrvenu, 1987. Definition of Communication, In Doctor, R. and A. Doctor, *Principles and Practice of Business Communication*, Bombay: Sheth Publishers.

Cartier, F.A. and K.A. Harwood,1953: Definition of Communication, *The Journal of Communication* November, 1953, In Doctor, R. and A. Doctor, 1977: *Principles and Practice of Business Communication*, Bombay: Sheth Publishers.

Catchcart,1966: Definition of Communication, In Verma, S.K. and N. Krishnaswamy, 1989: *Modern Linguistics: An Introduction*, Delhi: Oxford University Press.

Chappell, R.T. and Read, W.L. 1979: A Textbook of Business Communication, In Pal, R. and J.S. Korlahalli, *Essentials of Business Communication*, New Delhi: Sultan Chand & Sons.

Corder, S. Pit, 1973: *Introducing Applied Linguistics*, Penguin Books Ltd. U.K.

Davar, R.S., 1980: *Principles of Management*, Bombay ; Progressive Corporation Pvt. Ltd.

Davis, Keith, 1981: *Human Relations at work*, New Delhi : Tata McGraw-Hill Book Company.

Doctor, R. and A. Doctor, 1977: *Principles and Practice of Business Communication*, Bombay: Sheth Publishers.

Gerbner, 1956: Model of Communication , In Verma, S.K. and N. Krishnaswamy, 1989: *Modern Linguistics : An Introduction*, Delhi: Oxford University Press.

Hicks, H.G. and C.R. Gullet, 1974: *Modern Business Management*, New York: McGraw-Hill Book Company.

Little, Peter, 1977: Communication in Business in Doctor, R. and A. Doctor, 1977, *Principles and Practice of Business Communication*, Bombay: Sheth Publishers.

Lasswell, H. D., 1948: Model of Communication, In Verma, S.K. and N. Krishnaswamy, 1989: *Modern Linguistics : An Introduction*, Delhi: Oxford University Press.

Lyons, 1977: Definition of Communication, In Verma, S.K. and N. Krishnaswamy, 1989: *Modern Linguistics : An Introduction*, Delhi: Oxford University Press.

Miller, 1951: Definition of Communication, In Verma, S.K. and N. Krishnaswamy, 1989: *Modern Linguistics : An Introduction*, Delhi: Oxford University Press.

Newman, W. and C. Summer, 1977 : Process of Management, In Doctor, R. and A. Doctor, *Principles and Practice of Business Communication*, Bombay: Sheth Publishers.

Pal, R. and J.S. Korlahalli, 1979: *Essentials of Business Communication*, New Delhi: Sultan Chand & Sons.

Rai, V.S. and S.M. Rai, 1989: *Business Communication*, Bombay Himalaya Publishing Company.

Redfield, Charles E., 1954: *Communication in Management*, University of Chicago.

Richards, I.A., 1928: *Definition of Communication in The New*

Encyclopaedia Britannica, Vol-4, 1982 : The Fifteenth Edition. University of Chicago.

Rodriques, M.V., 1992: *Effective Business Communication*, New Delhi : Concept Publishing Company.

Scott, William, 1977: Organizational Theory, In Doctor, R. and A. Doctor, *Principles and Practice of Business Communication*, Bombay: Sheth Publishers.

Sekaran, U., Chicago, 1989 : *Organizational Behaviour*, New Delhi: Tata McGraw-Hill Publishing Co. Ltd.

Sharma, R.C. and K. Mohan, 1986 : *Business Correspondence and Report Writing*, New Delhi : Tata McGraw-Hill Publishing Company.

Tead, Ordway, 1959 : *Lecture at the School of Commerce, Accounts and Finance*, New York, Delivered on 11th February, 1959.

Terry, G.R. and S.G. Franklin, 1984: *Principles of Management*, Delhi: All India Traveller Bookseller.

Thomas, D.A. and M. Fryar, 1988: *Business Communication Today*, National Textbook Company, Lincolnwood Chicago, Illinois.

Vogel, R.A. and W.D. Brooks, 1977 : *Business Communication*, California: Cummings Publishing Company.

Wofford, J., Gerloff, E. and R. Cummuins, 1977: *Organizational Communication*, Tokyo : McGraw-Hill Kogakusha Ltd.

3

THE TENOR OF COMMUNICATION CHANNELS

"Let your likght so shine before men,
that they may see your good works and
glarify your Father in heaven."

—St. Mathew 5:16

Introduction

The channels of communication are the formal and informal ways of communicating with other people. A channel can be defined as the tone of media used in communication. It may be formal or informal, polite or impolite. In fact, the tenor is encoded along with the meaning of the message. It is the part of the contextual meaning, which is already encoded. The media should transmit not only the message but also the tenor of the message — the channel of communication. The communicator must know the relative merits and limitations of both the formal and informal channels of communication before selecting one which is appropriate for the kind of message and the context of communication. Every business organization has to maintain the internal as well as external communication. The internal communication is concerned with the transmission and reception of information, orders, suggestions, warnings, etc. within the organization, whereas the external communication is concerned with the transmission and reception of messages with the banks, government offices, insurance agencies, expert consultants, customers, export and import agencies, other business houses, etc. For both the internal and external communication, the company has to build up its communication systems. The organizational setting and the hierarchy of officers, authorities, clerks, operators, etc. form a context for all kinds of communication that takes place in the organization. In other words, we can say that the patterns of communication depend on the structure of the organization. If one has to understand and manage the 'How' of communication, he has to understand the informal and formal communication systems.

A communication channel runs along with the hierarchical line of authority in the organizational pattern which is designed with the view of carrying out organizational activities (Doctor, *et al*, 1977). In business organizations, usually the policy matters are decided by the Board of Directors and information regarding it is transmitted to the Managing Director who is supposed to execute the policy decisions. He issues the directives to the assistant departmental managers. The supervisors receive instructions from the assistant managers. In their turn, the supervisors pass the relevant instructions to their subordinate clerks or to the operators who are actually concerned with the operational function. When the information is communicated through the hierarchical lines of authority, it is called as 'formal communication'. The formal communication puts obligation on all those who communicate internally, to follow the prescribed channels and not to by-pass the authority. For example, a supervisor is not expected to communicate directly with the Managing Director. He must impart the message to the departmental manager who will pass it on to the Managing Director. These lines of authority are actually the channels of communication, which generally follow the upward, downward and horizontal directions. These lines must be kept as short as possible so that the original message does not get distorted. The communication channels can be divided under the following subheads :

1. Downward Channel,
2. Upward Channel,
3. Horizontal Channel,
4. Grapevine,
5. Consensus.

DOWNWARD CHANNEL OF COMMUNICATION

Downward communication is a supervisory communication, which is initiated by the upper management. It flows downward through the hierarchy of command. "Downward Communication in an organization means that flow is from higher to lower authority. This usually is considered to be from management as a group to first-level employees, but much of it also is within the various levels of management." (Davis, *et al,* 1989: 80). The effective dcwnward communication is crucial to the success of the organization. The management or the supervisory staff has to communicate with the subordinates in order to organize, coordinate, and direct the operational aspects of the organization. It is a very suitable channel to the organization in which the 'chain of command' is arranged in the ranks that are distinctly one below the other.

Media of Downward Channel

The downward flow of communication is dominated by oral media. It is convenient for a departmental head to give oral instructions and orders to the supervisor. Instead of issuing lengthy written instructions, the Managing Director usually convenes a meeting of the departmental managers in order to impart the essential directives or to gather their suggestions on various issues. Yet, the management may use both oral and written media for downward communication. There are various alternatives of communication media at the disposal of every management. Some typical alternative devices of communication media which are effective for downward communication are letters, circulars, notices, memos, company journals, video and audio recordings, telephone calls, meetings, face-to-face conversations, speeches to the employees and the posters.

Message Redundancy

It is found that using a combination of media tends to give best results because it increases the effectiveness of communication. When the same message is sent through more than one media, it creates redundancy. Redundancy is helpful in receiving and memorizing the messages. The busy people in business organizations require more message redundancy in order to act on the directives they receive from their superiors. On the other hand, the law of diminishing returns is also applicable to the organization in which the employees are overburdened with the overflowing downward communication. The increasing number of phone calls, memos, letters and meetings may make each employee much busier but as it requires adequate time to attend each of these messages, the employee will not be able to give proper justice to the every piece of work in his hand. Therefore, the management has to remember the proverb "More is better, up to a point".

The Objectives of Downward Channel

The superiors communicate with their subordinates with the objective that the employees may do their work with accuracy, neatness, sincerity, steadiness, thoroughness, honesty and punctuality. Katz and Kahn (1966: 239) ascribe five goals to communication. According to them, the downward communication purports to provide specific directives in respects regarding jobs, furnish information in respects of procedures and practices, give information regarding rationale of the job, provide knowledge to the subordinates of their performance, and furnish information to facilitate the indoctrination of goals. The superiors give specific directives or instructions to the employees that clarify the ways and procedures of the job performance. They expect that the employees should maintain the standards of work quality. The employee is instructed with the view that he does not commit mistakes in his operative or supervisory works. The downward communication is also required to check, assess and appreciate the performance of the employees.

The employees are also required to be well informed regarding the policies, procedures, rules and regulations of the organization and these are communicated through the downward channel. Frequently, some workers are found uncooperative and antagonistic. They may have little willingness to work and little interest in the associates. They may usually help the others, but grudgingly. They may be tolerant, but not friendly with their colleagues. In case of such employees, the downward channel is used to instruct and advise them. Sometimes, the superiors have to warn or reprimand the workers for their undesirable behaviour. Sometimes, the managements use the downward channel to motivate the employees for better productivity by imparting propaganda message. If a worker's comprehension of work details is inadequate, the supervisors use this channel to educate him and to assist him for the improvement of work.

Limitations of Downward Communication

It is essential to take care that the message is reliably transmitted through each level of the downward authority. Fred Luthans (1973: 249) observes that a communication system which merely provides specific directives regarding job instructions and organizational procedures and which does not give information in respect of the job performance or provide ideological type of information to facilitate indoctrination of goals, is conducive to an authoritarian atmosphere which adversely affects the upward and horizontal systems of communication as well. According to him attempts should be made to communicate to the subordinates the rationale for the job, the contribution of the job to the overall attainment of organizational goals and knowledge of job performance appropriately through the downward system of communication. However, there are certain difficulties that come in the way of achieving exact reproduction of the message from the source.

1. Delay: A message has to pass through a number of levels which involve the time limitations. When the line of downward communication is long, it take much time to reach the message at its destination. According to Galbraith (1956) and Dwivedi (1989), the problem of the flow of messages through communication channels is very acute especially in the Indian nationalized industrial enterprises controlled by a complex system of boards, corporations or government departments. The private sector has a major feature in the form of a short chain of command and fairly close relationships between the worker department and boss. It is the public sector which suffers under the impersonality and the frustration of an extremely distant boss.

2. Message Abbreviation: At each level, at least some part of the message is likely to be lost because of the lack of understanding or by shoddy handling. It also occurs that the participant abbreviates the message because he does not want to spend much time in transmitting all the contents of the message. The abbreviation of message has always an adverse effect on its fidelity.

3. Message Distortion: The downward communication has to go through some filter points, therefore, the chances for distortion are more. The more filtering points assure more distortion of the message. Slanting, interpreting, condensing and twisting are the possible ways to distort the message. The fidelity and authenticity of the message is affected both in quantity and quality by the successive judgments of the several members in the chain of communication.

4. Message Overload: A real danger of message overload is found in the business organizations which generate a very high volume of messages and impose them on the employees. It is like an electric circuit in a house which operates normally with the appropriate amperage demand. When the amperage demand overloads the circuit, a fuse blows. When the superiors overcommunicate with the subordinates, the balance of handling the messages is disturbed. The major cause of message overload is the increasing complexity of business life. Overload, according to Myers & Myers (1982), is the amount of message which exceeds the handling ability of the person or subsystem. It may either be the amount of data arriving to be processed; or it may be related to the complexity of the data assigned. Either quality or quantity can cause overload.

5. Incomplete Information: If an employee does not receive enough information to do the job, the possible outcomes are disfunctional. The incomplete information or the lack of sufficient instructions to the subordinates result in errors and unsatisfactory performance. The management then has to use up the additional time for correcting the errors and also for assessing them.

Essentials of Effective Downward Communication

1. The superior or the communicator must have a clear and complete idea of the message.
2. The communicator must be well informed about the policy decisions taken by the management in the past.
3. The communicator must know the past performance and achievements of the organization.
4. The communicator should have a clear idea of the aims and objectives of the organization.
5. Adequate volume and substance of the information must be well-organized before its transmission.
6. The substance of the message to be imparted must be prepared by keeping in view the competence and understanding ability of the subordinates.
7. The message must be channelised at proper time.
8. There should neither be over-communication nor under-communication.
9. The information must pass through the hierarchical structures of the organization. There should not be by-passing of any authority.
10. The lines of communication should be shortened in order to minimize the possibility of distortion.
11. The language in downward communication must be simple.
12. The subordinate employees must be conditioned to expect that most of the important messages regarding their work come to them from their immediate superior.

UPWARD CHANNEL OF COMMUNICATION

The behavioural scientists have shown the relationship between the communication and performance. The findings related with it have a tremendous effect on the managerial practices today. The business managements have become concerned more than ever before about what is going on at several levels below them. They have employed some fairly new techniques like open-door policy, suggestion schemes, etc. and they are still anxious to know any new or revolutionary method to get information from the lower ranks. It is generally found that the superiors are better talkers and writers than their subordinates. The subordinates are generally more cautious and less confident than their superiors when they are to pass some information through upward channel of communication.

The two-way flow of communication in any business organization is supported by efficient and effective upward communication. "Not only is an organization interested in the much of a message is received and acted on, but frequently the superiors want information about activities normally engaged in by subordinates". (Myers, *et al,* 1982: 136). The management can keep itself in touch with the needs, requirements, difficulties and grievances of the employees when it receives messages from the employees. The management is also helped to make sound decisions on the basis of the sufficient information secured from the subordinates. In order to improve the productivity, it is not necessary to put pressure on the employees or try to motivate the employees towards more loyalty and hardwork, or to put articles in the company magazines. But, on the other hand, it is necessary for the management to develop the procedure for encouraging upward communication to receive the information regarding production, quality-control, absenteeism, inventions, advertising, sales, complaints, research, etc., and constructive suggestions regarding various other matters that promote the welfare of the organization, etc. When the management receives information and suggestions from the subordinates regarding the matters given above and many other, it is able to issue the fresh directives to the employees regarding their work and procedures. The management can also get an idea of how the subordinates receive the directives and how the directives are followed. When the management realizes the problems, difficulties and grievances of the employees, they can try to find out the solutions. The upward communication gives an opportunity to the employee to express his frustrations of the work situation and helps him to relieve the pressures of the pent-up emotions, which are associated with their daily problems. Finally, it must be noted that the employees' sense of participation in the enterprise is enhanced by the upward communication.

Methods and Policies of Upward Communication

1. Meetings: The meetings with the employees are found to be very useful in building upward communication. The higher-ups are to encourage the employees to talk about their constructive suggestions, job problems and needs. They are also to be encouraged to express their views on whether the managerial practices help the job performance or interfere with it. The meetings enable the management to ascertain the worth of their directives imparted to the workers.

2. Counselling: The workers can be encouraged to seek the counsel of their superiors. When an employee comes to his superior with his personal or official problems and difficulties which adversely affect his working in the organization, the superior can earn the trust and confidence of the employee by encouraging him to talk freely and by taking firm steps to solve his problems. The managers get valuable information by the method of counselling, if they can successfully encourage the employees to talk freely about themselves and also about the organization.

3. An Open-Door Policy: The purpose of an open door policy is to remove the blocks in the way of upward communication. The employees are encouraged to walk into the manager's cabin without any hesitation for having a problem and without being afraid that they would invite disfavour of their manager. Though the open-door policy has good purpose, it is very difficult to be implemented because of the socio-psychological barriers that come between the manager and the employees.

4. Correspondence: The employees are encouraged to write letters. First the management sends enquiry letters to the employees and the replies are encouraged. This is a direct and personal way for the employees to transmit the information to the management.

5. Participation of Social Gatherings and Group Events: Some casual events provide opportunities for arranging social gatherings in different departments of the firm. The informal atmosphere during the sport events, picnics and parties offer spontaneous information from the employees to the firm.

6. Reports: The management may ask the subordinates to present the reports. The reports are the basic tools used by the management in decision-making. In the large business organizations, where a large number of employees are engaged in different activities, the reports from the subordinates are extremely important and indispensable for the success of managerial functions. As the senior managers cannot keep a personal watch over all the business activities, he requires reports about the progress of the work done by the employees.

7. Suggestion Boxes: The employees are encouraged to drop their suggestions and new ideas in the suggestion boxes. The managements which are aware of the fact that the small problems and complaints of the employees that go unnoticed have way of mushrooming into major problems, encourage the employees to drop their complaints also in the suggestion boxes. These suggestions or complaint boxes are placed at some convenient places in the firm. These boxes are opened at regular intervals. The management is supposed to reward the positive and constructive suggestions.

Problems of Upward Communication

1. Positive Encouragement: The upward communication goes to minimum if the management does not positively encourage it. What goes unrewarded does not thrive in the organization. Lack of rewards for employee feedback stands as a problem in the upward communication. The management must take positive action to initiate the employees to communicate upward. Simply waiting for the employees to come in with some information is of no use.

2. Concealing Unfavourable Facts: The employees tend to conceal their difficulties and the on-the-job problems from their superiors. Especially, they conceal the ignorance and inability from the boss. They feel the risk in imparting unfavourable information to the boss because of the belief that the surest way to get ahead is to agree with the boss. 'Deliberate distortions in organization are usually based on the needs and ambitions of certain organization members in relation to others in the chain of command. For example messages set to a manager may combine the basic information with what the subordinate thinks the manager wants to hear' (Myers, *et al*, 1982: 123).

3. Delay, Distortion and Filtering: Usually, the upward communication is subject to delay, distortion and filtering, especially when the lines of communication are long. Each level in the hierarchy is reluctant to take a problem to the higher authority, because in sodoing, he is afraid that he may lose the favour of his superior. At each level, an effort is made to solve the problem. All this results in delay, distortion and filtering.

4. Bypassing and Suspicion: Some workers become so bold in the process of upward communication that they by-pass their immediate-superior authority, which results in the bypassed authority's getting suspicious about the intentions of the subordinate (Doctor and Doctor, 1977; Pal and Korlahalli, 1979).

5. Poor Listening: Poor listening skills of the superior often discourage the speaker to communicate his message. Listening does not mean just hearing a message. It requires careful attention and exact decoding of the signals received from the speaker. If the superior goes on shuffling the papers while listening to his subordinate, he pays divided attention to the speaker's message. This divided attention is usually interpreted as his lack of interest in the message. The superior's divided attention can adversely affect the superior-subordinate relationship. Poor listening skills of the superior does not allow him to attend and interpret the message accurately. If the superior does not develop his listening skills, it will surely minimize the opportunity for both the superior and subordinate to benefit from the upward communication.

6. Communicating Criticism: The subordinates carefully screen or filter the information before transmitting it to the persons of a higher status. It is very difficult for any subordinate to communicate criticism on the superiors and management policies.

Effective Upward Communication

The following are the essentials of effective upward communication:

1. The lines of communication should be kept as short as possible to avoid the distortion by filtering, screening and editing.
2. To find out how employees feel about their jobs, it is always convenient to conduct the employee attitude surveys.
3. There should be a formal system to handle the suggestion objectively and seriously.
4. Positive efforts must be taken by the superiors to eliminate the fear and awe of the authority from the mind of the workers.
5. Constructive suggestions for the improvement of the organization must be suitably rewarded. If the information transmitted by the employees is ignored, they will quickly abandon this channel. Therefore, the upward communication must be reinforced and rewarded with adequate attention.
6. The management must ensure the workers that they feel genuinely concerned for the problems and grievances of the subordinates.
7. It is essential to build a corporate atmosphere of trust. There must be mutual trust in the relationship between the superiors and the subordinates. If the workers think that they are going to be rewarded with punishment for their feedback, they will never provide it.

HORIZONTAL OR LATERAL CHANNEL

The complexity of today's business organizations has made 'horizontal communication' a vital subject for management studies. It takes place between and among the people who belong to the same level of hierarchy. We have now realized that the survival of any modern business organization depends on the degree of specialization achieved by it. Because of this specialization existing in the business organizations today, each unit of the same organization is differentiated from others. The horizontal channel of communication is the primary method of coordinating inter-dependent units and departments. Horizontal communication studies have shown that managers frequently engage in horizontal communication. Wickesberg (1968: 253-62) in his study of communication networks found that two-third of management communications were either horizontal or diagonal while merely one-third was vertical within their chain of command. To keep the organization running efficiently, it is essential to coordinate or integrate all its diverse units. For example, if the sales manager has to give exact date of delivery to the customer, he must get certain information from the head of the stores and packing department as well as from the head of the department of transportation. Horizontal or lateral communication, if effectively used, socialises people into the system and gives them a sense of belonging to the organization. "It is necessary for job coordination with people in other departments. It also is done because people prefer the informality of lateral communication, rather than going up and down the more official chain of command" (Davis, *et al*, 1989: 89).

Although many business organizations generally consider horizontal communication to be unproductive; it is, in fact, the most productive form of communication because almost all of the employees exchange information regarding different aspects of the company with their fellow-employees through horizontal channel. Secondly, it is possible for them to judge their performance by comparing it with the performance of the other employees in the organization. But the autocratic organizations tend to discourage the horizontal communication. Such managements are afraid that the employees may get friendly and their union may pose some problems to the company. They believe only in the downward communication which is dominated by the directives, orders and warnings. They should realize the role of horizontal communication in preventing the inter-departmental conflicts which may arise due to slanting, misconceptions, distortion of message, misunderstanding or lack of understanding. In order to facilitate the process of problem-solving and to promote friendly and cooperative spirit among the employees of the organization, the horizontal channel must be used effectively.

Methods of Effective Horizontal Communication

1. Telephone and Face-to-Face Communication: The telephone conversations and face-to-face conversations are the primary means of horizontal communication which facilitate the coordinating activities of the organization. The telephonic communication cannot be as effective as the face-to-facc communication because people cannot use facial expressions and gestures in telephone conversations. But it is possible to make it effective through modulations of voice.

2. Meetings: The meetings of the employees belonging to different departments is a means of achieving horizontal communication. It can bring about the organizational integration. The activities and discussions in the meeting can be well-directed if the purpose of meeting is specific and the agenda is strictly followed. The meetings help to heighten the team-spirit and assure the necessary information flow by encouraging two-way communication. The horizontal communication can also be channelised by the meetings of the standing committees which are designed to integrate the inter-dependent departments. As the employees are associated with the decision-making process of the committee, their relationships are improved. The useful knowledge and experience of the employees is mutually shared by them. If a committee consists of departmental heads, it promotes coordination, the spirit of understanding and cooperation.

3. Written Media: The letters and memos are also used for horizontal communication.

GRAPEVINE

What is Grapevine?

Grapevine is an informal communication network which ignores formal channels of communication and spreads rumours and gossips at all levels of the organization. "Gossip, hear-say, rumours go to make up that 'Personal communication' that we call grapevine" (Doctor, *et al*, 1977: 41). Although every business organization has its formal channels of communication, the informal channel of communication called grapevine also operates in it. "In addition to the organized formal channels of communication, there is a secondary channel of personal, informal communication in every organization. It has no definite pattern or direction though it is largely horizontal". (Rai, *et al*, 1989: 25). It can be easily found that a large portion of the communication in almost every business house is not formal or preplanned. The employees communicate through informal channel as they do their jobs. It is neither preplanned nor deliberately motivated by the management. It is neither written nor documented or recorded. Therefore, it refers to any communication that takes place outside the prescribed and preplanned channels of formal communication. It is not set with the lines of organizational hierarchy. As it has no set rules and regulations, it is not confined to a particular direction. It just spreads like grapevine.

Significance of Grapevine

Though the structure of grapevine is not so well-defined as that of the formal channels, it should not be taken for its weakness. The messages flowing through grapevine have greater speed than that of the messages flowing through the formal channels. The grapevine may carry equally vital message through it for the achievement and success of the organization. It is not correct to underestimate the grapevine by saying that the vital messages pass only through the authorized, formal channels. On the other hand, though the formal channels are systematic, preplanned and documented, it is authority-laden. It can never be as speedy and spontaneous as the grapevine. The employees communicate through grapevine, not because they are compelled to communicate but because they earnestly want to communicate with their associates.

The method of formal written communication is slow and expensive method of information transmission. The grapevine, on the other hand, is non-expensive and most rapid oral method of transmitting the information to the communication receivers. Being a multi-directional channel, grapevine is a convenient means to cross the hierarchical boundaries. The grapevine is not restricted to any particular line of hierarchy or to the vertical and the horizontal directions. It can flow wherever the participants wish it to flow, therefore, the manager can use the properly cultivated grapevine in dealing with the problems that require crossing the boundaries between the departments.

Grapevine originates from the psychological need of the employees to talk about their jobs and their associates as the subjects of their main interest. The absence of grapevine surely creates the dull, sick and unfriendly atmosphere in the organization. Grapevine is also described as the barometer of public opinion in the organization. If the manager is sensitive to it, he can gather information about the ideas, opinions, attitudes and interests of the employees.

The grapevine gives an opportunity to the employees to let off the suppressed air of anxiety, worries and frustration. When they talk about their associated, they get emotional relief. The fact that the employees talk about their associates or that they have the interest in their associates is a proof of the high morale. Thus, the grapevine not only promotes unity, integrity and solidarity of the organization but it also helps to raise the morale of the employees.

Limitations of Grapevine

1. The grapevine may carry some degree of error in it.
2. The baseless, imaginary and non-factual messages may prove harmful to the organization.
3. Often the grapevine is fed with self-serving information by the employees. They add to the facts rather than simply report.
4. The grapevine often carries incomplete information which leads to misunderstanding of the receiver.
5. The communicator does not take the responsibility of the message.
6. Sometimes the grapevine spreads the message so swiftly that it causes damage to the organization.

How to use the Grapevine Effectively?

The management can use grapevine to supplement the formal channels of communication. Though it carries some degree of error and distortion, efforts can be made to correct it. Ignoring the grapevine is nothing but to ignore a valuable source of communication. The management can eliminate its negative consequences and, at the same time, it can nourish its positive benefits. The managers have to learn to manage and control it.

1. The management can open up all the channels of organizational communication to present the facts positively before the employees and thereby can fight the negative messages with positive weapons of facts and figures.
2. Better job design and better quality of work life can easily bring the grapevine under the control of the management.
3. It also prevents the boredom, idleness and suspicions among the employees.
4. The negative consequences of the grapevine can be easily eliminated if the management is successful in creating trust-relationship with the employees.
5. The rumorus flourish beyond limits when the

employees are not well-informed by the management regarding the policies, objectives and the work procedures of the organization. The inadequate access to information and the feeling of insecurity are the reasons behind the negative outcomes of the grapevines. The managers but give their employees an adequate access to information and the feeling of security.

6. The rumours spread when the situations are unpredictable, unstructured, unplanned and are beyond the control of a person or the persons who are involved in them. Therefore, the best way to manage and control it is to provide accurate and substantial information of the situation to the employees. The managers should pick up the false rumours and dispel them by providing correct information.
7. Before taking any decision or action, the managers must consider its possible effects on the informal groups and systems in the organization.
8. The management can use the grapevine as a barometer of the public opinions in the organization or to feel the pulse of the employees in a particular situation. This will surely help them to take right policy decisions.
9. In the formal activities of the organization, the management should avoid threatening the informal groups which are responsible in spreading the grapevine effectively.
10. The management should find out the people in the informal groups who are more active on grapevine. These people should be accurately and adequately informed so that the false rumours causing excitement and insecurity do not spread among the employees.
11. The management should remember that the workplace community is maintained not only by the work itself but also by the informal human relationships. Therefore, the manager should honestly try to integrate their interests with those of the informal groups.

CONSENSUS

What is Consensus?

The concept of consensus has become quite familiar and desirable means of informal communication not only in the political fields but also in the commercial spheres as well. It is a common agreement of opinion on a given problem among the majority of people in a group or community. "When there is common agreement of opinions among a group of persons, it is known as Consensus" (Doctor, *et al,* 1977: 43). "A general agreement of opinion is known as consensus" (Rai, *et al,* 1989: 24). The board meetings of commercial organizations take certain decisions through consensus. Sometimes, merely a copy of resolution is circulated among the members of a particular group to get their approval. When the decisions are taken unanimously, the unity and uniformity of the group is recognized. It projects a good image of the business house and the status of the organization is raised. It also suggests high morale of the management to the employees, customers, shareholders and other people. Consensus does not mean that there exists no opposite views among the members of the group. Of course, perfect unanimity should not be expected because it cannot exist. As consensus does not imply perfect unanimity, it implies that the majority of people express a particular view which is accepted as the consensus by the members including those who actually oppose it. The dissent of the opposition is sacrificed in the interests of the harmony among the members or in the larger interests of the organization.

The consensus is sought through consultation. The problem is presented before the board meeting by the chief of the management in the form of the proposal or resolution. The problem is analyzed and some additional information regarding it is also collected. The chief listens to the divergent views and opinions of the members. He tries to discuss the issue with every individual member. At last, he is confirmed about the solution which is most likely to be accepted by the majority.

Significance of Consensus

1. The consensus communication projects a good image of the management.
2. The essential image of the management presented through consensus strengthens the confidence of the employees in their superiors.
3. There can be little or no chance for conflict among the employees because the instructions issued by the directors never conflict with each other.
4. The consensus is always based on the attitude of mutual respect which enables the members to accept and support the views of each other.
5. The decisions of consensus are promptly accepted by the members because they are derived after mutual consultations.
6. The process of consensus ultimately leads to an unquestioning acceptance of the authority of the chief.
7. The trust of the members in their chief help to avoid the splits and conflicts between the majority and the opposition.

Limitations of Consensus

1. While the superiors receptively listen to the ideas of the subordinates, the latter sometimes undermine the authority of the superiors.
2. The dissents are never encouraged. The views and opinions of the minority opposition are not attended.
3. A member of the group can be forced to accept the view which he does not hold.
4. A member who is accustomed to being consulted may misunderstand the chief if the latter fails to consult him.

Note : Please see the references of this Chapter at the end of Chapter 6.

4

THE VERBAL MEDIA OF COMMUNICATION

"To everything there is a season
time for every purpose under heaven."

—Ecclesiasfes 3:1

ORAL MEDIA OF COMMUNICAION

Nature and Significance of Oral Media

Our spoken words have graeater power than that of the sword taken out of a scabbard. The speeches given by Voltaire and Montesque gave birth to the world famous French Revolution. "Oral communication is one of the most important qualities of every manager for oral communication is an inseparable part of any business", (Michael, 1992: 28). The words can encourage the people to take over and complete the tasks beyond their ability. On the other hand, the words can dis-spirit and discourage the people from doing even their routine jobs. Oral communication is vital to human relationships in every business organization as well as in any other social organization. The employees disclose their feelings to one another, they exchange their views and share each other's knowledge and experiences. Of course, there are many people who do not go about belabouring the world with their personal thoughts, feelings and ideas. But, as even the verbal battles are useful when they serve to clarify certain messages, there is no need to speak about the importance of talking out the differences by breaking the barriers of silence. We talk with other people for many purposes. We may talk in order to escape boredom, to get acquainted with a newcomer, to warn the subordiate about his misbehaviour, to suggest novel ideas to the superior, to instruct the workers, and for a number of other purposes. Much of the professional and business communication through oral media takes place between two people. The success of the business organization depends to a large extent on managing the formal and informal oral communication between two persons. It is due to this fact, much face-to-face business communication takes place between two persons. The time factor and other difficulties that come in the way of arranging for a small group of busy people to take part in a meeting is also an important reason behind giving stress on the oral communication between two people. "Much of the oral communication that goes on in business is informal. Primarily, it is face-to-face communication that takes place whenever people get together" (Lesikar, *et al*, 1989: 615). In addition to informal conversation that goes on in business various kinds of formal oral communication also takes place. For example, the business people have to make formal presentations in speeches, oral reports, lectures etc. They have to conduct and participate in the committees, conferences, workshops, seminars and interviews.

Effective Oral Communication

1. Pronunciation: All the language units must be pronounced properly and clearly. The message cannot be intelligible without proper articulation of sounds. Sometimes, it happens that a person who is able to articulate a sound properly is unable to pronounce the words correctly. The words in English language must be stressed on the exact syllables.

2. Clarity, Conciseness and Completeness: It is essential that the message should be brief and concise, but complete in every respect. The brevity should not be achieved at the cost of clarity and completeness. Too much talking may lead to misunderstanding and overcommunication, but too little talking can lead to partial understanding and undercommunication.

3. Vocabulary: The communicator must have a good vocabulary. He should use choicest words to convey correct meaning. If the person who communicates orally has inadequate vocabulary, the listener will receive incorrect and confused meaning.

4. Self-Confidence: If the communicator lacks self-confidence, it is likely that he will not be able to impress the message on the listener. He must have a sufficient knowledge of the subject on which he has to talk. Secondly, he must plan his message carefully before imparting it to the receiver. The logical sequence of various ideas in the message is an outcome of the systematic organizing and planning the message. Adequate planning, preparation and organization of the message helps the speaker to raise his morale and self-confidence.

5. Variations in the Intonation Patterns: There are three intonation patterns, viz (i) the rising pitch, (ii) the falling pitch, and (iii) the dividing pitch. It is essential to use the correct pitch of sound. The variations in the pitch of sounds can help the speaker to create interest and hold the attention of the listeners.

6. Tone and Style: The message must make appeal not only to the intellect but also to the heart of the listener. The words impart the intended meaning when they are spoken with the tone and style that suit the occasion. The 'tone' of the voice gives the listener an idea about the 'feeling' associated with the words.

Advantages of Oral Communication

1. Adjustment of Message: The speaker gets immediate feedback from the receiver which helps him to find out how the receiver receives the message and how he reacts to it. The immediate feedback not only lets the communicator to know the kind of response from the receiver but it also helps him to modify his message in such a way it becomes readily and favourably acceptable to the receiver.

2. Immediate Clarifications: The communicator can clarify certain ideas in his message which are not properly understood by the receiver or which might leave some doubts in his mind. These doubts or the queries (in the mind) of the receiver arise from the defective message and these are communicated to the receiver in the form of feedback.

3. Time: Oral messages can be transmitted through telephone almost immediately whereas the written message take more time to reach up to the receiver by post. The written message takes comparatively longer time because it may require consulting, dictating, drafting, typing, posting, etc., which the oral transmission does not require. When immediate action is required, the oral communication is the best media.

4. Persuasion and Control: The speaker can judge the replies of the other party and can change his arguments in such a way that thereby he can influence the attitudes, feelings, opinions and beliefs of the receiver. The oral directives and instructions are effective in controlling the employees and the situations in order to ensure the fulfilment of the objectives.

5. Formality: Oral communication is less formal than the written communication. Informal talks can help in building friendships and personal relations between the communicator and the receiver.

6. Cost: Oral communication is not as costly a process as that of the written correspondence, especially when the message is to be communicated within the organization.

7. Group Communication: Oral communication is a convenient and reliable media for communicating in the committee, conferences and meetings where a number of people come together for discussion.

Disadvantages of Oral Communication

1. Future Reference: The oral message cannot be referred back in future if they are not tape-recorded. As compared to the written messages, oral messages do not constitute permanent record. Therefore, it has little or no value for legal procedures. It cannot become legal evidence in case of future disputes or lawsuits.

2. Speaker's Preparedness: Oral communication cannot be good and effective if the communicator is not a good speaker. He requires to be lively, enthusiastic, vital, earnest and keenly interested in the subject.

3. Lengthy Message: Oral communication is not a suitable media for any lengthy official message that constitutes minute details.

4. Distortion: The oral message is more likely to be received in a distorted meaning by the receiver due to his misunderstanding and misinterpretation of it.

5. Retaining the Message: It is found that people tend to have trouble in recalling correctly and completely the main ideas of the factual details which are communicated to them orally. Due to the imbalanced mental state of a listener or due to the listening barriers, the receiver may not understand the message completely and he may even forget the major part of message after a long time.

WRITTEN MEDIA OF COMMUNICATION

Nature and Significance of Written Media

The old-style business entrepreneurs were not particularly concerned with labour relations, advertising, quality control, income taxes, sales taxes, engineering, technology and many other aspects of modern business. They would converse with their employees almost daily and instruct them regarding the job requirements. The number of the employees working in the business houses of those days was relatively less as compared to that of the today's large business organizations. They could easily inspect, direct and judge the work of the employees. But today, the business houses require a team of specialists and each one of them is trained, experienced and most qualified person to carry out his specific assignment. They may be research people, purchasing agents, scientists, technicians, personnel people, sales executives, accountants, psycho-analysts, tax consultants, traffic experts, physicians, etc. These specialists and experts have to communicate their ideas to one another and also to the management. They assist the management in decision-making process. Their findings, advice and instructions are vital to business success. This flow of infomation which helps to operate the business is necessary to be maintained through written media because of the mounting complexity of business activities. The written media is like the human sensory organs and memory power which receives, analyses and records the information for the purpose of decision-making in future. Especially, the written reports are like the memory of the business. The management scrutinizes the information, acts on some part of it and stores up the remaining of it for future reference.

Written media helps to coordinate the knowledge and work of the staff specialists and the research specialists. The increasing research activities in every phase of business and the development of large organizational structures has made written media almost indispensable in every business house. The management has developed itself in every business house. The management has developed itself as a professional occupation. They need accurate written information to carry out their managerial duties related to different business and professional activities, which can be summed up under the following heads:

> Sales, Quality-Control, Accounting, Purchase, Wages and Salary, Complaints, Machinery, Production, Absenteeism, Company Relations, Supplying Agencies, Raw Material Storage, Overtime, Retirements, Shipments, Transportation, Appraisal and Assessment of The Employees' work, Education and Training of The Employees, Advertising, Grievances and Adjustments, Disciplinary Actions, Credit, Finance, Trade-Union Relations, Sales Reports, Market Surveys, Requirement of New Branches or Plants, Material Handling, Packing, Customer Study, Compensations, Productivity, Motivation of The Employees and Customers, Product-Analysis, Business Research, etc.

The Art of Written Communication

A communicator who aspires to get mastery over the

techniques of written communication, must keep his writing tools in enough of work and practice. "Good writing is based on clear objectives, effective audience analysis and effective structure" (Munter, 1987: 144). The action-oriented people may have the ability to get the things done, but they may find it difficult to put their thoughts in written words because they occupy themselves in their selected activities rather than in the practice of writing. Such a manager may have the ability to think logically and clearly and he may express his thinking through oral media. He may organize, analyze and evaluate the ideas of his own and those of others also, and he may really deserve to acquire the mastery of written media, but he would certainly require some of his devotion, time and practice to acquire it.

Everybody possesses the tools of the written media, but they have to learn to make effective use of their priceless possession. The tools of written media are used by all the individuals in the field of business, industry, science and education. These tools of written media are as follows;

(a) Memory
(b) Imaginative power
(c) Power of observation and study
(d) Units of language like words, phrases, sentences, etc.,
(e) Ability of thinking
(f) Ability of collect and analyze the information, and
(g) Ability of writing

A good writer is an artist who knows how to write a specific message effectively by making use of the above mentioned tools. He must keep his tools in good working order. It usually takes years of struggle and hardwork to learn and master the art of writing.

A wide and vast storehouse of information is the capital of writers' trade. It gives him the depth, perspective, balance and insight into the subject matter. He should always be alert to all the sources of information, which are related to his selected field of knowledge. He should also read widely the literature which does not belong to his limited field of specialization. For example, a manager must know broadly the socio-economic trends, problems and changes; the labour problems, government regulations, rules of the taxation, changes in the government policies, etc. Good reading indirectly helps to improve the skill of writing. A good writer can judge and evaluate the written message with ease and accuracy.

Besides reading, the business correspondent or the reporter should try to find a world of information with an inquiring mind and discerning eye. He can learn a great deal by asking some questions to the workmen performing an operation. They can give a piece of practical solution to his problem. Some of the basic problems that confront the business and industry can be understood when one tries to do things for himself and works with his own hands. The main purpose of written communication is to move, motivate and mould the minds and behaviour of the people in the organization. It is necessary for the communicator to study the people with whom he works. Finally, he should know the history, policies, procedures, hierarchy, regulations and customs of the company in which he works. It must be remembered that the art and skill of writing depends on the competence and knowledge of the communicator. Besides all this, the communicator should prevent his feelings from dictating his thinking and should organize his thoughts which are based on factual information.

Advantages of Written Media

1. Permanent Record for Reference: Written message can be kept in files as a permanent record of the general affairs, transactions and agreements of the business organization. It remains as an evidence of the company's performance which is useful for future reference. It forms a basis for new policy decisions and also for the fresh measures for the development and expansion of the business.

2. Legal Evidence: Written message provides tangible evidence of the agreements signed between the two parties.

It also gives a proof of the stages in which the transaction was carried out. It can show how the mistakes were committed in carrying out the transactions by either of the parties involved in it.

3. Accuracy: Usually, the written messages are organized more carefully than the spoken messages. The communicator uses standard language and tries to avoid colloquial words and expression. As compared to oral messages, the written massages are more accurate in grammatical structures. Accuracy in language helps to prevent any misunderstanding or misinterpretation of the message.

4. Lengthy and Complicated Messages: Written media is especially more suited for lengthy and complicated messages. The receiver can read it repeatedly till he properly understands it. Secondly, it assures retaining every vital details of the lengthy and complicated message.

5. Correspondence: Postal correspondence has given a really wide access to written media. This facility is available to almost all the communicators and receivers in the nooks and corners of the world.

Limitations of Written Media

1. Access of Literates: The access of the written media is limited to the literates only. There are millions of illiterate people who cannot use this media.

2. A Costly and Time-Consuming Process: In an organization, a number of people get involved in the process of collecting information, consulting, drafting, typing and posting the messages. It takes the total cost of an average business letter to not less than thirty rupees. Secondly, the oral message reaches almost instantaneously on the telephone, whereas a letter may reach to the receiver after 2/3 days. The communicator has to wait for the reply from the receiver. In oral communication, the feedback is almost immediate.

3. Formalism: Usually, the written communication is more formal, and rigid than the oral communication.

Note : Please see the references of this Chapter at the end of chapter 6.

5

THE NON-VERBAL MEDIA OF COMMUNICATION

"Then He put His hands on his eyes again and made him look up. And he was restored and saw everyone clearly."

— Mark 8:25

NATURE AND SIGNIFICANCE OF NON-VERBAL MEDIA

A noted anthropologist Ray Birdwhistell (1970) estimates that the non-verbal element accounts for 65 per cent of what gets communicated when we speak. The verbal media can be used to communicate almost any thought, feeling or idea; but the non-verbal media has comparatively very limited range. Especially, it communicates feelings of likings and dislikings and reinforces the feelings expressed through verbal media. Occasionally, it contradicts those feelings which are expressed verbally by the communicator. It is less conscious and deliberate; rather, it is more subtle and instinctive than the verbal communication. "Seven percent of the meaning in a face to face situation is derived from word symbol, 38 per cent from voice tone and inflection and 55 per cent from bodily movements, particularly facial and gestures" (Lesikar, *et al*, 1989 : 646).

There are five major forms of non-verbal media like, spatial, kinesic, chronemic, paralingual and artifactual.

1. Proxemics (spatial)
2. Kinesics

    Facial expressions,

    Postures,

Body movements,
Gestures,
Eye contact,
Haptics (touch),

3. Chronemics (temporal)
4. Paralingual (vocal cues)
5. Artifacts (objective language).

These different forms of non-verbal media help us to judge the intensity of feelings and also the contradictory feelings which contradict the verbal message of the communicator.

Charlie Chaplin, Harold Lloyd, Harry Langdon, Buster Keaton reached the non-verbal communication media to almost perfection in their own silent movies. Though each of these silent comedians had their own style of wordless communication, they were all able to communicate the complete sequence of human behaviour along with the isolated ideas. The managements and the employees may not be as well-skilled in silent, wordless or non-verbal communication as these actors, but much of the communication which affect their behaviour in the organization is never verbalized. They transmit their messages by their movements like a smile, frown, handshake etc. The non-verbal media is the most suitable means for the expression of the emotional messages. The manager's view regarding the suggestions of the employees become more clear by his attention and actions rather than by his words of encouragement for dropping the suggestions. The employees are motivated more by the manager's actions than by his words. Jurgen Ruesch and Weldon Kees (1956) say that we communicate non-verbal messages in three languages; sign language, action language and object language. Sign language is deliberately used to replace words, numbers or punctuation marks by the gestures. Action language includes all the movements which we do not use exclusively as signals i.e. walking, running, eating etc. Most of these actions are intentional non-verbal stimuli. Object language can be either intentional or non-intentional display of material things, i.e. clothing, jewellery, art objects. All these non-verbal languages help the communicator to talk without words. They give us the cues for interpreting human behaviour, cues for transmitting messages and the clue about intentions, emotions, views, social status and personalities of the people.

Often we spend a great deal of time in organizing verbal messages. It indicates that effective oral or written communication requires conscious efforts. We spend years together in learning how to read, write and speak. Non-verbal communication does not require that much conscious learning efforts. It is usually learnt by imitation. It also happens that many people are often unaware of their own non-varbal communication behaviour. Silence is a form of non-verbal communication which usually goes unnoticed. Manager's silence over the achievements and hardwork of an employee makes the latter feel discouraged.

KINESIC MEDIA

1. Facial expression
2. Posture
3. Body movements
4. Gestures
5. Eye-contact
6. Haptics

1. Facial Expression: Face is the best non-verbal conveyor of the message among all the other non-verbal aspects of kinesic importance, "Our face and eyes are probably the most expressive parts of our body" (Munter, 1987: 26). There are four component parts of the face, which are capable of independent movements. These movements produce a number of signals and they carry a variety of messages. We can look into the face of a person to know his real sentiments and reactions. One cannot command the expression on his face as one can command his language.

Face can be divided into four parts: (i) upper face, which includes eybrows and forehead; (ii) middle face, which indludes the eyes, eyelids and foot of the nose; (iii) the lower face, which includes mouth and chin; and (iv) the sides of the face including cheeks. Facial expression can communicate happiness, anger, surprise, embarrassment, boredom, fear, sadness, disgust, apology, favour, liking or disliking, etc. Sometimes different facial features require coordination in order to convey some message. Human face is so mobile that we unconsciously and effortlessly convey love, affection, sympathy, anger, boredom, disapproval, or surprise. All this is possible because of the proper coordination of the facial features. A smile on the lips is reinforced by smiling eyes. Half-raised eyebrows indicate worry. Half-closed eyes indicate boredom. An up-curved mouth indicates happiness and a down-curved mouth indicates unhappiness. But the eyebrows, eyes, cheeks, lips, etc., indicate a particular emotion through their simultaneous collective movements. In 'The expression of Emotions in Man and Animals', Charles Darwin says that most of the human expressive actions are instinctive and not learned. Darwin further argues that even those born-blind children blush from shame. The facial movements are instinctive, spontaneous and are, to a large extent, beyond our control.

2. Posture: "Because body shape and posture affect how we think about ourselves, how we relate to others and how others relate to us, this part of kinesic deserves our analysis" (Lesikar, *et al*, 1989: 651). Posture gives us an idea about the attitude of the bearer towards the other persons involved in the process of communication. "Although you may not be aware of it, your posture indicates your confidence, your openness and your attitudes" (Munter, 1987: 259). A good deal of relaxation in posture indicate disrespect, dislike and disinterest in the other person. A less relaxed posture indicates respect and liking for him. Generally, postures indicate superiority, fear, aggressiveness, confidence, rejection and anxiety. Anxiety, fear and lack of confidence is indicated by the total lack of relaxation in the posture. Superiority, higher status, confidence and even aggressiveness are generally indicated by a relaxed posture. For example, a man who sits expansively and stretches out his legs in front indicates that he is confident. There are some postures like looking down, slouching, bending head or biting one's nails, etc., which reveal anxiety, nervousness and the feeling of insecurity in the person. There are postures like forward leaning of the body or possible touching the other person which usually indicate nearness, intimacy, affection and other positive feelings towards the other person. We can communicate many moods through postures. 'Hunching shoulder', and `keeping head down' can be one's way of telling others to leave him alone. 'Crossing arms' may indicate that one is not ready to accept what the other is saying. The effect of impressive clothing, good grooming and other items of dressing is lost when one is not careful enough about proper posture. The traits of character or personality are also revealed by the postures. One is supposed to be lazy if he sprawls when he sits. Resting all your weight on your one leg while standing indicates that you are tired. But the postures do not tell the whole story. A man standing and resting his weight on one leg may not be tired and exhausted but such is the impression that his posture gives. A man who sprawls in the chair may not be lazy but such is the impression derived from his posture. A man standing tall, erect and straight may be tired and even exhausted, but he seems to be enthusiastic, self-confident and prepared to do something.

3. Body Movements: The individual tends to increase his body movements as the intensity of a particular emotion in him increases.

4. Gestures: The individual tends to increase his gestures as the intensity of a particular emotion increse in him. Every man or a woman is enabled to do a variety of works through his or her flexible hands. Flexibility of the human body and especially that of our hands is very useful in communicating a wide range of gestures. People can communicate their moods and 'talk' loudly with the movements of their hands. Sometimes, hand gestures can be substituted for the verbal communication. For example, one can give an order to another person to leave the room immediately solely by means of hand gestures.

The hand gestures also play a significant role of supplementing the verbal message of the speaker. "All people unconsciously use gestures to back-up what they are saying....Gestures not only reinforce what people say, they also reveal peoples attitude" (Munter, 1987: 259). An inexperienced public speaker often does not understand the way of using hand-gestures effectively. He seems to ignore those two arms attached to his shoulders. He pays very little attention to them, because he feels very awkward with them. He tries to hide them by putting them both behind his back. He does so merely because he is just ignorant about its use in communicating gestures. Sometimes, he tries to hide his useless hands in his pockets or folds them over his chest. Gradually, he comes to know that the hand gestures are not only supplementary to the verbal messages but they can also be the substitutes for written or oral media. A system of hand-signals used to communicate the messages to the deaf-mutes is so comprehensive that it is literally a substitute for the spoken language.

The hand signals used in the gestures are as arbitrary and conventional as those used in verbal languages. The words which are used as the linguistic signals are culturally determined and they do not have meanings but they represent the culturally accepted meanings. Similarly, the hand signals or gestures represent the culturally attached meanings and carry different messages in different cultures.

It is possible to feel confident in using the gestures by practicing them at home in front of a mirror. We can learn to move out hands to express the ideas with suitable gestures. While practicing gestures in front of the mirror, the movement of the entire arm up to the tips of the figures must be ensured. It is also essential to verify which gestures add to the meaning and which gestures distract and divert the meaning of the message. The movements of the entire body like stepping forward, pulling backward, crouching, hunching shoulders, turning on one side or another, etc., are the body gestures, which suggest non-verbal message of certain mood or feeling. "We refer to these movements as gestures — the physical movements of arms, legs, hands, torso and head" (Lesikar, *et al*, 1989: 650). The managers should observe the gestures of the people in the organization. He also needs to observe how well the gesture clusters fit in with the facial expressions and the verbal messages.

5. Eye-Contact: The area around the eyes is one of the most expressive part of the face. "By far, the face is where we look for most expressions of what is going on inside us. Within the facial area, the eyes tell us much more than other facial features" (Lesikar, *et al*, 1989: 649). The eyes hold the place of most significance among all the body expressions. Eye-contact gives us the clues to reveal a good deal of truth about the traits of someone's personality. Probing into an individual's eyes helps us to guess his mood. For effective management, the insights about effective eye-contact are essential. A research study in the role of eye contact in communication has found that we spend about 45 per cent of the time in eye contact with others during groups discussions, though twenty per cent of the eye contacts last only about a second. Some insights about eye-contact are as follows:

1. A looker's frank gaze can be interpreted as his positive attitude towards the other person.
2. Repeated mutual eye contacts indicate friendship, love and intimacy.
3. Generally, eye contacts are interpreted as the signs of honesty, confidence, interest, openness and friendship.
4. The embarrassed or nervous people try to avoid eye contact.
5. Seldom, avoiding eye contact indicates dishonesty and deception.
6. Those who seek eye contact are usually well-disposed towards the others.
7. It is easier to maintain eye contact at public distance than at closer range.
8. Usually the persons who seeks eye contact are regarded as more believable, trustworthy and earnest.
9. Speakers, especially the teachers, tend to believe those who look at them as being sincere to their purpose than those who do not care to look at them.
10. If the short and intermittent gazes are replaced by the constant and longer gazes during conversation, the receiver tends to perceive that the assigned work is less important than the personal relations between the communicator and the receiver.

11. A constant gaze or staring at another person can be interpreted as an invitation for interaction.
12. To avert the eyes of the looker is interpreted as a rejection of the looker's invitation for interaction.
13. Negative or poor eye contact of the audience results in poor performance of the speaker.
14. Eye-contacts have a number of different cultural associations in different countries.

6. Haptics (Touch): The observation of physical contact gives revealing clues of non-verbal messages. Haptics is the study of how physical contact or touch is used to commu- nicate the ideas and feelings. In one research study, it was observed that people seated in outdoor cafes in each of four cultures have different haptic behaviour, "They counted the number of touches during one hour of conversation. The results were: San Juan, Puerto Rico - 180 per hour; Pairs - 110 per hour; Gainesville, Florida - 1 per hour; and London - 0 per hour" (Knapp, 1980: 150). The Americans interpret positive or negative feelings from the quality of the touch through a shakehand. A limp shakehand indicates lack of interest or friendship for them.

PROXEMICS

"If you think about it carefully, you will conclude that the space around you and its contents communicate. They create meaning in your mind and in others minds" (Lesikar, *et al*, 1989: 653). The terms 'proxemics' refers to the study of how we use space to communicate message. Hall Edward (1959) describes human relationship in terms of four kinds of distances: (i) intimate, (ii) personal, (iii) social, (iv) public.

Intimate distance of six inches or less lends itself to non-verbal communication and the subject discussed between the two persons involved in communication is usually some top secret. The intimate distance of six to eighteen inches is used to discuss the confidential matters. Personal distance, ranging from 1.5 to 4 feet is a distance for close relationship and friendship. Social distance ranges from four to twelve feet. It is a suitable distance for business discussions or meetings in business office or conference room. Public distance ranging from twelve feet or more is suitable for public meetings.

The way people communicate with one another depends upon the proxemics of where the people are in relation to one another. If the chairman of the conference is the employer and the other participants are his employees, he keeps some distance from the participants in order to indicate the status difference between them. The observation of the way people sit at a meeting can reveal a good deal of secrets about who likes whom and who is competing with whom for position, profit or influence. Participants leaning backward or forward in the chair or his turning and pulling away from the speaker indicates his acceptance or rejection.

The distance maintained between people during communication in houses, offices and elsewhere throw light on their relationships. The appropriate distance between a communicator and a receiver depends upon the communication situation. The appropriate distance for communicating with colleagues need not be the same as the appropriate distance for talking with the superior. The structure and use of space conveys a non-verbal message for itself. The authority and powers, position and status can be indicated by the location of the office and its furnishing. The space speaks also when individuals come physically closer or maintain distance between them. They move closer with those whom they like and maintain distance from those whom they dislike. A greater distance is usually maintained from the people of high status.

CHRONEMICS (Use of Time)

The use of time is an important non-verbal element, which is also known as Chronemics. Time can be considered as a commodity that can be saved, wasted, earned or spent. Chronemics is concerned without study of how human beings communicate through their use of time. "In order to give meaning to time, we must perceive it, filter it and symbolize about it... Probably few of us would disagree that we have meaning for time" (Lesikar, 1989: 655). Almost everyone is usually sensitive and concerned about his or her use of time. In business world, time is money for everybody and every successful businessman seems to be very time conscious.

Delay in replying to a personal or business letter; a phone call early in the morning, late entrance at a committee meeting, meeting of a friend after long interval, and innumerable other examples of this kind communicate certain non-verbal messages. Use of the watches or time clocks throughout the working hours; agendas, setting completion dates for projects and allotted work, time scheduling, etc., show the importance of time in business organizations. Completing the work of a project within a specific recommended time communicates sincerity, hardwork, loyalty and reliability; whereas frequent late coming and absenteeism may communicate unreliability, laziness and disinterestedness of an employee. The conception of time and its associations vary from culture to culture. Indian host may politely invite the American or British guest to come at any time to his home. But the European guests would misinterpret this "any time". They might believe that the Indian host does not expect them to visit. They may not pay a visit to the house of the Indian unless he states a specific time for the visit. Most of the non-verbal communication by the chronemics depends on 'late' or 'early' arrival time and departure time. A participant arriving late for a meeting of the executive committee may communicate disinterest and lack of respect for the Chairman and other committee members. If he arrives ahead of time for the meeting, it may communicate interest and respect for the Chairman and the committee members. The employees are never expected to arrive late for an appointment with the employer.

PARALANGUAGE

Intonation Pattern Pitch Stress Intensity Range Rhythm Tempo Articulation Resonance Vocalizations. Paralanguage refers to something in addition to the language itself. It distinguishes the verbal message from the vocal message. "Paralanguage involves the 'how' of a speakers voice rather than the 'What' of the words" (Lesikar, 1989: 656). It makes distinction between what is said and how it is said. But it is concerned with how something is said rather than what is verbally said. Paralinguist studies the voice qualities such as intonation pattern, pitch, stress, intensity, range, rhythm, tempo, articulation control, resonance and some vocalizations such as sighing, yelling, yawning, laughing, grunting, crying, giggling, etc. "The spoken word is never neutral. It is always affected by our tone of voice, our emphasis and inflections, the breaks or pauses in our sentences, the speed of our delivery, how loudly or softly we speak and the pitch of our voice" (Myers, 1975: 143). The study of vocalizations and voice qualities gives us the vocal cues which differentiate emotions and gives us an idea of the speaker's social standing and personality traits. Every human being possesses a distinctive and unique contribution of voice qualities. A combination of paralinguistic vocal characteristics help many people to make some judgement about the personality of another person, which, in some cases, turns out to be accurate and reliable. The Deep-throaty voice of men indicates sophisticated and mature personality. But the same throaty voices in women indicate boring and ugly personality. Nasal voices indicate nagging and unpleasant personality in men and women. Breathy and high-pitched voices indicate pretty and feminine qualities whereas the breathy voice of a man may indicate his unmanly personality. Flat monotonous voice indicates the personality of a man who lacks interest in life.

ARTIFACTS

Artifacts refer to the object language which can either be intentional or non-intentional display of material things. Artifact means any article which is made by employing skill or craft. The artifacts include tools, implements, ornaments, utensils, religious objects, clothes, folk material and other art objects. They communicate the owner's cultural economic and social background as well as the style and standard of his living.

Note : Please see the references of this Chapter at the end of chapter 6.

6

OBSTRUCTIONS IN HUMAN COMMUNICATION

"Hearing you will hear and shall not understand,
And seeing you will see and not perceive."

— Isaiah 6:9

If one has to become a consistently successful communicator in any field, one has to develop his ability and skills of doing so effectively. But, his planning, preparation and practice of communication will be incomplete and unsuccessful unless he identifies and understands the barriers to communication. These barriers are linguistic, physical, sociological and psychological obstacles that interfere with the planning, organization, transmission and understanding of the message. There are a number of such obstacles that can occur in the process of communication. The natural result of such obstacles or interfering factors is the misunderstanding of the message. "There are many kinds of barriers that interfere with communication. Both the sender and the receiver in communication process need to be aware of them and guard against them" (Thomas, *et al*, 1988: 12).

These factors interfere with the self-confidence, self-disclosure and self-consciousness of the communication senders and receivers. The managers must contend with these barriers. They have to use communication in the managerial functions of planning organizing, staffing, monitoring and controlling. The barriers to communication are dangers to any business organization if they are not removed in time.

When the communicator transmits the idea in an unchanged and undistorted form to the receiver and the receiver responds to it, then, the process of the communication is supposed to have been perfect. But this process of 'perfect' communication can never exist due to the number of factors which stand in its way as the barriers. The communicator has to identify and understand the reasons for poor communication in order to communicate effectively. Unless he knows the ailments he cannot seek the remedies. Understanding the process of communication is the first step towards improving the abilities and skills of communication; but understanding the factors that prevent us in transmitting the exact meaning is very essential for effective communication. The executives may spend ninety per cent of their time in communication but a substantial part of their message is misinterpreted and misunderstood. In large-size, complex business organizations, messages get lost before they reach the receiver. The messages get distorted by the sender himself or by someone who carries the message or by the receiver or by the external environmental factors. There are lots of ways to go wrong and to misunderstand the messages, but attempts must be made to remedy the situation.

LANGUAGE AND SEMANTIC OBSTRUCTIONS

A. Lack of Common Language

Language uses oral or written arbitrary symbols to transmitt meanings from one person to another. Every human language has its own vocal symbol system and its own grammatical structures. If the communicator and the receiver belong to different language groups, their ignorance of each other's language or the lack of a common language will be a barrier to communication between them. It is not possible for them to communicate with each other unless they know some common language which is properly understood by both of them. An English speaking boss and a Tamil speaking worker will not be able to communicate without a good knowledge of each other's language. If both of them know a common language, say

Hindi, their knowledge of Hindi word, inflections, phrases, clauses and sentence-structure should be adequate to express their thoughts and feelings. According to Myers and Myers (1975), a great deal of misery that we experience in our daily communication comes from very common yet irritating mix-ups with languages.

B. Semantic Barriers

Words are said to have no meaning but they represent arbitrary meanings associated with them. "Words, of course are symbols and therefore limited because they cannot have precisely the same meaning for everyone" (Munter, 1987: 15). A word may have a variety of meanings and the meaning attributed to a word by the communicator may not be the same as that of the receiver's attributed meaning to that word. "Denotation is direct statement of meaning; to denote is to point with your words instead of with your fingers. Connotation is suggestion of meaning; to connote is to imply — to hint — what you think and feel" (Wolf, *et al*, 1979: 85). According to Lesikar and Pettit (1989), those meanings that are based on references to the real world are called denotative meanings and the meanings that exist only in the mind are connotative meanings. Most words have both forms of meaning. A word can have different meanings to different people at different occasions. It is found by experts that people attribute 14,000 different meanings to 500 commonly used English words. Therefore, the sender and receiver many a times likely to attribute different meanings to the same word. Sometimes, they may use different words to communicate the same meaning. There are many words in English such as light, cheap, etc. which can be used with favourable as well as unfavourable connotations. A word can stand for its positive or negative connotations. Sometimes, the intended meaning of the sender's word is misunderstood by the receiver by attributing negative meaning to it.

C. Poor Vocabulary

Poor vocabulary makes our message more difficult and

less effective. Our pen falters and tongue fumbles when we probe into our brain for a suitable word or phrase. The words have different connotative and denotative meanings. The communicator needs to know them clearly in order to use them with clarity and precision. Words stand not only for their meanings but they are also charged with action and emotions. When the communicator and the receiver understand these word-associations, they are capable of using them as living entities. Poor vocabulary does not allow the communicator to write or speak effectively. It does not allow the receiver to understand the message clearly and completely. If the receiver does not understand the words, the sentences cannot be properly comprehended by him.

D. Poor Know-how of Grammar and Punctuation

Poor knowledge of grammar and punctuation is a barrier to verbal communication. A good vocabulary is useless unless the communicator acquires the knowledge of how to use it in a sentence. More than ever before, the job applicants, business report writers, business correspondents and all those who are involved in written and oral communication today must have superior grammar skills because an understanding of grammatical structures provide excellent basis of effective writing, speaking, listening and reading skills. If the communicator is not able to choose the correct verb form that agrees with a given noun or pronoun; if, he is not able to use nouns and pronouns precisely to indicate who does what; if he is not able to select exact adjective or adverb; if he is not able to use conjunctions and prepositions to join words correctly, he will not be able to communicate his ideas, thoughts and feelings fully and correctly. In addition to a good grammar, a knowledge of punctuation is essential for effective communication. Many of us do not pay adequate attention to it. But it must be remembered that the faulty and improper punctuation can change the intended meaning of the sentences. The absence or misplacement of a comma or a period can prove misleading to reader.

E. Roundabout Verbiage

Roundabout verbiage consists of the use of overworked, troublesome and exhausted words and phrases which usually cause a considerable amount of misunderstanding and confusion. It is a long winded way of saying the meaningless padding. By avoiding such roundabout verbiage, we can add a good deal of liveliness and simplicity of expression to our written as well as oral communication. For example, instead of saying 'in the majority of cases' or 'in a number of instance', we can say 'some' or 'usually'; instead of saying 'commence', we can use 'start' or 'being'; instead of saying 'prior to', we can say 'before'. Roundabout verbiage should be avoided to achieve clarity and simplicity of the message. By omitting such words and phrases, we can save our message from hollow pomposity.

ORGANIZATIONAL OBSTRUCTIONS

A. Hierarchical Barriers

In an organization, communication transmission must flow through certain formal channels which are established by the organizational hierarchy. The employees are expected to contact the superiors and the subordinates through their immediate superiors or subordinates. This often results in hardships and difficulties in maintaining free flow of communication. Some managements disapprove with the barriers of hierarchy and propose that everyone in the organization should be free enough to communicate directly with anybody else who can help him to solve his problems.

Usually, the subordinates do not find it easy to communicate their problems to their superiors. They experience an awe of authority in communicating with their superiors. Sometimes, the upward communication is deliberately distorted and suitably edited in order to make it pleasant, palatable to the boss. The long lines of hierarchical communication are responsible for the loss of information and also for the exaggeration and understatements. Frustration is caused among the employees when their communication is restricted to the formal channels only. They try to find the resources of the informal groups which communicate through informal channels of communication like grapevine.

B. Specialization of the Work-force

In large-size complex business organization, increasing specialization of the workforce is posing a serious barrier to effective internal communication. The tasks are specified and the procedure are structured in such a way that workforce can hardly come out of their compartments to communicate with the people in other functional groups. They look only at those things that need to be done by a functionalized group. Everyone of them is assigned with a special kind of job. This makes it increasingly difficult to see and converse with the people outside one's specialization. In such organization, the right hand can never find access to know what the left hand is doing. So far as possible, the work of each employee is confined to a single function. But this is not always possible. Therefore, generally the people who are involved in related functions are grouped together in the form of a functional department which is headed by a common superior. This separates the group of people belonging to one department from the people belonging to other departments in the organization.

C. Wrong Choice of Medium

There are many ways and devices of communication. It may be oral communication through interviews, conversations, speeches, telephone talks, conferences, radio speeches, etc. It may be face-to-face communication, written communication or non-verbal communication. All these ways or media of communication are suitable for communicating at different times and for different purposes. Therefore, it is essential to think about their relative merits and limitations, before selecting one of the media for communication. The sales manager must think over if it would be better for him to hold a face-to-face talk with the prospective buyer than talking to him on the telephone. The oral communication may be a wrong medium for the smuggler at certain occasion and he may communicate safely and quickly by flashing a torch-light as a signal. Again, the oral media will be wrong one for a policeman who should blow his whistle or use hand gestures to stop the vehicles. Audio-visual media vehicle better to instruct the uneducated workers, especially in rural area, rather than using the written media for that purpose, which is merely an audio-aid to communication. Sometimes, it is better to communicate on telephone than to write a letter but there are certain messages which are more effective if they are communicated through written media.

D. Communication Load

Communication load is one of the major barriers to communication. It refers to the amount and the complexity of messages received by the receiver. The increasing specialization and complexity of the modern business world has resulted in our growing needs of boundless information. Through the astonishing variety of communication media, we are continuously bombarded with messages from morning till night. In a busy organization, a person who is connected with all the formal and informal channels of communication, is bound to be very busy in receiving and imparting the messages rather than a person who is supposed to receive the message through a single channel. He has to process a large amount of information. He can handle a lot of information, provided it consists of routine and simple messages, but it is very difficult to handle the information which is relatively more complex and unpredictable. Even communication underload can be a barrier to communication. An employee who is under communicated gets bored because of his uninvolvement and ultimately starts communicating with the help of gossips, rumour, chitchat, etc. which may prove harmful to the organization.

PHYSICAL OBSTRUCTIONS

A. Noise

It interferes with the transmission of the signals. It also refers to the 'unwanted' signals of messages which interfere and disturb the reception of the wanted signals. This disturbance is usually in the form of sounds, but it need not be always the sounds. It can be in visual, audio-visual, written, physical or psychological form also. There are many people who communicate with a little signal and much noise. In fact, they communicate extraneous matters which may diminish the interest of the receivers or may even annoy them. Anyway, they tell the receiver something more than they are required to communicate. Their extraneous distracting signal can be the result of their wandering minds — it can be because they try to communicate something more about themselves.

Technical or physical noise refers to loud noise of the machines or blaring noise of the stereo and such other noises which makes it difficult for any listener to receive the 'wanted' message. Visual noise can be experienced when a committee member arrives late at the meeting hall and all the committee members are distracted by his arrival. Poor telephone connections which interrupt conversations, smudged typescripts and bad handwriting are some examples of the technical noise.

B. Time

The frequency of communication encounters affects the human relationships, and the intensity of human relations is affected by the amount of time that passes between these encounters. If the employee does not communicate with his superiors for a long time, or if the husband and wife stay away from each other for a long time, it may create a communication gap between them which may affect their relationship. Time can act as a barrier to communication in some other ways also. A guest who arrives at midnight will not be able to communicate well with the host who might feel embarrassed or disturbed in his sleep. Time will not allow two communicators to talk with each other if they work in different shifts. A phone call at midnight can irritate or embarrass the receiver. A husband who keeps his wife waiting for a long time will not find it easy to communicate with her.

C. Distance

The distance between the communicator and the receiver can be a strong barrier to communication, if the technical devices of communication such as telephone, telex, etc., are not available to link them. Faulty sitting arrangement in the office can create a kind of communication gap which can be eliminated by adjusting the distance. Distance between the work-benches in the offices or in the modern production departments and half partitions between them are the distance barriers which severely limit the communication among the employees. By minimizing the physical distance down to the personal distance that ranges from 1.5 to 4 feet, the boss can minimize the status difference between himself and his employees. A friend or a colleague who ceases to maintain the personal distance, i.e. 1.5 to 4 feet, and keeps himself always beyond the distance of 12 to 25 feet is a friend who keeps communication gap.

D. Age

The age, maturity, educational background and the eras in which a person grows up make a generation which inevitably comes in the way of human communication. The generation gap becomes obvious in their use of vocabulary and style of speeches and the values of life to which they stick or adhere. Considering his age and maturity, we tend to apply different standards of judgment to judge the statements of the speaker. In an organization, older workers gradually form their social groups, which often remains apart from the younger workers. Their likings and interests are different and they take less interest in sports, cocktail parties and movies. Gradually, the older workers feel socially isolated and insecure because of the widening gap of communication between the older workers and the younger workers.

E. Sex

Men and women communicate with one another according to their sex. "We can see that sex is one of the factors leading to differences in interpersonal communication effectiveness" (Thomas, *et al*, 1988: 21). When they work together in a group, men tend to be more assertive, acquisitive, self-confident and aggressive than the women. This may be because a five year Billy is encouraged to 'hit back' by his father, but Billy's sister is told that girls 'don't fight'. Thus, sex stands as a barrier to a direct, honest and appropriate expression of a female's thoughts, opinions and beliefs. On the other hand, men are more assertive of their thoughts and opinions. It is also found that women are more likely than men to express their emotions and feelings about a situation. But, it must be remembered that these are general tendencies of sex-typed communication behaviour and not the rules. The girls tend to be less aggressive because they receive negative results such as rejection, criticism for such behaviour. They are brought up with the feeling that assertiveness is unfeminine. A girl who is brought up with feminine conceptions about herself may try to avoid a frank eye-contact with the interviewer and may even speak in a voice that is almost inaudible.

SOCIO-PSYCHOLOGICAL OBSTRUCTIONS

A. Status Barriers

Status is a position or social rank of a person in a group. It depends on the person's abilities, amount of pay, job-skills, seniority, type of work assigned, age, etc. When the employees are status-conscious, it becomes one of the major barriers to communication. The high-status employees within a group enjoy more power and influence than the low-status employees. Thus, status reflects the degree of power, authority, importance and responsibility placed on an individual by the other people in the organization. The subordinates are usually afraid of communicating unpleasant and unfavourable information to the high-status people. They get scared of entering into the air-conditioned cabins with rugs on the floor and a number of telephones on the table. They become conscious of their own status in relationship with the status of their superiors. This status consciousness is harmful in the process of upward communication. The employees fear that the unpleasant facts communicated to their superior might bring adverse effects on them, if the information displeases the superiors. They are reluctant to communicate their problems, shortcomings, mistakes and other unfavourable information to the higher-ups because of the fear that the superior might consider them incompetent and unworthy to do their jobs. They do not show courage of offering suggestions and plans of improving the organization and its procedures for the fear of being called 'arrogant' by their superiors. The high-ups too are strongly conscious of their status. "A member of a higher status block (a Dy. General Manager) may not give due cognisance, weightage, and importance to a message sent by a salesman (lower status block), though the message is of a priority nature" (Michael, 1992: 35). In order to safeguard the dignity of their status, they avoid accepting suggestions from the subordinates and presume that their higher status stands for better knowledge and competence than any of their subordinates. These assumptions prove serious barriers to communication between them. Therefore, it is essential that every superior should encourage his subordinates to talk freely. If he earns confidence of the employees, it can later on help him to earn the respect from them.

B. Attitudes and Values

The attitudes serve the personal needs of the people. They provide need satisfaction to the individuals. When the message is unfavourable to the receiver, he cannot be easily persuaded by it. The messages are interpreted by the people in terms of their attitudes and values. Their attitudes and values are different not merely because they are physically different but also because they have different backgrounds. They deal with the individuals and events according to their attitudes and assumptions. Their personal attitudes, values and opinions are the barriers to effective communication. The most agreeable information for anybody of us is the one which is favourable and palatable to our opinions, values, norms and attitudes. "If you concentrate on the message to be communicated rather than on yourself in the act of public speaking, you will develop communication attitude" (Thomas, *et al,* 1988: 106). The message which runs contrary to our views and beliefs is not easily acceptable to us even when it is factual and true. We promptly accept the government policy if it is favourable to our business, but we express our strong resentment towards it if it adversely affects our business. Even the process of interpreting the message is consistent with the existing attitudes and values. It is due to the fact that our thinking is coloured and characterized by our attitudes and values. Sometimes, these attitudes and values can have emotional basis. Such attitudes are extremely difficult to change.

C. Different Perceptions of Reality

Francis Bacon has said, "Man prefers to believe what he prefers to be true." The individual experiences and their interpretations are never identical because their perceptions are different. If two friends see a movie together, their interpretation of the events and the characters in it will certainly be different. The communication barrier arises as a result of different selective perceptions of the same object or idea by two or more people. "Every individual has his own perception of various situations and perception differs from person to person" (Michael, 1992: 31). Our physical senses like hearing, sight, taste, touch and smell are our contacts with the physical world. Some people have limited range and power of their senses, whereas some people have very acute and strong senses. These physical differences are also responsible for different perceptions of the existing things. Human needs are strong motivating factors which can very easily alter our perceptions. Poor children tend to estimate a coin of 50 paise to be physically larger than the children coming from the rich families. We create our own reality through selective perception which hides certain things that are there and see certain more things than are there. If a salesman treats all his customers, colleagues and others as if they were the same, then he is sure to get into a real communication difficulty. He should remember that his communication difficulties arise because his perceptions differ from those of the other people, and that each one of them conceives a different picture of the reality.

D. Inference

Our everyday life is full of various activities based on inference. When we get up in bed at 8.10 a.m., we infer that mummy might have already started her housework. When we sit down at a table to write, we infer that the chair will support our weight and ink will flow from the pen. Thus, the statements which are based on the facts and go beyond the facts are inferences. We may have good reason to expect that our inferences will be correct but they may prove incorrect due to some unpredicted probability. As inferences go beyond the facts in making certain statements, they can give wrong signals also. We are to interpret symbols on the basis of assumptions which usually prove correct, but we must be aware of the probability that they may sometimes prove incorrect. When we travel in the state transport bus, we infer that we may reach safely at our destination, but this inference may not prove correct if the bus is caught in some accident. The inferential statements involve certain amount of risk, but in every imaginable context, we cannot avoid them. The inferences drawn by the specialists are many a times reliable because they are based on verified facts, but the inferences of the non-experts should be accepted after receiving more feedback from the concerned people. If a girl comes out crying from the defendant's room and she has her dress torn and cheeks bruised, one may infer that the girl and the defendant had been brawling. But this inference may not be the actual fact. Therefore, it would be risky to accept the above inference without verifying the facts.

E. Abstracting

We use language to communicate our experiences and feelings, but we cannot communicate every detail of it. We cannot communicate every detail of our experience to others. "Because of its symbolic nature, language is a poor substitute for the realities which it attempts to represent. The real world is more complex, more colourful, more fluid, multidimensional than the pale words or over simplified signs used to convey meaning" (Katz, *et al*, 1947: 250). Secondly, we focus our attention on some details and do not bother about the rest. We prepare a business report on our observation of the various events in the market. While preparing it, we abstract the reality and report only the valuable characteristics of the market. We observe partially and communicate partially because our experience of the event is also partial. When we try to convert our observation and experiences into words, we further abstract it by using selected words, which involve leaving out the details. If we try to completely describe a simple object like 'shoe', we would require several volumes for it which would still be insufficient to describe the object.

F. Allness and Closed-Mindedness

A person may close his mind to communication receptions, if he considers himself to be a person who knows 'all' about a particular subject. "More specifically, allness is an attitude implying that what one knows or says about something is all there is to know or say about it" (Lesikar, *et al*, 1989: 81). It is very difficult to communicate with a man who has deeply rooted prejudiced mind. Such a man is not prepared to receive any message on a subject about which he assumes to know everything. His mind is closed to new ideas, facts and revelations. If an employee approaches his closed-minded boss with some suggestions to improve the work of a business unit, the boss would not entertain the suggestion, but, on the other hand, he would retort the employee by saying that he knows better than the latter regarding what should be done for the betterment of the organization. Perhaps, he may further warn the employee that the latter should never try to teach him again. Thus, he completely rejects the information and recommendations of the communicator even before he knows the real facts. The reason behind his closed-mindedness is his deeply rooted prejudices. He may preclude all possibility of communication unless the humbles himself down and admits that he has a great deal to know about himself, his occupation and also about the other people and their occupations.

G. Distortion, Filtering and Editing

When a message is transmitted through translations, interpretations, explanations and simplification, some part of it gets distorted or lost. The legally worded resolutions made in the management committee meeting cannot be transmitted in the same words to the operator on the machine. It requires translation of it into simple language. The translated message does not exactly replicate the idea of the original message on the receiver's mind, but, on the other hand, it interprets and simplifies the message for him. The accuracy of the message is lost and the transmission becomes imperfect as the message goes through the filters of translations and simplification.

The upward communication also tends to be distorted and filtered. Most of the employees bear in mind what their boss would like to hear from them and shape their messages accordingly. They are reluctant to communicate the information which might expose their faults and inefficiencies. The horizontal channel is also subjected to such distortions and filtering. The negative effects of the informal channel like grapevine are due to distortions and filtering. No one knows where it begins, but everybody seems to be anxious to repeat and impart it to others. The message in grapevine receives fresh additions with every repetition until it gets worst. Thus, often the original information communicated through formal or informal channels get lost or distorted to a large extent and very little of it is retained.

H. Past Experiences

Our manners of thinking, feeling and acting are influenced by the way of our living and also by our experience in the past. Even the attitudes and values depend on our background of experiences. Every human being has his own set of experiences. His style and way of living and personal background separates him from the rest of the society. If the individuals do not have similar experiences and expectations concerning any given communication situation, they will not attribute similar meaning to the symbols of the message. The experience and expectations attached to the language symbols by a farmer are bound to be different from those of the doctor, banker and a scientist. The process of communication between them becomes hard and difficult because they cannot exchange each other's ideas and feelings quickly, smoothly and readily even though they use the same language.

I. 'Bad' Listening

Bad listening is one of the major communication problems. Misunderstanding and conflicts can be reduced if people would listen the message with enough of attention. Most people do not listen very well due to various distractions, emotions, excitement, indifference, aggressiveness and wandering attention. One of the major reasons for bad listening is an individual's continual thinking about his own problems and worries. The poor listeners always feel that the thought in his mind is more interesting than what the speaker is saying. A college student involves himself in thinking about his girl-friend rather than listening to the lecture of his professor. Bad listening can also be due to some strong reason for worrying. An employee may get engrossed in worrying given by his departmental manager. Some listeners mentally argue with the speaker before comprehending the complete message. This usually leads to misunderstanding and conflict. Their impatience to talk out their thoughts and their lack of interest in the message contents are strong barriers to communication.

J. Emotions

Negative emotions are obstacles in the communication. Emotions are our feelings about the world around us. Usually, the positive emotions such as joy, love or affection do not interfere with communication, but the negative emotions act as strong barriers to effective communication. "Emotional excesses stand in the way of effective oral communication. Emotion — charged discourses are bound to generate emotion in the listener. Negative emotions produce negative reaction in the listener, positive emotions produce positive reactions" (Michael, 1992: 32). Emotionally excited communicator is unable to organize his message properly. His excited or nervous state of mind does not allow him to think clearly. He expresses his blurred thoughts with gesticulations and keeps on repeating the same words. He cannot even grasp the message sent by the communicator in its true sense. This is especially true when one's negative emotions are uncontrolled and misdirected. Emotions make him blind to the reason. "Emotions get in your way, especially when you attempt to evaluate the message — but they may also prevent you receiving the message or cause you to distort the meaning you assign to it" (Thomas, *et al*, 1988: 40). When everything seems to go wrong with someone on some bad day, he gives vent to his negative emotions. Almost anybody who comes across such an irritated person becomes a victim of his unfocused negative emotions. The perplexed, nervous and excited state of mind never allows smooth flow of communication.

K. Halo-Effect

The halo-effect is a psychological barrier to the listener's trust or distrust of the speaker. "The halo-effect is the effect of an oral communication on the listener on the basis of his impressions of the speaker" (Michael, 1992: 30). Trust is an essential dimension of all human encounters. What two people would say to each other and how they would interpret it depends on the level of trust between them. If the psychological climate between two people is uneasy, there would be more distortions and misinterpretations of the messages communicated between them. Distrust distorts mutual understanding and takes always pleasurable and acceptable aspects of communication. It may even interfere with the efforts of introducing attitude changes and motivating actions. If we trust the speaker, we may change our attitudes easily and readily according to whatever the speaker proposes. Our readiness to change our views and values is a result of our acceptance of the speaker's statements as reliable 'truths' or 'whites'. If we distrust the speaker, everything that he says can motivate no action from us, nor can it bring any change in our attitudes, views and values. Our negative reactions are the result of the fact that we do not accept whatever the speaker says as 'true' or 'white'. The picture of our life is multi-coloured and it should not be painted just in black and white. We must be sensitive to its mixed tones and tunes. We must try to see and understand the 'gray' tones (the halo effect). If a departmental head believes that his subordinates are dishonest and will take disadvantage of him if they can, his communication with the subordinates will be characterized by suspicion and distrust. If he believes that people are basically honest and helpful he will communicate with trust and confidence.

L. Inattentiveness

The communication receivers are inattentive to the messages that have no emotional value for them and the messages which they do not expect to hear. As such, messages are likely to be transmitted by many communicators, in which the barrier of inattentiveness can be found frequently. A receiver can exercise a considerable voluntary control over what he has to receive. However, selective attention is not always a conscious process. We are inattentive to certain messages even without our conscious efforts of controlling the reception process.

If we do not like the exposure to the message which does not support our views and opinions, we prefer to be inattentive. But in face-to-face communication, it is somewhat difficult to be directly inattentive. When it comes to a theatre show or TV programmes it is easier to walk out of the theatre or to switch off the television set if we dislike the performance or the programme. Distractions are also responsible for inattentiveness of the receiver. A clerk may not be able to concentrate his attention in his work if he is distracted by some appealing movements of a lady typist. A person can be inattentive because of his tiredness, anxieties, worries and sleepiness which may not allow him to concentrate his attention on the message.

M. Resistance to Change

If we receive a message which proposes a new idea, we tend to be inattentive to it. The new idea is rejected consciously or sometimes unconsciously if it conflicts with beliefs, morals, values, attitudes and opinions of the receiver. The average adult human mind ignores the new idea, especially when he feels insecurity and uncertainty about its aftermath. He feels that the things go along just fine with him and he would be insecure if the changes are introduced. He is also suspicious about its success in future. Because of its uncertainty, he hastily concludes in his mind that the proposal would make things worst for him. The new idea is considered as a drastic proposal which is not needed. Thus, the average human mind which resists change does not accept the new ideas from the communicator.

References

Birdwhistell, Ray, 1970: *Kinesics and Context,* Philadelphia: University of Pennsylvania Press.

Davar, R.S., 1980: *Principles of Management*, Bombay : Progressive Corporation Pvt. Ltd.

Davis, Keith and J.W. Newstrom, 1989: *Human Behaviour at Work*, New York : McGraw Hill Book Company.

Doctor, R. and A. Doctor, 1977: *Principles and Practice of Business Communication*, Bombay: Sheth Publishers.

Dwivedi, R.S., 1989: *Human Relations and Organizational Behaviour*, New Delhi: Oxford & IBH Publishing Co. Pvt. Ltd.

Galbraith, J.K., 1956: *Problems of Communication*, Bangalore: In the Symposium on Organization and Management of Public Enterprises Organized by Indian Statistical Institute, Bangalore, on 17th and 18th April, 1956.

Hall, Edward, 1959: *The Silent Language*, New York : Doubleday.

Kazt, Daniel, 1947: Psychological Barriers to Communication, from *the Annals*, Vol. 250.

Katz, D. and R.L. Kahn, 1966 : *The Social Psychology of the Organizations*, New York: John Wiley & Sons Inc.

Knapp, Mark L., 1972: *Nonverbal Communication in Human Interaction*, New York: Holt, Rinehart and Winston, Inc.

Lesikar, R.V. and J.D. Pettit, Jr. 1989: *Business Communication, Theory and Application*, New Delhi : All India Traveller Bookseller.

Luthans, Fred, 1973: *Organizational Behaviour*, New York : McGraw Hill Book Co.

Michael, V.P., 1992: *Communication and Research for Management*, Bombay: Himalaya Publishing House.

Munter, Mary, 1987: *Business Communication, Strategy and Skill*, New Jersey : Prentice - Hall Inc.

Myers, M.T. and G.E. Myers, 1982 : *Managing by Communication*, Tokyo: McGraw Hill Book Company.

Pal, R. and J.S. Korlahalli, 1979: *Essentials of Business Communication*, New Delhi: Sultan Chand & Sons.

Rai, U.S. and S.M. Rai, 1989 : *Business Communication*, Bombay: Himalaya Publishing Company.

Ruesch, Jurgen and Weldon Kees, 1956: *Non-verbal Communication*, Berkeley: University of California Press

Thomas, D.A. and M. Fryar, 1988 ; *Business Communication Today*, National Textbook Company, Lincolnwood Chicago, Illinois.

Wickesberg, A.K., 1968 : Communication Networks in The Business Structure, In *Academy of Managements Journal*, September, 1968.

Wofford, J.E., Gerloff and R. Cummins, 1977 : *Organizational Communication*, Tokyo, McGraw Hill Kogakusha Ltd.

Wolf, M.P, D.F. Keyser, and R.A. Aurner, 1979: *Effective Communication in Business*, Cincinnati, Ohio, South-Western Publishing Company.

7

THE ESSENTIALS OF EFFECTIVE COMMUNICATION

"Bless those who curse you,
Do good to those who hate you,
And pray for those who spitefully use you."

— Mathew 5:44

Effective communication is the key of sure success in all the areas of human life. The increasing specialisation and the expansion and complexity of today's tradefare have also brought about a revolution in the systems of communication. The businessman who wants to survive in the competition has to develop his communicating skills. He must know how to communicate with the help of new and speedy technical devices of communication. The efficient management executives spend more than ninety per cent of their time in communication. Their efficiency depends on their skills and effectiveness of communicating with others. He has to communicate with other traders and dealers for purchase and sell. He has to communicate with his superiors in order to decide the objectives and directives. He has to communicate with his subordinates in order to get their cooperation and improve the productivity. He has to deal with banks, transport agencies, government officials, legal advisors, insurance companies, experts, customers etc. The delay and lack of effective communication can result in heavy loss of money for any businessman. Therefore, it is very important for every businessman to know the art of how to communicate effectively.

'How we say' is equally important as 'what we say'. We want that people should listen to what we say; they should understand it, believe in it, appreciate it, and finally, get activated by it. The response of the other party depends upon how our personality is judged by them. It is the judgement of our manners, outward appearance, dress neatness and it is also the judgement of our style, tone, clarity, completeness, correctness, consciousness, objectivity, integrity, attractiveness, purpose and of many other essentialities of effective oral and written expressions.

CLARITY

A. Clarity of Purpose and Objectives of Communication

Communication is maintained at various levels of organisational hierarchy for the achievement of several objectives, but all these objectives originate from the purpose of achieving the general welfare of the organisation. The manager cannot plan, organise and control, if he does not communicate effectively to get the information about the facts and circumstances relevant to his daily responsibilities. If he has to take correct decisions, the information received by him must be complete, correct and concise. The administrator must be very clear about the exact purpose behind his communicational needs. In an organisation, he has to use communication media for the objectives like issuing orders, and warning, raising the morale, giving advice and suggestions and for some other purposes of persuasion, education and instructions, etc. He can motivate his workers effectively, if he tries to satisfy their basic human needs and healthy social relationships. Warning is very effective means of communication, but it ought to be used discreetly and sparingly. It should not be given to a person in the presence of others. The morale of the labours can be raised if the superior appreciates their good work, encourages them and gives them a sense of belonging with the organisation. The order can be very effective authoritative communication, if it is clear, complete and given in a friendly manner. In an organisation, an advice is effective, if it is related to a particular work of the worker. It should not create in him the feeling of inferiority.

Suggestion can be used as a mild and subtle form of communication. Workers are to be encouraged to drop their suggestions in suggestion boxes. Persuasion is always better than repression and compulsion in order to change views, beliefs, attitudes, habits and actions of the people. The persuasive art is usually effective and successful as it is suggestive and the appeal is indirect.

B. Clarity of Thought and Expression

The cycle of communciation starts at the origin of an idea in the mind of the communicator. It is the origin and source of the message to be communciated. The communicator must be very clear about all the aspects of the idea in his mind and about the purpose for which it is to be communicated. Next to it, he must be clear about the selection, suitability and usage of the medium. The signals of the encoded message must be carefully composed of and transmitted. It must be clear enough to replicate the exact meaning in the mind of the communication receiver. The words and sentences must be short, simple and common, so that the message is understood easily and readily. The clarity of thought and expression cannot be maintained if the communicator himself fails to understand his subject thoroughly. Sometimes, he may know his subject but he may fail to distinguish between its major and minor aspects. In order to maintain the clarity of thought and expression, the communicator can discard the use of well-turned phrases, elegant sentences and utopian-luxurious language. Good language should not call attention to itself. On the other hand, it should strive to transfer ideas and thoughts from mind to another. The communicator need not desire to captivate the receiver with the prose but should see whether his message is clear or not. The message must be so clear that even the dullest man in the world should readily understand it. It should not consist of any ambiguities or misleading meanings. It should not be faulty and it should not produce any confusion in the mind of the receiver. It should be free from syntactical errors. The communicator must plan and organise his material before communicating it to the receiver.

The encoded message should be grouped under the major and subordinate heads. While placing related ideas together, there should be no fault in punctuation and pause in the written and spoken communication respectively. The special trade and professional language which is popularly known as jargon is difficult to be understood by a common man. If we avoid jargon, it adds to the clarity of the message. These precautions should be taken before transmitting the message. When our objectives, thoughts and expressions are clear and simple, the imparted message becomes easier to be understood by the receiver and the purpose of communication is effectively served.

Clarity is the first characteristic of today's business English. Business communicator develops his ideas clearly and completely in order to promote understanding. He tries to take the reader step by step through his reasoning process. Clarity of expression depends on the use of words, phrases and sentences in their proper significance and accuracy. It is essential to be sure that each idea follows logically from the previous one. Business communicators must use the words and expressions carefully. "You must, as far as possible, avoid the use of foreign or unfamiliar words, abbreviations and expressions which tend to distort meaning." (Ramesh, *et al,* 1986: 9).

CONCISENESS

Conciseness is an important factor in effective communication. It means saying all that needs to be said and no more. The aimless verbiage, unnecessary details and heavy paragraphs make our communication ridiculous and ineffective. We must omit those words and sentences from our message which are not likely to bring good results. The message which can be expressed in fewer words is more impressive and effective than the same message expressed in a number of words. It must never ramble on and on unncessarily. It cannot persuade the receiver to take action if it bores him by its length and heaviness. The communicator must organise his message in such a way that every word in it is meaningful and of interest to the receiver. There should not be needless repetition of the same ideas and words. Even a single word or a sentence which does not contribute to accomplish the purpose of the communication should be carefully omitted. As time is precious in the business world, the businessmen do not have time to read irrelevant details. Brevity, which is a part of conciseness is desirable, but it must not be achieved at the cost of clarity and completeness. To be concise means both to be brief and to be complete. The message should be as short as possible, but it must consist all significant ideas and necessary details. By conciseness, it also means that only relevant ideas should appear in as few words as possible. The message must consist of only those sentences which are related to a specific unit of thought. The communication receiver should not feel that he is wasting his valuable time in receiving the lengthy message.

"Brevity is the soul of a business letter. "The old style of writing long letters is steadily disappearing" (Bapat, *et al*, 1973: 20). The speedy growth of modern business with its innumerable engagements and activities, needs every piece of business writing in its briefest possible way. Business letter writers try to keep every commercial document as concise as the subject matter will permit. They avoid repetition of words and ideas. They cut out verbosity of the language. They do not use extravagant expressions like 'immensely pleased' 'exceedingly glad', 'most supreme' etc. They try to avoid unnecessary words and phrases as far as possible. But, sometimes, they achieve brevity at the cost of completeness and grammatical accuracy.

COURTESY

Courtesy or politeness is considered as one of the significant attributes of effective style in business communication. "That a polite form of language should be used in all commercial writing needs no emphasis because a remark that might pass unnoticed in conversation may, if reduced to writing, be sufficient to mar business relations" (Ramesh, *et al*, 1986: 8). Business communicator's polite style does not mean the use of superfluous words. On the other hand, he should take every care to avoid superfluous flattery, empty phrases and personal irritation.

Our personality is understood by the stule and tone of our language and by our overall behaviour. Our communication can be effective if we are courteous in our language and conduct. Courtesy can be defined as the considerate, friendly and sympathetic approach towards others. In order to be courteous in our language and conduct, we must not become sarcastic, unfriendly, impatient and irritated. In business, the important objective of communication is to build goodwill by establishing better customer-company relationships. We can create the new customers and hold the present ones by our courtesy. By our courteous and thanking nature, we shall not only be able to create new friends in the business world but we shall also be able to avoid enimity and wrath of others. Courtesy is a matter of polite tone, good manners and thanking nature. A courteous man neither criticises the other party for his mistakes nor uses harsh and bitter words in his speech. He maintains goodwill by keeping 'You' attitude in his mind and on his tongue. When the 'You' attitude is kept in mind, a courteous tone naturally comes in written as well as oral communication. He wins the trust and reliability of the other party by promptly attending to their complaints and requests. He wins their favour by using the sweet sounding words like 'thank you', 'please', etc.

Courtesy is obviously an important factor for both the verbal as well as non-verbal media. A businessman can never afford to ignore courtesy in his manners and etiquettes. While writing a business letter, the importance of courtesy does not need to be mentioned. We can say that a businessman should not write a letter unless he is in a right frame of mind. In fact, when he is in an irritated and perturbed state of mind, he is likely to write in an unfriendly and insulting manner. His discourtesy may be quite unintentional, but the reader will fail to realise that it was unintentional and unsought.

The words 'please' and 'thank you' show courtesy when

dealing with all sorts of people. A businessman who wants to promote goodwill of the customers need not consider that the meaning of courtesy is limited to the use of words like 'please' and 'thank you'. He has to understand that "The basis of true courtesy is consideration for the other person" (Clark, *et al*, 1988: 20). A sense of fair play and 'You' attitude can help to make courteous sentences.

For example —

> You are entirely correct in saying that ....
> We appreciate your .....
> We very much value your .....

Doctor, R. and Doctor, A. describe courtesy as a matter of "frame of mind" rather than the use of polite and oily phrases. (Doctor, *et al*, 1979: 165).

COMPLETENESS AND CORRECTNESS

Completeness is an essential factor for effective communication. A message must be organised appropriately in the sense that it must include all the important ideas and its details. The contents of the message must be checked in order to verify that there is no omission of the relevant details. An incomplete message can do little to convey the information and to persuade the receiver. All the aspects of the message must be grouped and brought together in logical sequence to prepare meaningful thought units. The communication effort can be more fruitful and effective if the receiver easily reacts to the sender's message. The successful business communicator provides complete message with all its necessary details. When the message is fully understood, it becomes easier for the receiver to give prompt reply. The incomplete message may create doubts in the receiver's mind. It necessitates further inquiries and correspondence. The incomplete message is difficult to understand and many a time, it results in misunderstanding. The receiver of the incomplete message feels angry, confused and irritated by it. The completeness adds to the clarity of the message. An incomplete information can be provided when the communicator strives too much for brevity. In such cases, another letter or inquiry is needed to get the necessary details. It results in delay and more expenses on further correspondence. Clarity and completeness of message save time, money and energy of both the parties.

"In business communication, completeness of facts is absolutely necessary. Incomplete communication irritates the reader, for it leaves him baffled" (Pal, *et al*, 1979: 63). Sometimes a wrong action can follow an incomplete information which may prove expensive to any one or both the parties involved in the transaction. The business letter writers take care in organizing their message in such a way that the recipients will not have any doubt about anything contained in the letter. Occasionally, incompleteness is the result of excessive brevity and conciseness.

Correctness

Business communication must be correct on various levels. It must be correct in tone and style of expression, spelling, grammar, format, contents, statistical information, stress-unstress, intonation pattern, etc. There should not be any inaccurate statements in the message. Efforts must be made to avoid the errors of typography, capitalisation, spellings, punctuation, etc. The incorrectly written documents lower the readers' confidence in the writer. In the same way, the incorrect statements and other miscellaneous errors of the speaker lower the listeners' confidence in him and it may tarnish his image and reliability too. When communication receiver finds one error, he suspects that there can also be other errors in the message. Then he starts searching for other mistakes almost automatically. Therefore, a businessman must give every detail correctly in his message. The external as well as the internal communication can be considered effectively only when it brings good reputation, status, profit and goodwill to the communicator. The errors in business message may bring down the status, profit, reputation and goodwill of the communication. The decisions taken by a businessman will be wrong and disastrous if he receives incorrect information from internal and external sources. Therefore, it is essential that the sender should verify the correctness of the information before transmitting it to the receiver. And before accepting the information for important decision-making, the receiver should clarify his doubts regarding the accuracy and correctness of the message.

Correctness and accuracy arc the essential features of business writing. A business letter writer must feel sure that he is using correct facts and expressing them in correct language. It is realized that improperly worded documents, spelling errors and disregard of the rules of punctuation create a bad impression of the writer and of the organization to which he belongs. Business correspondence requires correctness in layout appearance, spelling, grammar, punctuation, style and diction. "It is taken for granted that business letter writer has a good command over the English language and he uses correct language for communicating the message" (Bapat, *et al*, 1973: 26).

CONCRETENESS

Using concrete expressions is one of the important features of modern business English. "Concrete expressions create visual images that are easy to comprehend" (Pal, *et al*, 1979: 61). 'Goods will be soon dispatched' is a generalized statement. It is always expected to be definite : 'Goods will be soon dispatched on 19 August 1991 through M/s India Transport Service'. 'This Diamond is inexpensive', does not give a definite idea about the extent of inexpensiveness of that diamond. It is better to say 'This Diamond costs only Rs. 1900'.

A POSITIVE AND CHEERFUL APPROACH

A positive and pleasant way of oral and written expression can easily build a goodwill in the customer-company relationship. With it, any businessman can win good reputation and friendly relations for his organisation. There are always many occasions when a businessman is likely to lose his temper. He has to refuse certain offers and requests of the people. Sometimes, he disagrees with the people in his organisation and also with the outsiders who are in someway linked with his organisation. Sometimes, he finds imperfections and mistakes in the business transactions. Sometimes, he has to suffer inconveniences and even financial loss. Naturally, he has to complain against some people. In these circumstances, the businessman stands on trial. It is very easy for him to become plainly negative in his approach towards these people. But, his anger and impatience might bring adverse results because nobody likes the negative approach and harsh words.

He can tactfully use the sugar-coated words to express his regret, disagreement and complaint. People accept these words with smile and without any grumble. When a businessman has to refuse something, he is likely to break the goodwill of the party. He can retain the goodwill even after his refusal by the only way of his positive and pleasant approach. He should never spoil the atmosphere of goodwill by using bitter words and complaining undertone. A businessman should look at every situation with optimism and should try to make the best of it. He may not find everything agreeable, he may come across several problems, but he should always believe in the fact that every situation can have the advantages of its own. He has to find out those advantages. Michael E. Adelstein says:

> "It is not a matter of overstating or overselling, but of accentuating the positive, and minimising the negative. Every cloud may not have a silver lining, but there usually is some sort of hopeful or optimistic prospect in a business transaction."

The tone and style of business writing is expected to be positive, optimistic and cheerful. "A businessman will have occasions when he has to refuse, say "no", regret, disagree, complain, or say 'sorry'. To say this in plain words and a straightforward style is not difficult, but its effect on the reader's mind and the repercussions on the firm are bad and far reaching" (Pal, *et al*, 1979: 11). It is realized that a negative opening or a negative connotation irritates the reader and makes him feel that the writer lacks business mannerism and gentlemanliness in his approach. It is possible to ensure that all business documents breath a spirit of optimism, cheerfulness and goodwill towards the reader. Though tone of business communication is always expected to be friendly and convincing, the communicator tries to avoid phrases that can be possibly regarded as flattery. Following are the examples of positive and negative approaches —

Positive and Cheerful :	*Negative :*
Thank you very much for order of G/37 dated 31 November 1990. The goods will be dispatched to you soon after	We regret to inform you that we shall not be able to consider your order until .....

THE 'YOU' APPROACH

We must remember that the receiver is primarily interested in himself and in his gains. His own achievements, success and well-being is more important to him rather than those of his communicator's. If he is a businessman, his main goal will be to make profit for himself. Therefore, out communication is effective only when we communicate from the receiver's point of view. Our message must be organised in such a way that it makes appeal to the issues of his own interest. While organising the message, we must not forget the truth that the receiver loves his name, his position, his property, his status, his fame and his profits. By adopting the 'You' attitude, a business communicator must look at the things as the receiver does. If he does not view the things from the receiver's point of view, his arguments will not be effective. The word 'You' is magnetic and highly effective in both the oral and written media of communication. The listeners as well as the readers of the message like themselves personally addressed by the communicator. We can make our communication effective and persuasive by using the word 'You' as many times as possible and by truing to avoid the pronouns 'I' and 'We' in our message.

To use the pronoun 'You' frequently would be an over simplification of the 'You' approach in business communication. What is important is that the communicator thinks, speaks and writes in terms of the reader and his needs. He ought to speak and write in terms of the receiver's interests and desires. The receiver (the reader or listener) is not primarily concerned about communicator (the writer or the speaker) and his company. He is not basically interested in the difficulties or predicaments of the communicator's company. Like all human beings, every businessman who receives message, wants to be flattered a little, courted a little, liked and noticed a little. The 'you' approach makes the difference in all business communications. By remembering 'you' approach the communicator can direct his message positively at the receiver and can be more apt to display goodwill toward him. But, excessive use of 'You' is not expected in business writings. "The 'you' approach should not be thought of as a gimmick guaranteeing success with a reader. It is not a device; the writer should not sprinkle 'you's throughout his sentences" (Adelstein, *et al*, 1971: 271). Though 'You' approach obviously results in the use of 'you' and 'your', they are relatively unimportant in themselves. It is essentially a way of thinking that turns the communicator's attention from himself to his receiver.

APPROPRIATE TONE, PITCH, QUALITY, FORCE AND INTENSITY OF VOICE

A small child is always conscious of the fact that the voice he listens does not always say what the words mean. He often experiences this fact when he is remonstrated by his parents. He looks into the eyes of his daddy or mommy and judges what the tone of their voice means. It is clear that words have meanings, but a different tone of voice conveys a different shade and colour of the meaning, which comes from the emotional involvement of the speaker. The tone of voice gives an idea of the depth and intensity of the emotions. The facial expression, gestures and postures are complementary to the tone of voice in conveying exact meaning to the communication receiver. The sound symbols (words) carry the ideas but the tone, pitch and force of voice communicate emotions of love, affection, hate, jealousy, fear, anger, etc. The pleasant and acceptable quality of our voice depends upon our emotional control. Pitch variations in our speech help us in emphasising certain points, whereas vocal monotony is useful in short formal speech. There are some people, who tend to speak rapidly. They find it difficult to change the pace of their speech. This monotony of pace is tiresome of the listeners. The variation in vocal pitch and rate helps the communicator to hold the attention and interest of the listeners. It must be remembered that the tone of our writing and speech invariably gives a cue to our personal attitudes. The receiver not only receives the words of the communicator but he also realises the mood of the conveyor between the lines. While listening to a public speaker, we first listen to the tone of his voice and then to the meaning of his message. Therefore, the communicator must strive to sound natural, friendly, sincere and pleasant.

Adequate Knowledge of the Subject

An adequate knowledge of the subject matter is essential for effective communication through both oral and written media. Before writing a letter or delivery a speech, the communicator should thoroughly know the subject on which he is going to express his thoughts, ideas and feelings. A salesman who works in a TV shop must have some knowledge of the TV sets. He will be able to raise the interest in the mind of the customers and focus their attention on the various points of merits in every TV set kept for sale in the shop. He must know how to operate the sets and how to make different appeals in order to generate interest in different types of customers. In generating interest and creating desire in the mind of a customer, the salesman has to dwell at length upon the various advantages and merits of the article he has to sell. The salesman should know not only the advantages of the product, but he should be able to compare it with other similar products available in the market. He should also know the facts and figures pertaining to the product. This statistical information can make an effective appeal to the educated. He should be able to judge the economic status and ability of the customer. In case of rich customers, he should make appeal to their pride of possession; and in case of the lower and middle class customers, the instinct to economise appeal is more effective. All this knowledge is essential to the salesman if he has to communicate effectively with the customer. An administrator, in a business firm, must know the background and policies of the firm. He requires the knowledge of buying, making and selling the article. He also requires the knowledge of why to communicate, what to communicate and how to communicate with different agencies, banks, insurance companies, government officials, etc., in order to be effective in his communication with them.

ADEQUATE KNOWLEDGE OF THE COMMUNICATION RECEIVER

A communication receiver has a very important place in the communication cycle. When the receiver is absent, the communication situation itself cannot exist. Therefore, the message must be prepared by keeping in view the type of person who is the receiver of it. It is very essential to see that every attempt is made to get maximum information regarding his educational qualifications, his status and designation, the nature of his work and responsibilities, his intellectual level and other aspects of his personality. The communication sender has to organise his message in such a way that it becomes pleasing, suitable and acceptable to the receiver. The language of the communicator must be persuasive, adaptable and intelligble to the receiver. The colloquial and informal language is likely to be unsuitable while communicating with the superiors, but it might, sometimes, be more acceptable while communicating with the equals and subordinates. The style, manner and content of the language must be carefully used to create goodwill in the mind of the receiver. It must be remembered that we should not use the same language with the illiterate worker and office clerk and with the manager of the organisation.

THE OBJECTIVE AND REALISTIC APPROACH

The mental set, attitudes, opinions and prejudices of the receiver towards the sender and towards the organisation have a marked effect on the meaning of a message. The hostile, suspicious and prejudiced receiver is likely to draw a negative, slanted and distorted meaning from the message. It is, therefore, very essential that the message should be objective, factual and realistic and it should exclude the emotional expression of the sender. The sender should not allow his opinions, attitudes and emotions to distort the objectivity and factuality of the message and at the same time, he should be aware of the feelings and responses of the receiver. Adequate care should be taken by the sender that the information provided in the message does not mislead the receiver or hurt his feelings. A high level of trust and mutual respect between the sender and the receiver facilitates clear and objective communication.

SELF-CONFIDENCE AND CONVICTION

Lack of self-confidence can be a critical barrier to effective communication. A person must have the self-confidence to communicate his achievements, his personal capabilities and his prospects. The communicator must build and develop in himself a justifiable self-confidence. The feelings of anxiety and worry are closely associated with the low self-confidence. A person with such feelings perceives himself unable to communicate with the people in any situation. He feels it difficult to face the different faces in his practical life. Anxiety is a negative emotion. It is natural that a person with negative emotions reacts negatively to the situations. In business, such a person tries to avoid the situations of challenge in finance, marketing, personnel management, etc. If he is in the management body of the organisation, he would give little time for communicating on unfamiliar and difficult problems. He would spend more time in dealing with the problems of which he is confident to find the solutions. The self-confidence is essential to generate positive outlook in the person.

It is also essential that the manager should make some

efforts to build the self-confidence among his subordinates. Stanley Coppersmith has suggested three conditions to which high self-confidence is related: (i) total acceptance of subordinates by the manager; (ii) clearly defind and enforced limits; (iii) managerial respect for individual action within the defined limits. The manager should be attentive to the needs of the people working in the organisation. When he shows the concern about the welfare of his subordinates, the total acceptance of the subordinates by him is communicated. The manager has to inform his subordinates about his expectations of work from them. Thirdly, the manager has to motivate and encourage the subordinates to act freely within the structure formed by him, the high self-confidence among the people working in the organisation can establish social relationship which is conducive to effective communication.

ORGANISATION OF MESSAGE

The message is transmitted through the signals of vocal and written symbol system, which is also accompanied by the non-verbal signals. The organisation of message involves the selection of suitable media and the composition of message by the systematic arrangement of symbols. When a message is to be communicated through written media, the words, phrases, clauses and the sentences must be simple and correct so that it may replicate the exact meaning to the receiver. Secondly, the handwriting, typing or printing must be orderly, neat, attractive and in suitable format. The sentences must be properly punctuated to bring clarity and to avoid ambiguity. The paper on which the message is written should have pleasant appearance. The appearance and the form of the letter is as important as the contents of the message in it. While communicating orally, the voice must be loud enough to be heard easily and clearly. We are to make use of the pauses to stress some ideas. The tone must be confident, vibrant and enthusiastic. The pitch of the voice should be suitable to the situation and to the content of the message. It is also essential that the message should be brief and concise. In face-to-face communication, the non-verbal aspects of communication like eye-contact, body posture, gestures, facial expressions, touch, silence, etc., are very effective in revealing trustworthiness, sincerity, intensity of emotions, enthusiasm, etc., of the persons involved in the process of communication.

The message must consist of an introduction, a body and a conclusion. The message can be organised in chronological pattern. The messages consisting of the historical accounts and the description of processes can be organised in a chronological order. The message can be organised in cause and effect pattern also. In this pattern, the communicator moves from the cause to effect or from the effect to cause. The third pattern of message organisation is that of a spatial order. In it, the message is organised by space, i.e., top-bottom, left-right, east-west, etc. The fourth pattern of message organisation is that of comparison. It points out the similarities and differences between the items under the study. Problem-solution pattern is often used in the business communications. It describes the problem, describes the solution, discusses the advantages and disadvantages of solution and finally, proves how the proposed solution is better than the other. Analytical pattern of message organisation analyses or divides the subjects into parts and sub-parts. A well organised message is always systematic and effective.

PROPER SELECTION AND USE OF MEDIA

A manager can communicate through a variety of media. The media available to him can be divided into four groups: (i) audio-visual, (ii) non-verbal, (iii) oral, and (iv) written. Audio-visual communication includes television, video cassettes, cinema films. Visual communication includes gestures, facial expressions, graphs, charts, diagrams, slides, posters, etc. The oral communication includes telephone conversation, face-to-face communication, interviews, seminars, conferences, group discussions, meetings, speeches, etc. And written communication includes a variety of letters, reports, memorandums, circulars, telegrams, minutes, questionnaires, etc.

All the communication media have their own advantages as well as disadvantages. Before selecting the media, it is essential to think over its relative suitability in communicating the message. If the manager has to communicate certain directives to the departmental heads, it would better for him to convene a meeting rather than talking with them over telephone separately. If he wants to inform common policies of the company to the employees, it is better to use speech. While communicating with the departmental or assistant manager, he can talk face-to-face with him, or he may talk to him over telephone. If he is desirous to record the message for future reference, he may send a memorandum to the assistant manager or to any other concerned authority in the company's hierarchy. He has to communicate with the local government officials also. He can get some clarification in certain matters by talking with them over telephone. But he has to communicate with the government authorities, insurance agencies, banks, etc., mostly through written correspondence.

Audio-visual media which is most suitable for mass communication is very suitable and effective in educating and training of the workers. When the manager wants to communicate with the general public, he can reach upto to them through advertisements on television, video tapes, cinema-films, radio, newspapers, magazines etc. The silence also can be an effective media of communication in certain circumstances. Silence talks loudly when a beloved blushes and indicates her consent to the proposal of her lover. The visual media can be effective only when it is used in combination with other media. The charts, diagrams, maps etc., are to be associated with the written media, and the facial expressions, postures and gestures, etc., are to be associated with the oral media in order to be effective in communicating the message.

APPROPRIATE FORMALITY

In almost every organisation, there are always some people who prefer to communicate with 'people' rather than with 'positions'. Formality in communication connects position and not people. The unplanned informal channels of communication are convenient for many people to interconnect them for a variety of reasons. Informal communication is essential in the organisation because it bridges people closer together and helps them to share their work experiences and common problems among themselves. But, if the group which had come closer by informal communication does not trust management, the morale of the organisation is threatened. The formal communication brings about some obligatory discipline by its network which sets the lines of communication with the lines of authority as they are structured by the management. The message passes formally and slowly from managers to departmental heads, departmental heads to supervisors, etc., and the communication links between the positions are maintained. But, in the organisation, when the people work near each other and share each other's experiences and problems, they are likely to come together for common purposes. When they come together, the informal group is formed. In order to coordinate and control such groups, the informal channels are more effective. The formal and informal ways of communication must go hand-in-hand in every business organisation.

PATIENCE IN LISTENING

The ability and patience to listen is a managerial skill which helps the manager to improve his relationships with the people in the organisation. To him, the auditory source of essential information is an important requirement for effective decision-making. The reception of information and its further processing are the important elements of communication circle. Therefore, it is obvious that effective communication requires effective listening. When the listener carefully listens to the message, he can understand, judge and evaluate the contents of it in a better way. Effective communication is impossible if the receiver does not listen to the message and does not comprehend it thoroughly. The receiver must be able to concentrate on the information imparted by the communicator. He must not be carried away by the distractions. It is likely that he might be distracted by the manners, etiquettes and physical appearance of the communicator. He must be positive and open-minded towards the communicator. He should not let his mind wander away from what the communicator is saying. Thus, if the receiver is a patient listener, with positive and flexible mind towards the speaker and understands the message by keeping himself mentally alert, the communication is bound to be effective.

ADAPTABILITY AND ATTENTIVENESS

A person must give adaptive responses to the changing circumstances. In any business organisation, the successful implementation of the technological as well as economic innovations are possible if the significant flow of information is involved. The adaptive responses of the receiver facilitates the incoming flow of the information at various levels in the organisation. The communicator also has to adapt his communication to the needs and requirements of the receiver. He has to adapt it to the intellectual, academic and linguistic competence of the receiver. The receiver's state of mind and overall psychological make-up also deserves adequate consideration.

In our 'struggle for survival' with the other species on this earth, we have survived not only because we have faster birth rate, nimble body and teeming brain but because we are more adaptive to changing circumstances. In human society and especially in our complex business world today, adaptability is an essential factor in effective communication with the different people in different circumstances.

Attentiveness

The receptivity of our mind decides our attentiveness and concentration on the message which is either to be composed, written and transmitted by the sender or to be read, listened and seen by the receiver. The sender must be attentive enough in composing the message correctly, clearly, precisely and completely before transmitting it to the receiver. And the receiver must be attentive enough to listen and see every aspect of the message received by him. A successful businessman keeps his eyes and ears open to keep himself abreast of the knowledge in his field. He must keep his mind open to new ideas. But in practical life, it is found that people are inattentive to receive a message which is against their belief and unsuitable to their taste and likings, they are also inattentive to the message which seems monotonous and boresome to them. Inattentiveness is actually an ignorance of the message. When the message is ignored, the communication circle remains incomplete. When the message is receivfed, the receiver is attentive to it. He can send the feedback to the communicator if he attentively comprehends the message. There cannot be effective communication unless both the communicator and the receiver are attentive to each other's message and feedback.

THE TIME CONSCIOUSNESS

In business, no matter how busy you are, you must communicate promptly and at approriate time. It is essential to answer a business phone after first ring. In written communication, the promptness in answering the business letter is a matter of courtesy. This timeliness may not be always possible but the communicator and the receiver must make the effort to be prompt and timely. Any businessman cannot afford to abandon his customer by not attending the phone call. He is likely to suffer the loss of goodwill and money, if he does not reply promptly to the letter of enquiry and order. Therefore, it is important to reply the letters and answer the phonecall promptly and courteously. A reply to the letter may be delayed sometimes, because the writer may require some clarification and explanation from some other concerned people. He may also require the consent of his higher authority. But whenever possible, a reply must be transmitted within 48 hours. When some more time is needed to make inquiries and to collect information in order to give full and satisfactory answer to the enquirer; atleast an acknowledgement receipt must be sent immediately. The promptness in replying is essential in business because it creates a goodwill and friendliness.

The message must be communicated at the appropriate and suitable time. If it does not reach its receiver at an appropriate time, it may not bring the expected and desirable results. If the receiver is seriously occupied with some other work, he will not be able to pay proper attention to the message. If a message is passed at the time when the receiver has lost his temper on some irritable issue, the communication cannot be good and effective.

References

Adelstein, Michael E., 1971: *Contemporary Business Writing*, New York: Random House.

Bapat, S.G. & Datar, S.G. 1973: *A Textbook of Business Correspondence*, Poona: Anomal Prakashan.

Bowman, J.P. and B.P. Branchaw, 1984: *Business Report Writing*, Tokyo: The Dryden Press, Holt-Sounders, Japan.

Brown, C.A., 1975: in *Write Better, Speak Better*, Reader's Digest Publication, p.278.

Clark, L.R., Zimmer, K., Tinervia, J., 1988: *Business English and Communication*, New York : English Language Series. McGraw-Hill International Editions.

Doctor, R. and Doctor, A. 1979: *Principles and Practice of Business Communication*, Bombay: Sheth Publishers.

Jayatilleke, C.L.V. and S. Sivasegaram, 1979: *Technical Report Writing*, New Delhi: Tata McGraw-Hill Publishing Co. Ltd.

Pal, R. and Korlahalli, J.; 1979: *Essentials of Business Communication*, New Delhi: Sultan Chand and Sons.

Rai, U.S., Rai, S.M., 1989: *Business Communication*, New Delhi: Himalaya Publishing House.

Ramesh, M.S. and C. Pattanshetti, 1986: *Effective Business English and Communication*, New Delhi: Published by G.S. Sharma, Prop. R. Chand & Co.

Rodriques, M.V., 1992: *Effective Business Communication*, New Delhi: Concept Publishing Co.

Sharma, R. C. and Krishna Mohan; 1986: *Business Correspondence and Report Writing*, New Delhi: Tata McGraw-Hill Publishing Company Limited.

Thomas, D. A. and Fryar, M.; 1988: *Business Communication*, New York: National Textbook Company.

PART - II

COMMUNICATIVE COMPETENCE

8

SPECIFICATION OF COMMUNICATIVE COMPETENCE

"Competence, like truth, beauty and contact lenses, is in the eyes of the beholder."

— Laurence Peter & Raymond Hull

Our communicative competence enables us to express our thoughts and feelings in novel propositions to deal with the interactive situations which are never quite the same. On the other hand, our language competence is a faculty of linguistic creativity that helps us to construct the sentences most of which have never been constructed by us or anyone else in past. The demands that we place on our communicative competence may be virtually limitless, but there is no doubt that the number of sentences we can create in English are too literally limitless. Human competence of linguistic creatively is a means of all social interactions including business communication which indispensably depends on the speaker's communicative competence in the target language. Nowadays, our entire elaborate business structure, for its complex interactions, rely on most advanced tools and methods of spoken and written communication. For understanding this process of communication, we must closely examine the human capacity for language use, at initial stage.

Communicative competence is not a feat of memory. We apply our knowledge and experience of language quite unconsciously to meet the communicative demands of our everyday life. According to Wilkins (1974,) we never know that we are going to need to communicate and yet when the time comes, as mature speakers of the language, provided the necessary knowledge and experience itself is not lacking, we have no difficulty in expressing whatever it may be we have the need to express. When we are involved in day-to-day interactions with the members of society in complex explanations of unforeseen events, in emotional reactions to unexpected happenings in the familiar and unfamiliar situations, we can quite unconsciously apply our knowledge of language to meeting the demands of what we need to say or write. It is obvious that our linguistic expression is a natural, spontaneous and unconscious application of our language competence.

SPECIFYING COMMUNICATION COMPETENCE

"For specifying communicative competence of a foreign language participant, it would seem inappropriate to work within one particular linguistic theory" (John Munby, 1978: 6). Therefore, it would be appropriate to survey the linguistic, psycholinguistic, socio-linguistic, socio-philosophical and socio-semantic theories to provide sufficient basis for specifying communicative competence. The ideas and activities involved in the study of communicative competence cannot be satisfactorily explained with the help of the existing linguistic theories and transformational generative (T.G.) grammar. While stating inability of such theories in this concern, Jakobovits (1970) says that there is no guarantee that generative transformational grammar, or for that matter any other linguistic theory, will be able to account for all facts about language which the native speaker possesses.

The Linguistic and Psycholinguistic Approaches

Grammatical competence was upheld and gained currency through work of Chomsky (1965). Many linguists and language teachers, after interpreting Chomskyan linguistic theory, arrived to the conclusion that the grammatical competence was an exclusive aim of language teaching and learning. According to Chomsky an ideal speaker who knows his language perfectly, is able to apply his knowledge of language in actual performance without getting affected by the psychological conditions as distractions, shifts of attention and interest, memory limitations etc. The 'ideal' speaker's 'perfect' knowledge of language refers to his knowledge of abstract system of rules which enables him to understand and produce well-formed sentences. Gradual acquisition of this knowledge by which the speaker is enabled to understand and produce any and all types of sentences of his language, helps him to build his communicative competence. According to Chomsky (1970), a person who has learned a language has acquired a system of rules that relate sound and meaning in a certain specific way. He has, in other words, acquired a certain competence that he puts to use in producing and understanding speech.

Widdowson's Reflections on Chomskyan Theory

H.G. Widdowson (1972) differs from Chomskyan theory of linguistic competence in saying that the ability to compose sentences is not the only ability we need to communicate. According to him communication takes place when we make use of sentences to perform a variety of different acts of an essentially social nature. Thus, we do not communicate by composing sentences, but by using sentences to make statements of different kinds, to describe, to classify and so on, or to ask questions, make requests, give orders (Widdowson 1972). Widdowson considers it a radical mistake to suppose that a knowledge of how sentences are put to use in communication follows automatically from the knowledge of how sentences are composed and what significance they have as linguistic units. He does not agree with any equation between linguistic forms and communicative functions.

Psychological and Socio-Cultural Constraints

Chomsky's views on competence and performance are concerned with the psychological constraints like memory, attitude, shifts of attention, interest, perception etc., rather than with the socio-cultural constraints. Hymes (1971) does not agree with Chomsky's omittance of almost everything of socio-cultural significance. According to Jakobovits (1970) social context selection rules and the rules of syntax are the essentially equal parts of the linguistic competence. Fodor and Garrett (1966) point out that Chomsky's theory of competence and performance does not account for an important linguistic ability to produce or understand utterances which are not so much grammatical but appropriate to the context in which they are made. This ability of the speaker belongs properly to his linguistic competence which provides the means of reacting appropriately in an indefinite range of new situations. Though Chomsky (1965) agrees with this view, he fails to provide for this in his theory. In order to enlarge this notion of competence to include contextual appropriacy, the opinion of Hymes (1971) that, "there are rules of use without which the rules of grammar would be useless," must be considered seriously. Johnson, K. (1976) expresses similar opinion to that of Hymes when he says that the language learner must have the 'structural' as well as 'functional' knowledge of the language. Though there are certain views that separate grammatical competence from communicative competence, K. Johnson maintains that grammatical competence is a part of communicative competence. He says that grammatical competence is a part of communicative competence and the language teacher is clearly committed to ensuring that his students are able to manipulate the language structurally (entailing grammatical knowledge) as well as use it appropriately (entailing functional knowledge).

Communicative Competence and Grammatical Competence

Chen-Si-Quing (1990) considers language proficiency to comprise competence and performance. Competence includes grammatical competence and communicative competence. Performance is said to be the realization of competence. Canale and Swain (1980) had proposed that grammatical competence is the sub-component of communicative competence. Chen's view runs contrary to the view forwarded by Canale and Swain (1980). He says that grammatical competence is not to be considered as a subcomponent of the communicative competence. Rather, it is thought to have the same status as does communicative competence in linguistic theory and language learning (Chen-si-Quing, 1990). Thus, with the discovery that language is constrained by many social and cultural factors (Hymes, 1972) and learning a language involves more than memorizing rules of grammar and lexis, the concept of communicative competence has evolved to complement grammatical competence. The grammatical competence and communicative competence have their own respective status and the one cannot replace the another. The statement of Hymes (1971), "there are rules of use without which the rules of grammar would be useless," and the statement of Canale and Swain (1980) that "there are rules of language use that would be useless without rules of grammar", support our view that communicative competence complements the grammatical competence.

THE SOCIO-LINGUISTIC APPROACH

Hymes (1972) takes competence as the most general term for the capabilities of a person. He says competence is dependent upon both (tacit) knowledge and (ability for) use. Individuals differ with regard to their knowledge and their ability to use the knowledge. Hymes takes performance models studied in psycholinguistics as the models of the aspects of ability for use. He says that the performance of a person is not identical with a behavioural record, or with the imperfect or partial realization of individual competence. It takes into account the interaction between the competence (knowledge and ability for use) and the cybernetic and emergent properties of the events themselves.

Cooper, Campbell and Wales, Widdowson, and others have rejected Chomskyan restriction of the concept of competence — the perfect knowledge of an ideal speaker-listener, in a homogeneous speech community, unaffected by socio-cultural or psychological constraints — because it cannot account for the communicative function of language. Although Cooper (1968) is concerned only with the sociolinguistic and grammatical parameters, his view of communicative competence is similar to that of Hymes. He supports Hymes' view that effective communication requires more than linguistic competence. To communicate effectively, a speaker must know not only how to produce any and all grammatical utterances of a language, but also how to 'use' them appropriately. The speaker must know 'what' to say, with 'whom' and 'when' and 'where' (Cooper, 1968).

Campbell and Wales (1970) accept Fodor and Garrett's (1966) distinction between competence and performance. Competence in any sphere is identified with capacity or ability, as opposed to actual performance which may only imperfectly reflect underlying capacity. Widdowson too disagrees with the Chomskyan view of performance and shares the Hymesian view of communicative competence. To him, a speaker's competence includes knowing how to recognize and how to use sentences in a particular social situation. He distinguishes speaker's knowledge of the rules of use in a particular situation from the speakers knowledge of the rules of grammar.

Linguistic Competence and Cultural Contextualization

Just as culture and its language are inseparable, the linguistic competence of person and his culture are also intertwined and inseparable. Linguistic competence is at once an outcome and a result of the culture as a whole. When we acquire language, we not only learn a system of communication, but we also learn the multiple facets of culture which are shaped and communicated through language. Our linguistic competence reflects our cultural patterns and value systems. Most of the cultural attitudes which a speaker has built into him are reflected in his speech patterns. J.R. Gladstone (1969) says, our culture rewards us for producing certain behaviour patterns and for ignoring others. This training develops in us a cultural perspective by which we judge all acts — a cultural sieve through which we pour all we perceive. Usually this cultural filter performs below the conscious level. Linguistic competence and culture are so intimately and dynamically connected that the culture gives a viewpoint to the communicator and the language gives an oral or written expression to this viewpoint. J.R. Gladstone feels that materials in a language programme should take cognisance of the relationship between culture and language. If a teacher uses the materials in language programme which take cognisance of the relationship between language and culture, he will be able to teach the linguistic items within their cultural context in an effective manner.

According to Nancy Isenberg (1990), in the context of learning English as a foreign language, the learner's understanding of the text will depend on the following factors, 'What exactly that will be depend on many factors, not least of which are his general knowledge of the language of the text is written in and his familiarity with cultural references.' In the communicative competence of the learners she includes learners specific intellectual ability of synthesizing information. While discussing psychological aspect of communicative competence she says that the individual's ability to store information in an effective way, within a mental classification system (procedural knowledge and informational knowledge) enables learner to utilize what is already stored in his personal encyclopedia to help him deal with new problems. A similar notion of communicative competence is expressed by Cheryl and Roberts (1990). He agrees with the view of Canale and Swain (1980) and says that the communicative competence is the speaker's ability to use language in real life situations.

Communicative Competence and Pragmatic Competence

What is new in the Bachman's (1989) notion of communication competence is the concept of pragmatic competence. This deals with the illocutionary and sociolinguistic components. This idea of illocutionary competence is derived from the Speech Acts theories of Austine (1962) and Searle (1969), and Halliday's (1973, 1976) description of language functions. Illocutionary competence means the speaker's knowledge of how to perform the language functions. The language functions are grouped into four macro-functions: Ideational, Manipulative, Heuristic and Imaginative.

i. *Ideational Function*: Ideational function refers to the use of language to express meaning of one's experience of the real world.
ii. *Manipulative Function*: The manipulative function refers to the use of language primarily to affect the world around oneself.
iii. *Heuristic Function*: The heuristic function is used to extend one's knowledge of the world.
iv. *Imaginative Function*: The imaginative function refers to the use of language to create an environment through creative language use, as in literature and humour.

Socio-linguistic competence refers to the speaker's ability to use the language appropriately in a given language community and in varying socio-cultural contexts or situations. Firstly, sociolinguistic competence allows the speaker to use the language appropriately in different registers and dialects. Secondly, it allows the speaker to use the cultural references and figures of speech which are incorporated into language with the set of meanings. Thirdly, it allows him to determine if an utterance that is grammatically correct is phrased in a 'nativelike' way. Pauley and Syder (1983) have called these functions as three aspects of sociolinguistic competence.

THE SOCIO-SEMANTIC APPROACH

Halliday (1971, 1992) is concerned with language use to account for the language functions realized by speech. These language functions are defined in the terms of formal features of language which enable the speakers to communicate. The distinction between competence and performance is rejected by Halliday. To him, the Chomskyan distinction between language competence and language performance is of little use in a sociological context. He does not draw any distinction between competence and performance; but, on the other hand, he considers such distinction as either unnecessary or misleading. According to him we shall not need to draw a distinction between an idealized knowledge of a language and its actualized use: between the 'code' and 'the use of code' or between competence and performance (Halliday, 1970). Later (1971, 1972) he developed a socio-semantic approach to language and the speaker's use of language. John Munby comments, "At the heart of Halliday's socio-semantic approach is his language defining notion of 'meaning potential', the sets of options in meaning that are available to the speaker-hearer. This 'meaning potential' relates behavior potential to lexicon-grammatical potential: What the speaker can do - can mean - can say —" (Munby, 1978: 13). According to Halliday's socio-semantic approach to 'language' and the 'use of language', the speaker's behaviour options are determined by social theory (What he can do). These behavioral options are translated linguistically as semantic options (What he can mean). Finally, the semantic options are encoded as options in linguistic forms (What he can say).

THE SOCIO-PHILOSOPHICAL APPROACH

To Habermas (1970), communicative competence means the speaker's mastery of an ideal speech situation. According to him to participate in normal discourse, the speaker must have in addition to his linguistic competence basic qualifications of speech and of symbolic interaction (role-behaviour) at his disposal, which we may call communicative competence. (Habermas, 1970). But, he does not equate this mastery with production. To him, communicative competence is defined by the ideal speaker's mastery of the dialogue constitutive universals irrespective of the actual restrictions under empirical conditions. Thus, communicative competence comprises knowledge of the universal formal features of language that make human communication possible.

In order to grasp how the various notions of the candidates communicative competence, i.e. linguistic, psycholinguistic, sociolinguistic, socio-semantic and socio-philosophical etc. discussed so far are interrelated, a constellation of communicative competence devised by Munby (1978) is reproduced in the Figure 8.1.

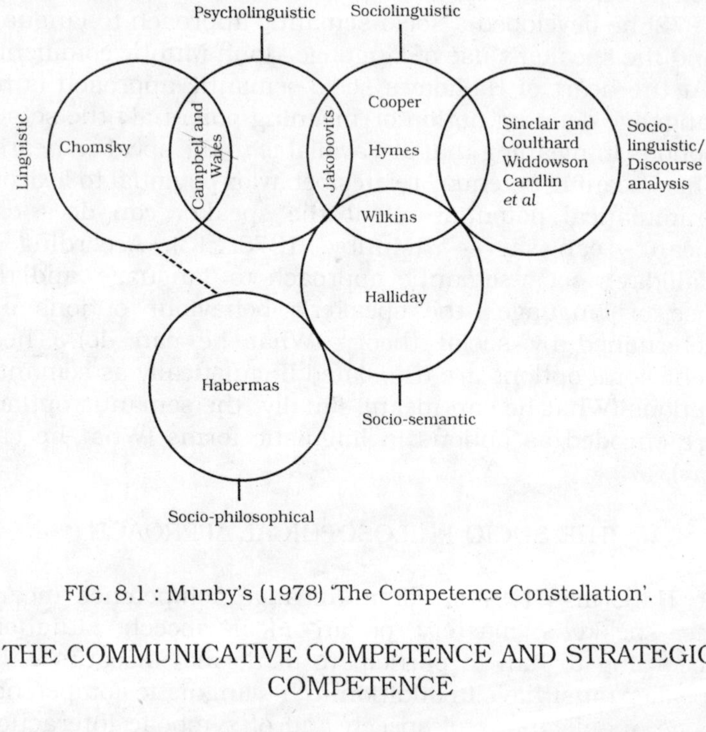

FIG. 8.1 : Munby's (1978) 'The Competence Constellation'.

THE COMMUNICATIVE COMPETENCE AND STRATEGIC COMPETENCE

Faerch and Kasper (1983) and Chen-si-Quing (1990) are of the opinion that the learner's communicative needs cannot be predicted exhaustively and accurately. But, Chen-Si-Quing also points out that the most popular way to develop the learner's competence today is to analyze and predict their communicative needs and then to relate theses to teaching goals and syllabus structure. It is possible to develop the learner's communicative competence, firstly, by analysing their communicative needs and syllabus structures, and secondly, by building up their strategic competence. The strategic competence of the learners is their ability to use the communication strategies that allow them to cope with various communicative problems. The assumption that strong strategic competence leads to high communicative competence has been theoretically proved by Canale and Swain (1980), and Canale (1983). The communication strategies have been generally defined by Faerch and Kasper (1983), Corder, P. (983) and Paribakht (1985) as devices employed by L2/L3 learners when they face problems in L2/L3 communication because their communicative ends have overrun their communicative means. While comparing various factors of communicative competence, Fouly, *et al.* (1990) have stated that Strategic competence consists of verbal and nonverbal strategies that are used to compensate for breakdowns in communication due to performance factors or insufficient grammatical or sociolinguistic competence.

A MODEL OF THE STUDENTS' COMMUNICATIVE COMPETENCE

Though various notions of communicative competence have been discussed so far give us a clear idea of communicative competence, there is a need to specify the students' communicative competence in business situations. Business communicative competence is a part of social communicative competence. The present study is concerned with the evaluation of communicative competence of the MBA-I students in communicative syllabus. Therefore it is essential to develop a model of communicative competence specification of the students in communicative syllabus. Before specifying subjects' communicative competence in communicative syllabus, it is necessary to specify business communication situation in which they have to communicate.

In business, communication flows upward, downward and horizontally. When the messages flow from the subordinates to the superiors, it is an upward channel of communication; when it flows downward through the hierarchy of command, it is the downward channel of communication; and, when communication takes place between and among the people who belong to the same level of the hierarchy, it is the horizontal channel of communication. The informal communication flows in one or all of these directions as it does not follow the set rules of formal communication in business. A business communicator requires knowledge and skills of using these channels.

Secondly, the messages that pass upward, downward and horizontally, are sent through written, oral and non-verbal media. A business communicator requires knowledge and skills of using these media.

Thirdly, there are linguistic, sociological and psychological obstacles that interfere with the planning, organization, transmission and understanding of the messages. If one has to become a consistently successful business communicator he has to overcome the communication barriers and has to develop his ability and skills of communication.

Fourthly, the efficiency of a businessman depends upon his ability to communicate effectively. Therefore, he requires to know the essentials of effective communication and to develop his communication skills accordingly.

The media used, the barriers to communication, and the essentials of effective communication are common to all the channels of business communication.

In every business communicative situation, the channels, media and some barriers to communication always exist. The effective business communication depends on those essentials of effectiveness which are common to all the channels of business communication in which different media are used.

When messages have to pass through some channel, the suitable media are chosen. When the chosen media carry the messages, some barriers are present at different levels of communication cycle. The efforts are made to overcome the barriers and to communicate the messages effectively. These messages perform the intended communication functions.

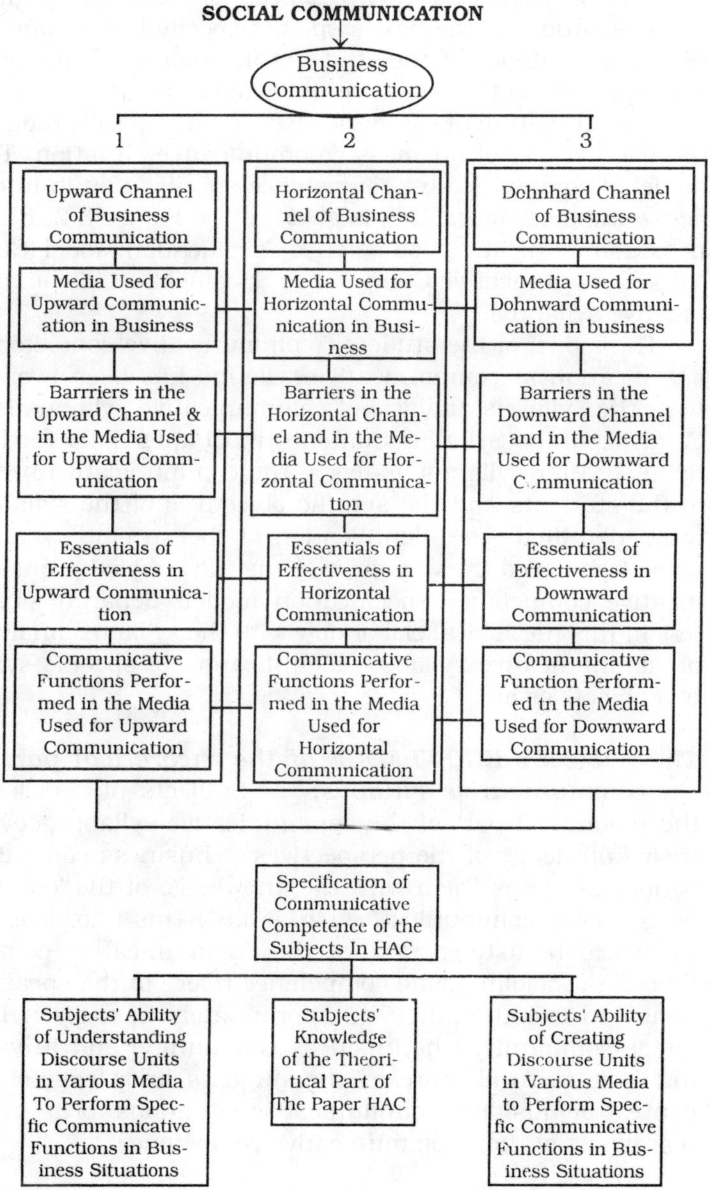

FIG. 8.2 : Business Communicative Competence Specification Model (Subjects, Communicative Competence Specification in HAC)

After specifying all the five aspects of business communicative situation, the next step is to specify the communication competence of the students in business situations. The specification of the required communicative competence of the students is derived from the specification of the five aspects of business communicative situation. The model of communicative competence specification in interactive business situations is given in the Figure 8.2. Business Communicative Competence Specification Model (Subjects' Communicative Competence Specification in communicative syllabus).

The model of the students' communicative competence specification in communicative syllabus has been evolved from the syllabus analysis of communicative syllabus (see 'Analysis of the Syllabus Contents' in Chapter 7 for further details). After syllabus analysis, the communicative needs of the students and the specific objectives of the syllabus were identified. The identification of the specific syllabus objectives paved the way for evolving the subject's communicative competence specification model. Separate chapters in this thesis deal elaborately with the syllabus analysis of communicative syllabus, identification of specific syllabus objectives etc.

The Subject's KNOWLEDGE of the theoretical part of the communicative syllabus: The Subjects' of knowledge the theoretical part of the communicative syllabus covers their knowledge of the perspectives of business communication. It equips them with the knowledge of the 'context' or 'business communicative situations'. This knowledge is the sociolinguistic aspect of the communicative competence. As sociolinguistic competence refers to the speakers ability to use the language appropriately in a given language community (the business community) and in varying socio-cultural contexts, the students' knowledge of the context or business communicative situations form an integral part of their communicative competence.

Subjects' ability of UNDERSTANDING of the discourse units in business communicative situations: The students' ability of UNDERSTANDING the discourse units in business communicative situations consists of the sociolinguistic, pragmatic and socio-semantic aspects of communicative competence. As the speaker's communicative competence includes knowing how to recognize and how to use utterances in a particular social situation, the students ability of 'Understanding' or recognizing the communicative utterances in business communicative situations forms an integral part of their communicative competence.

Subjects ability of CREATING the discourse units in business communicative situations: The students' ability of CREATING the discourse units in business communicative situations consists of the socio-linguistic, pragmatic and socio-semantic aspects of communicative competence. As the speaker's communicative competence includes knowing how to recognize and how to use utterances in a particular social situation, the students ability of 'Creating' or using the communicative utterances in business communicative situations forms an integral part of their communicative competence.

Sociolinguistic aspect: The sociolinguistic aspect in the above model refers to the notion of sociolinguistic competence which was propounded by Fodor, *et al* (1966); Cooper (1968), Campbell, *et al* (1970), Hymes (1972) Canale, *et al* (1980), and Cheryl, *et al* (1990). According to them the sociolinguistic competence comprises the speaker's knowledge of how to recognize and how to use the language in a particular social situation.

Pragmatic aspect: The pragmatic aspect in the above model refers to the notion of pragmatic competence which was derived the Speech Act theories of Austine (1962) and Searle (1969), from Halliday's (1973, 1976) description of language functions, and Bachman's (1989) concept of pragmatic competence. The pragmatic competence comprises the illocutionary and sociolinguistic competence. The illocutionary competence means the speaker's knowledge of how to perform the language functions. As described earlier, the language functions are grouped into four macro functions: Ideational, Manipulative, Heuristic and Imaginative. The Micro functions of the language in business communicative situation are dealt with in a separate chapter of this thesis.

Socio-semantic aspect: The Socio-semantic aspect in the above model refers to the notion of socio-semantic competence which was propounded by Halliday (1970, 1971, 1972), Willkins (1974), Munby (1978). The socio-semantic competence comprises the students knowledge about 'what a speaker can do — can mean — can say (Halliday, 1972) in varying socio-cultural contexts.

Thus, having dealt with the multiple dimensions of 'Communicative Competence' in this chapter, we shall deal with 'Communicative Competence Testing' in the next chapter.

References

Austine, J.L., 1962: *How To Do Things With Words*, Oxford, UK: Clarendon Press.

Bachman, L.F., 1989: Language Testing - SLA Research Interface, In *Annual Review of Applied Linguistics*, 9,193-209, 1989.

Chen-Si-Quing, 1990: A study of communicative strategies in Interlanguage Production by Chinese EFL Learners in Language, Learning, *Journal of Applied Linguistics*, Vol. 40, No. 2, June 1990.

Chomsky, N, 1965: *Aspects of the theory of syntax*, MIT Press.

Chomsky, N, 1970: Remarks on Nominalisation. In Jacobs, R. and P. Rosenbaum, (Eds.) *Readings in English Transformational Grammar*, Ginn.

Campbell Robin and Roger Wales, 1970: The Study of Language Acquisition, In Lyons, John, (Ed) *New Horizons in Linguistics*, Penguin.

Canale, M., 1983: Communicative Competence of Communicative Language Pedagogy London: Longman, In J. Richards and R. Schmidt (Eds.) *Language and Communication*, pp 2-27.

Canale, M. and Swain M., 1980: Theoretical Bases of Communicative Approaches to Second Language Teaching and Testing In *Applied Linguistics*, 1 pp 1-47.

Cooper, R.L., 1968: *An Elaborated Language Testing Model*. In *Language Learning* - Special Issue No.3 on Problems in Foreign Language Testing.

Corder, P., 1983: Strategies of Communication, London : Longman, In Faerch, C. and G. Kasper (Eds) *Strategies in Inter-language Communication*, pp 15-19.

Faerch, C., Kasper G., 1983, *Strategies in Interlanguage Communication*, London: Longman.

Fodor, and Garrett, 1966: Some Reflections on Competence and Performance, In *Psycholinguistic Papers*, Edinburgh University Press.

Fouly, K.A., L.A. Bachman and G.A. Cziko, 1990: The Divisibility of Language Competence: Confirmatory Approach, In *Language Learning* 40:1 March , pp 1-21.

Gladstone,J.R., 1969: Language and Culture, in *English Teaching* XXIII - 1, pp 114-117.

Habermas, J., 1970: Towards a Theory of Communicative Competence, In Dreitzel, H. (ed.) *Recent Sociology*, No.2 Collier, Macmillan.

Halliday, M.A.K., 1970: Language Structure and Language Function, In Lyons, John (ed.). *New Horizons in Linguistics*. Penguin.

Halliday, M.A.K., 1971: Towards a Sociological Semantics, In *Explorations in the Functions of Language* — Edward Arnold.

Halliday, M.A.K., 1976 : The Form of Functional Grammar, In G.R. Kress (ed.), *Halliday: System and Function in Grammar*, Oxford University Press, UK, pp 7-25.

Hymes, Dell, 1971: On Communicative Competence, In Pride and Holmes, (eds.) *Sociolinguistics*, Penguin.

Hymes, Dell, 1972: Models of The Interaction of Language and Social Life, In Gumperz and Hymes, (eds.) *Directions in Sociolinguistics*, Holt, Rinehart.

Isenberg, Nancy, 1990: Literary Competence and TEFL, In *ELT Journal* Vol 44/3, July 1990.

Johnson, K., 1976: The Production of Functional Material, In *ELT Documents*, The British Council, 1976/1 pp 19-20.

Jakobovits, Leon A., 1970: *Foreign Language Learning: A Psycholinguistic Analysis of The Issues*, Rowley, Mass - Newbury House.

Munby, J., 1978: Communicative Competence and a Theoretical Framework, In *Communicative Syllabus Design*. Cambridge University Press.

Paribakht, T., 1985: Strategic Competence and Language Proficiency, In *Applied Linguistics*, 6 pp 132-146.

Pauley, A. and F.H. Syder, 1983: Two Puzzles for Linguistic Theory: Nativelike Selection and Nativelike Fluency, In J.C.Richards and R.W. Schmidt (Eds.) *Language and Communication*, pp 191-226, New York : Longman.

Roberts, Cheryl A., 1990: The Art of Circumlocution : Teaching Strategic Competence, In *Forum* Vol. XXVIII, No. 4, Oct. 1990.

Searle, J.R., 1969: *Speech Acts*, Cambridge University Press, UK.

Widdowson, H.G., 1972: *The Teaching of English as Communication*, London: Oxford University Press.

Wilkins, D., 1974: *Second Language and Teaching*, Arnold 1974, pp 1-4.

9

COMMUNICATIVE COMPETENCE EVALUATION

"For with what judgement you judge, you will be judged; and with the same measure you use, it will be measured back to you."

— Mathew 7:2

The objective of this study is to test comprehensively the communicative competence achievements of the selected University MBA-I students in communicative syllabus. Therefore, it is necessary to take a survey of the trends in modern language testing, the testing devices of linguistic and communicative competence, the testing devices of communicative skills and the evaluation systems of communicative competence in general English, and finally, to evolve a most comprehensive and scientific way of evaluating the students communicative competence achievements in communicative syllabus.

Further, the objective of this study is to test the three dimensions of the students' communicative competence achievements in communicative syllabus, i.e., (i) to test the students' knowledge of the theory part of business communication; (ii) to test the students' competence of understanding the discourse units which are used in the business communicative situations; and (iii) to test the students' ability to create the discourse units in the business communicative situations. The present chapter merely surveys the communicative competence testing techniques from 1975 onwards. The following two chapters deal with the development and formation of the comprehensive communicative competence testing design.

THE TRENDS IN MODERN LANGUAGE TESTING

At the 1975 AILA (Association International de Linguistique Appliquee), World Congress, 1975, in a Keynote speech entitled, "Language Testing: Art or Science?" Bernard Spolsky identified three trends in the history of modern language testing :

(1) **The Prescientific Trend:** This period relied heavily on teacher's subjective assessments of the learner's ability to speak and/or write the language. During this period, generally before the 1960's, there was little concern about the statistical reliability or validity of language assessment. It was assumed that anyone proficient enough to teach a language was also qualified to assess the learners' proficiency.

(2) **The Psycho-structuralist Trend**: The publication of Lado's Language Testing in 1961 marked the beginning of the psychometric — structuralist period. This second era was primarily concerned with constructing tests which measured knowledge of the discrete linguistic structures and rules. The psychometric structrualists constructed tests which had demonstratable statistical reliability and validity.

(3) **The Psycholinguistic—Sociolinguistic trend**: Recently, there has been a reaction against the psychometric — structuralist approach which resulted in what Spolsky has termed the 'intergrative-sociolinguistic' approach to language testing. This approach does not discount the importance of psychometric reliability and validity, but it places major emphasis on testing language as a functional communicative tool which is used in genuine communicative settings.

TESTING LINGUISTIC AND COMMUNICATIVE COMPETENCE

Discrete — Point Tests

The accuracy of learner's command of linguistic elements

like vocabulary, structures and pronunciation etc. is determined by the test of linguistic competence. Discrete point tests are used to evaluate learner's linguistic competence. "Tests of linguistic competence are equated with discrete point tests, in that the leaner is evaluated on specific aspects of the second language" (Valette, 1977:12). On the other hand, the test of communicative competence focuses on the learner's ability to communicate in specific situations. In discrete-point test, learner's score depends on the linguistic accuracy. The discrete— point tests "measure knowledge of individual language items, such as a grammar test which has different sections on tenses, adverbs and prepositions. Discrete — point tests are based on the theory that language consists of different parts (eg. grammar, sounds, vocabulary) and different skills (eg. listening, speaking, reading and writing) and these are made up of elements that can be tested separately" (Richards, 1985: 84). Though integrative means of testing and evaluation are used extensively to assess the overall communicative performance of the test-takers, the objective test items i.e. multiple-choice forms, are ideal to measure the multiple facets of communicative competence separately.

A. Multiple Choice Tests

A.1. ***The characteristics of Multiple-choice items***: A multiplechoice item consists of a 'stem' or 'lead' and a list of suggested solutions of the problem given in that stem. The problem in multiple-choice item is given in the form of a direct question or an incomplete statement. The suggested solutions are called 'alternatives' or 'choices' or 'options'. The test-taker is directed to read the stem and the list of alternative solutions and to select one alternative which is correct or best. The correct alternative is the 'answer' and the other alternatives are the 'distractions'. The intended function of the incorrect alternatives is to distract the test-taker who are not sure about the correct solution. As the most versatile type of test item, it has such a wide applicability and uses that many designers of standardized test use multiple-choice items exclusively. Multiple-choice items can measure a variety of learning outcomes in the knowledge area — the knowledge of terminology, the knowledge of specific facts, the knowledge of methods and procedures etc. Secondly, multiple-choice items are especially adaptable to measure various aspects of understanding and application—the ability to interpret various relationships among facts, the ability to identify correct application of facts and principles, the ability to select the correct justification of a particular method or procedure.

A.2. ***The Uses of Multiple-Choice Tests***: Multiple-choice test item types were developed to overcome a number of the weaknesses and limitations of composition tests. The multiple-choice item can measure not only the simple learning outcomes, but it can also measure both the knowledge and understanding levels. Therefore, multiple-choice item is useful to measure not only the discrete components of language but also a variety of more complex outcomes of the communicative competence of the test-taker.

A.3. ***Limitation of Multiple-Choice Items***: Like all other paper-pencil tests, multiple-choice test is limited to learning outcomes at the verbal level. Even the application which the leaners are asked to make are verbal applications. The Multiple-choice test item, like other paper-and-pencil tests, measures whether the pupil 'knows' and 'understands' what to do when confronted with a problem situation, but it cannot determine how the pupil, actually 'will' perform in that situation (Gronlund, *et al* 1990: 177). Harris (1974) mention the most common objection to this testing method — 'the examinee does not have to think of his own answers; he "merely" makes choices' (Harris, 1974, 8). Multiple choice tests require considerable skill and time to prepare them. Multiple choice items are not well adaptable for measuring the ability to organize and present the ideas. Finally, in multiple-choice items, the test-designer has to find out incorrect but plausible distracters.

Using Error — Analysis Technique

In the tests of communicative competence, the learners demonstrate their language skills used to meet the specific communicative situation. They use language components in oral and written self-expressions to communicate their thoughts and feelings, but, the given test cannot predict which sentences the learner will produce. Therefore, standard item analysis techniques or the preparation of diagnostic answer keys are not suitable for testing communicative competence. Using error analysis technique is supposed to be one of the most appropriate way of interpreting learner's performance on communication test. The error analysis technique was primarily used by Albert Valdman (1975: 219-258). Error analysis helps the test giver to reveal learner's strategies and later, to prepare more effective learning materials. The main goal of error analysis technique is to classify the types of errors and identify those which hinder communication.

All the 'slips of tongue' or 'slips of the pen' are the subject of investigation for some linguists. Such typical slips are transposition, substitution or of an utterance like speech sound, morpheme or a word. This investigation aims at discovering the patterns of regularity in the slips. According to Boomer and Laver (1968), by studying these slips, linguists are able to infer relevant properties of an unobservable system on the basis of its output characteristics. S. Pit Corder (1973) labels these slips or false starts or confusions of structure as 'Lapses'.

The speaker or the writer may also produce 'inappropriate' utterances. These are some sort of error of judgment. Corder says, 'They are failures to match the language to the situation. The most obvious examples of these failures are 'social gaffes'; but they may be more subtle, the selection of the wrong term in some technical discussion — I understand the Navy do not like their ships to be referred to as "boats". Such mistakes, as I shall call them, are a case of the selection of the wrong style, dialect or variety' (Corder, 1973, 259).

The speech and to some extent writing is liable to

breakdowns and failures. These breakdowns are not just random but systematic; and, they arise from physiological and psychological causes or from imperfect knowledge of the linguistic norms of some group.

According to Chomsky, the object of linguistics is the characterization of the competence of the native speaker-hearer. Both the speaker and the hearer require knowledge of the formation rules. If they have inadequate knowledge of these rules, this 'inadequacy' will show itself in their expressive and the receptive behaviour. But, as compared to the receptive behaviour, it has been understood that it is much easier to detect imperfect knowledge in the case of expressive behaviour. 'Expression leaves traces transient, but recordable, in the case of speech, permanent in the case of the writing. The receptive behaviour most often has no observable behavioural concomitants. The hearer does not always demonstrate unambiguously that he has understood fully what we say. Much speech and most writing requires no overt response from the recipients; some is satisfied with smiles, grunts or other paralinguistic behaviour; some demand specific non-linguistic activity: the executing of orders or the following of instructions, and only a small part expects linguistic activity: answers to questions, denials and agreements (Corder, 1973, 261). He further says that even when we have reason to suspect a failure of comprehension, we still may have great difficulty in determining which particular linguistic features of our utterance have been misinterpreted.

It is the systematic nature of any code system like 'language' that makes communication possible. The assumption which underlies the description of errors is that they are evidence of a system, not the system of the target language, but a system of some 'other' language. The theoretical objective of error analysis is to describe that 'other' language precisely. 'The key, then, to error analysis is the systematic nature of language and consequently of error. No one would attempt the task unless he worked on this assumption' (Corder, 1973, 270). It must also be remembered that something may appear unsystematic only because one has no inkling of the nature of its regularity. A single occurrence of an error is an insufficient evidence upon which to base any hypothesis of a system. Before hypothesizing one needs a fair quantity of data to assure that the observed regularity is not a chance one.

S.Pit Corder classifies the errors in two groups: predictable errors and unpredictable errors. Yet he admits that this classification is not adequate. The interlanguage is instable, therefore prediction is an uncertain thing.

In the present study, the errors are classified in 3 groups — syntactic, semantic and pragmatic.

Testing Communicative Competence — An Artful Task

Communication allows and indeed encourages creativity on the part of the language learner; therefore, in communicative competence tests, it is usually difficult to predict how the learner will respond. It is possible to develop objective test items to evaluate the listening and reading comprehension, but the test of the productive skills like written and oral self-expression draws out free responses which are difficult to be scored objectively. Elliott Eisner (1967) who was providing the classic humanistic defense of liberal teaching and subjective artful evaluation of the learners understanding of language use, has opined that the "construction of curriculums" were "artful tasks". M.J. Benson (1987) supports Eisner's view that construction of curriculums in ESL and EFL, and testing its consequences are the "artful tasks". However, an appropriate scoring procedure can be developed to evaluate the learner's performance with a good degree of objectivity. Regarding subjectivity of such test, Valette (1977) opines that the teachers of the foreign language course must give the learners an opportunity to demonstrate their communicative ability. "If communication is one of the major goals of the foreign language course, teachers must give the leaners the opportunity to demonstrate the ability to communicate. Even such tests are not totally objective" (Valette, 1970: 10).

INTEGRATIVE APPROACH TO COMMUNICATIVE COMPETENCE TESTING

The Meaning of Integrative Testing

The tests of communicative competence which focus on the learner's ability to communicate in specific situations are also called as 'integrative', functional or 'global' tests. These tests measure the learner's ability to understand and use language in different contexts. While preparing a language test, the test designer generally takes into account the elements of both the psychometric strucuralist trend and the psycholinguistic sociolinguistic trend. He tries to find out, in as objective manner as possible, whether the learner has mastered the vocabulary and structures in a specific lesson. He is also concerned with how well the learners have assimilated the elements of language and to what extent they can use the second language for communication. Psycholinguistic-sociolinguistic trend gives more emphasis on testing of communicative competence.

Global tests take into account the total communicative effect of the message. The psycholinguistic sociolinguistic trend concentrates attention on the global or integrative tests. The psycholinguists uphold the concept of "overall language proficiency or language competence". They are of the opinion that knowing a language is more important than just knowing several thousand discrete elements. The sociolinguists have introduced the concept of a situational approach to testing and have given stress on communicative competence.

"The dictation test based on unfamiliar material is a global test. So is the reading test in which random words have been omitted (the cloze test). Tests in which leaners are presented with a situation and must express themselves, and in which their performance is evaluated in terms of their communication effectiveness, are also termed global tests" (Valette, 1977: 12). In these tests the learner is scored, not on linguistic accuracy, but on his or her ability to produce or comprehend a message. In this context, learner's linguistic errors are counted only if they interfere with communication. According to Rebecca Valette (1977) the global test also includes indirect measures of language proficiency. The global tests are essentially different from the discrete point tests. In discrete point testing, "We need to test the elements and skills separately" (Lado, 1961: 29). It includes the items that test the learner's vocabulary items, structural patterns and the like. It is a test which measures knowledge of individual language items, such as a grammar test which has different sections on tenses, adverbs and prepositions. Discrete point tests are based on the theory that language consists of different parts (eg. grammar, sounds, vocabulary) and different skills (eg. listening, speaking, reading and writing) and these are made up of elements that can be tested separately (Richards, 1985: 84). Usually, the discrete-point tests are the tests consisting of multiple choice items. However, "Multiple choice interpretation questions based on a longer listening or reading selection can focus on global aspects of the language. Longer speech and writing samples, in themselves global measures, can be scored on the basis of specific elements in a manner that parallels discrete point items" (Valette, 1977:12). Global test designer does not isolate the elements and skills, but he uses tasks that are fundamentally analogous to normal communicative exchanges. On the other hand, the discrete point test designer sees language competence as a collection of relatively independent components. The advocates of global testing see language competence as a functional totality, a psychologically real grammar. According to Oller (1973:8) the global tests are based on the assumption that in any normal use of language, the sequence of linguistic elements that occurs is restricted by various kinds of contexts. Groot (1975) is of the opinion that in global testing the learner is expected to show his ability to understand the target language which is spontaneously produced by educated native speakers at normal conversational speech in a variety of communicative situations, and secondly, he is required to produce appropriate oral feedback. In global testing, learner's linguistic creativity may cross the rules of grammar and it may even modify the very generative mechanism. However, in discrete-point testing this creativity of language has no scope beyond the limit of well-formedness of sentence structure. According to Oller (1973), learner's linguistic creativity is more than just the ability to generate an indefinitely large set of mental objects, such as well-formed sentences. Linguistic creativity also entails the capacity to modify the very generative mechanism itself. This aspect of learners communicative competence allows him to use different varieties of language and to modify his utterances according to the audience concerned in a variety of communicative situations. Therefore, it can be said that, "the sole criterion in a test of communicative competence is intelligibility" (Allen, 1975: 6). In global testing, there is direct predictive validity which is assessed by an external criterion which can be applied after some time has elapsed following the administration of the test (Moller, 1975:7-8). On the other hand, in discrete point testing, the predictive validity is determined on the basis of the test's concurrent validity.

The global tests of communicative competence, particularly the cloze and dictation tests have been found to be useful measures of the learner's communicative competence, and, according to Oller (1979, Chapter 10,12) these tests are relatively easy to construct and administer. These tests produce inter individual variation which is fairly reliable.

However, the scores generated by these tests usually cannot be interpreted in a criterion referenced manner. It is usually not possible to identify in any meaningful way the level of proficiency represented by a particular test score. Since the total scores obtained in such tests may represent many different patterns of responses, the total test scores may not be easily comparable among individuals. Gary A. Cziko (1982) points out another difficulty with global tests of cloze and dictation that there is no way to know if a particular prose passage on which the test is based will be too easy or too hard for a group of language learners until after they have the test. A test used for a typical cloze or dictation test which is either too easy or too difficult for the examiners will result in a restricted range of score and reduced sensitivity to individual difference.

Global or integrative tests are based on the cognitive view that language is more than the sum total of its constituents. The aspects of phonology, syntax, semantics, morphology, the language skills of listening, speaking, reading and writing, are not isolated in integrative testing as they are specifically isolated in discrete point tests. In psycholinguistic approach of Campbell and Wales (1970), Psycho-Sociolinguistic approach of Jacobovits (1970), sociolinguistic approach of Cooper (1968), Hymes (1971), Sinclair, Forsyth, Coulthard and Ashby (1972), and in sociosemantic approach of Halliday (1971, 1972), Wilkins (1972), all of them, have put more premium on language in 'context'. Therefore, integrative testing also came to be known as integrative of context. Integrative tests are a way to test language proficiency. Cloze tests, dictation tests, composition tests and dialogue tests are all tests of integrative skills.

The Cloze Tests

The cloze technique is derived from gestalt psychology which views language as a whole and not in its parts. Therefore, cloze test is widely accepted as a test of integrative language skills. The cloze procedure was originally designed by Taylor in 1953 to test the reading comprehension of the leaners. It refers to the learner's ability of filling in the gaps in an incomplete pattern (Hinofotis, 1987). According to Taylor (1953), cloze procedure is a method of intercepting a message from a transmitter (communication sender), mutilating its language patterns by deleting parts and so administering it to the receivers (readers or listeners) that their attempts to make the patterns whole again potentially yield a considerable number of cloze items.

Though cloze procedure was originally developed by Taylor to test the difficulty of reading passage for native speakers, it received particular attention of number of researchers in 1975 (Oller, 1973; Anderson, 1979). They used cloze procedure as a possible measure of overall ESL proficiency. Oller (1988) points out that the cloze tests measure elements of language ability which is not tapped by traditional discrete point tests. Stabbes and Tucker, (1974:241) suggest that the cloze procedure provides 'a powerful and economical measure' of EFL proficiency.

A. Random Deletion, Rational Deletion and Cloze-Elide

In cloze procedure, every 'n'th word, usually every fifth, sixth or seventh word is deleted from the selected reading passage (Anderson, 1979; Brown, 1983; Klein-Braley, 1983). The first sentence is retained without any deletion. Sometimes, even the second sentence is not touched. The intention is that the subject of the passage be established. After this, every 'n'th word is deleted throughout the remaining passage. The learner is asked to fill in the blanks. Rational deletion is an alternative form of deletion. In this form, deletion is limited to content words rather than function words. MacLean (1984) and Bachman (1985) have preferred 'rational deletion' because the nature of the deleted item can be controlled and the semantic relationships tend to be less distorted. Cloze-Elide technique is the third variation of cloze tests (Manning, 1986). In this technique, the learner is asked to identify the incorrect words inserted into a passage.

B. What Does The Cloze Test Measure ?

Cloze test has been accepted as a very good test of integrative skills and it measure both achievement and proficiency of the learner in the target language. According to Oller (1973, 1988), Bachman, (1982, 1985), Brown (1983), Heilenman (1983), Chavez-Oller, Chihara and Weaver (1986), Hinofotis (1987), Laesch and Van Kleeck (1987), cloze test measures the learner's advanced skills and global proficiency, because it correlates well with the other tests like dictation, reading tests, essay tests and standardized proficiency tests. According to Farhady (1979) the cloze and other integrative tests are statistically similar to discrete point tests because there exists no statistical difference between them. According to Alderson (1979), the cloze procedure is useful to measure only basic skills of language because it correlates more with grammar tests than with the tests of reading.

As compared to various discrete point tests, the cloze test is easy to construct and score. In random deletion, it involves equal deletion of content and function words. It tests the learner's lexical control and reading comprehension. Cloze tests have high correlations with other measures of language skills and they test all abilities involved in language use (Farhady, 1979; Oller, 1973, 1988, Brown, 1989, Bachman, 1982, 1985, Hinofotis, 1987, Fotos, 1991). And the measurement of leaners' abilities of language skills through cloze procedure helps the test-giver to discriminate the population.

C. The Validity of Cloze Tests

The issues regarding validity of cloze tests have been explored by different researchers. Alderson (1979), Bachman (1982), Heilenman (1983), Klein-Braley (1983), Upshur (1983), Hanania and Shikhani (1986). Alderson (1979) studied the effects of different deletion rates on three different texts in a total of twelve cloze tests. Then, he compared the leaner's performance on these cloze tests with their performance on a standardized discrete point test of English proficiency. The twelve cloze tests varied significantly with each other and with the standardized discrete point test of English proficiency. This led Alderson (1979) to conclude that "the cloze procedure is not a unitary technique, since it results in tests which are markedly different" (Alderson, 1979: 225-226).

However, Heilenman (1983), Hanania and Shikhani (1986), Laesch and Van Kleeck (1987), Brown (1988, 1989) have found that the use of cloze tests as a proficiency measure can yield parallel and reliable forms with content validity. For this purpose, there are certain steps which must be followed carefully in preparing the test material. These are: (1) The alternative tests of appropriate reading difficulty must be selected and prepared carefully. (2) These tests must be given for pretesting to determine which have the best reliabilities and difficulty indices. The tests having best reliabilities and difficulty indices will provide the best discrimination among the test takers. (3) The final selection must be rewritten to ensure that all language functions are examined equally. (4) There should be the last pretesting of the chosen form.

Bachman (1982, 1985) and MacLean (1984) have found that both content validity and the equivalence of items across different cloze test forms appear to be better handled by the rational deletion procedure. On the other hand, Brown (1989) suggests language functions representatively, as long as the samples are large enough for it. There exists a considerable body of research (Stubbs and Tucker, 1974; Oller, 1973; Bachman, 1982; Brown, 1983, 1988, 1989) that demonstrates criterion-related validity and its two components concurrent validly and predicative validity of various cloze tests.

Dictation Tests

There are a number of practical reasons for the renewed popularity of the dictation procedure as a measure of second language proficiency. The dictation, despite the criticism against it that it is uneconomical and uninformative as a testing device and has a problematic scoring procedure, is still a very good test of how well the leaner can handle language. A dictation test is easy to construct because it requires only to locate a passage of appropriate difficulty, style and its division into segments (of usually 7 to 12 words) for presentation (Cziko and Lin, 1984). According to Oller (1979), a dictation test is considerably easier to construct than the multiple choice tests, and secondly it is highly adaptable to the needs of individual classes. Though dictation tests are easy to construct and are adaptable to the needs of individual classes, there are a number of factors that limit its usefulness. Some of these are: There is no simple and uniform formula for deciding the level of difficultness of the dictation passage. The usual procedure of scoring in dictation is to subtract one point for different types of errors. This equal weighing of all types of errors is illogical as it does not stand on any empirical basis.

As compared to other tests of written responses like multiple choice tests or cloze tests, a dictation test requires more time and care to score.

Composition Tests

Though composition is considered as a test of integrative skills, it is very difficult to score and hence it is not always reliable. According to Harris (1969), there are two chief difficulties in using and assessing compositions as a measurement device — (i) It does not elicit the specific language items that the test writer particularly wishes to test and, (ii) It does not find a way to evaluate these free responses reliably and economically.

Dialogue Tests

As an integrative test, in a dialogue, the learner is asked to imagine a situation and produce an oral composition. However, like composition the dialogue is also problematic for scoring due to subjectivity.

TESTING LEARNER'S COMPETENCE OF USING COMMUNICATIVE SKILLS

Understanding Aspects of Communication

"It will be generally acknowledged that the ultimate aim of language learning is to acquire communicative competence, to interpret, whether this is made overt in talking or corresponding or whether it remains covert as psychological activity underlying the ability to say, listen, write and read" (Widdowson, 1978: 67). Because of the increased emphasis today on direct communication in English as a second and foreign language, the skills of listening, writing and reading have also become the objects of growing attention. It is, in fact, impossible for two persons of different linguistic backgrounds to carry on a productive conversation or correspondence in which each speaks or writes his or her own language.

Testing communicative competence is essentially the assessment of the levels of communicative competence and it requires the construction of a test in one or more than one of the four skills. i.e., reading, writing, listening and speaking. It assesses the learner's use of language in communication particularly the relationships between sentences and contexts and situations in which they are used. In business communicative competence tests, learner's understanding of the following aspects of communication are tested:

i. How the interpretation and use of utterances depend on the knowledge of the real business world.
ii. How speakers use and understand speech acts.

According to Patil D.K. (1984:191) communicative competence testing aims at measuring the learner's ability to function in a given environment in that target language. He says that the test should aim at indicating whether the learner is proficient enough to use the language in a real life situation. Anyway, the test should indicate the learner's level of communicative competence with reference to the prescribed objectives in the curriculum of the course. It should aim at measuring the extent of learner's achievement of the instructional goals (Harris. 1969:2-4).

Communicative competence test designer does not concentrate on testing the learner's ability to handle elements of the language such as phonology, vocabulary and grammar, but on the other hand, to a greater extent, he concentrates on testing the integrated skills. J.B. Heaton (1975) gives more stress on including test items that measure the learner's ability in using second language. "It is generally advisable to include test items which measure the ability to communicate in the target language. How important, for example, is the ability to discriminate between the phonemes /i:/and/i/? Even if they are confused by the testee and he says : Look at the sheep sailing slowly out of the harbour, it is unlikely that misunderstanding will result because the context itself provides other clues to the meaning" (Heaton, 1975: 6). A learner cannot be described as being adapt in a target language simply because he is able to make a distinction between two sounds or because he has mastered a number of structures of the language. According to Heaton (1975), it can be argued that fluency in English or, a person's ability to express feelings, ideas, facts and attitudes with ease, clarity and completeness, in writing or in speech, and his ability to comprehend what he listens or reads can be measured by tests which evaluate performance in the language skills. Tests of auditory and reading comprehension, oral interviews and essays are generally used to assess performance in these language skills.

The Present Trend in Testing Communicative Competence as Comprising Sub-Skills

For testing communicative competence, the present trend is to regard communicative competence as comprising subskills which may develop differently and at different rates (Carroll, 1983: 104). In the case of speech and writing, attempts have been made to identify these components of communicative competence and to measure them separately. Margaret Mathews (1990) is of the opinion that this trend threatens to complicate administration of the test. In the first place, when oral skills are being measured, the burden upon the assessor is too great. This happens especially when the assessor plays a dual or even triple role. He acts as a plausible, sympathetic interlocutor and an efficient administrator as well as assessor. "It is simply not possible to participate in conversation, put candidates at their ease, watch the clock, check papers and consult criteria for a range of sub-skills; at least; it is not possible to do all these things satisfactorily" (Mathews, 1990: 117). In such a case Underhill (1987, 86) suggests that 'three or four' may be the maximum number of parameters an assessor can cope with at one time. It was opined by Underhill (1987) and Mathews (1990) that, if the present trend of assessing speech across multiple parameters continues, it will be necessary to delegate the roles of interlocutor and possibly administrator to others, thereby increasing administrative complexity and costs. Serious flaws are also found in the area of test validity. In the first place, the selected criteria are at times arbitrary and inconsistent. For example, within the same test of English language Testing Services (ELTS Non academic), the criteria for writing skills are accuracy and communication of meaning. In this context, Mathews (1990: 119) asks, "...if phonological clarity is held to be such a significant sub-skill as to carry one-third of the total mark, why is its graphic counterpart, handwriting, completely overlooked ?" Allocating equal marks for the various sub-skills is the another flaw. It is illogical to allocate equal marks because the relationship between them is not simple one of addition. Carroll's (1982: 3) delineation of performance levels refers to hierarchical abilities, but subsequent versions of his framework have confused the relationship between the parts. Margaret Mathews (1990:120) thinks that the validity of the current tests (RSA CUEFL the Royal Society of Arts Examination in the Communicative use of English as a Foreign Language, English Language Testing Services (ELTS) etc.) could be improved by greater attention to the selection and description of categories. Descriptions of sufficient accuracy to allow objective distinctions to be made are simply not available. This is not a call for a return to the old, safe, discrete-point type of test. Rather I think we must explore the possibility of still other test designs, where neither reliability nor validity are too obviously compromised (Mathews, 1990:120).

Though increased interest in the teaching of the communicative skills has brought about greater emphasis on both the teaching and the testing of oral communication, oral performance in communicative situations is one of the most difficult skills to assess. Shohamy, Reves and Bejarano are of the opinion that the main reasons for this difficulty stem from the fact that, "Communicative speaking tests tend to have low rater reliability and low content validity and construct validity" (Shohamy, *et al*, 1986:212).

Testing Listening

The skill of listening has become an object of growing attention due to increased emphasis on direct communication. If the listening skill is considered a course objective it becomes necessary to assess learner's achievement in auditory comprehension, "Auditory comprehension of a foreign language means recognition and control of the signaling elements of the language in communication situations" (Lado, 1961: 206). According to Valette (1977), the skill of listening requires proficiency in three areas: (i) discrimination of sounds, (ii) understanding of specific elements, and (iii) overall comprehension.

The auditory comprehension tests can be divided into two types :-

(A) Auditory comprehension tests for evaluating linguistic competence, and
(B) Auditory comprehension tests for evaluating communicative competence.

A. Auditory Comprehension Tests for Evaluating Linguistic Competence

In order to assess the learner's auditory comprehension for evaluating his linguistic competence, the test designer has to assess the following abilities of the learner —

i. Ability to discriminate sounds
ii. Ability to understand vocabulary
iii. Ability to understand structures

The main object of a listening test is to measure learner's degree of comprehension. The learner's degree of comprehension depends on their ability to discriminate phonemes to recognize stress and intonation patterns and to retain what they have heard (Valette, 1977: 74-75). However to understand a message in conversation, the listener also requires a knowledge of vocabulary and grammar of the target language. As the ability to understand the target language greatly depends on one's knowledge of vocabulary, many commercial listening tests can rightly be called as modified vocabulary tests. In such listening tests, the vocabulary to be tested is introduced in a natural conversational framework. A wide variety of oral quizzes are used to assess the learner's comprehension of key lexical terms. According to Wilga Rivers (1975) these are primarily the tests of "skill-getting".

B. Auditory Comprehension Tests for Evaluating Communicative Competence

In these tests the objective is to evaluate the learner's communicative competence. The test-designer is concerned to find out if the learners exactly replicate the sender's intended meaning of the message. He is not concerned to find out whether the learners are able to discriminate sounds or to identify specific structural signals. According to Wilga Rivers (1975), the communication items are tests of "skill-using". Usually these tests include passage comprehension items. "The recorded passage is usually a contrived dialogue read by native speakers or a monologue or talk read by one native speaker — the questions follow a multiple choice format" (Valette, 1977: 104). Since the aim of such a test is to assess the learner's ability to follow a dialogue or monologue or talk, the questions are framed in an easily comprehensible format. Taking notes in outline is a test that evaluates a learner's ability of note taking and organizing the message. But it is not a pure listening test as it also tests the learner's command of the written language.

As compared to 'taking notes', 'taking dictation' is a precise measure of listening comprehension. The dictation test is effective as a listening comprehension test with the learners who can handle the written media.

Testing Oral Production

The development of communicative competence being the goal of the second language teaching programmes, emphasis is placed on the development of correct speech habits.

However, "... all too frequently the speaking skill is more or less ignored when tests are being planned. While many teachers claim that they can assign overall grades for speaking ability according to class performance, such scores are to a certain extent subjective" (Valette, 1977: 119). In addition to this, if all formal tests are of the pen and paper variety, the learners realize that their preparation should depend on reading and writing rather than on acquiring oral communicative competence. But over the past thirty years, language test designers are placing more emphasis on the speaking tests. They have realized the fact that one of the major reasons for which the learners have been enrolling in language classes is to acquire the ability to communicate with the people of a different linguistic background. Therefore, "Behind the development of new instructional programmes and the dissemination of audiovisual materials is one aim: teaching the learners to speak the language" (Valette, 1977: 119).

The aspects of learning to speak a second language are: (i) Mastering a different sound system, (ii) Mastering Vocabulary, (iii) Mastering the grammatical patterns of the language, and (iv) Acquiring oral communicative ability. The learner is expected to make accurate pronunciation of an individual vowel, diphthong and consonant sounds and to control the intonation rhythm and stress patterns of the target language. His vocabulary acquisition is the second important aspect of the speaking skill. Thirdly, he is expected to handle the grammatical patterns of the target language with ease and accuracy. Finally, the main emphasis focuses on the transmission of a message or series of messages.

While testing the first aspect, the test-giver evaluates the production of the segmental phonemes, vowels, diphthongs and consonants of the target language. He also prepares items that permit the evaluation of specific aspects of intonation and stress system. While testing the second and third aspects via speaking he uses the visual and oral cues in the native and target language.

When the learners are being evaluated on their ability to communicate orally, the essential consideration is whether they are able to make themselves understood (Valette, 1977). The prominence is given to the meaning of the message, rather than on its grammaticality. The learner is instructed about the message he has to transmit. However, the choice of words and structures is not specified and is left to the learner. The learners are assigned roles and are given precise directions regarding the type of conversation they are to engage in. Their performance is rated simply on the basis of the amount of relevant information transmitted. A wide variety of directed conversation tests are written by Gerald E. Logan (1973) and Hilda Bals (1976). Leon A. Jacobovitz and Barbara Gordon (1974) introduced tests of reporting conversation. In these tests, the learner listens to a live or recorded conversation between two native speakers of the target language. Then the learner reports the contents of the message. Learner's performance is rated on the basis of the accuracy of information, amount of relevant information, fluency of speech, naturalness of discourse organization, style of expression, clarity of expression and gestural fluency. The emphasis is given on the transactional competence rather than on correctness of syntax and pronunciation. In the tests of 'getting information' (Bartz, 1974), the learner plays the role of an interviewer and tries to obtain certain information from his teacher or the other learner. The learner uses only the target language in conducting interview and then writes down the information obtained. Bartz (1974) developed the rating scale which was based on fluency, quality of communication, amount of communication and the learner's effort to communicate.

In a free expression oral test, the learner determines what to say and how to say it. "Although a general topic or conversational direction may be suggested, the teacher cannot predict the actual content of the learner's talk" (Valette, 1977: 151). A free expression oral test includes a role play test, test of acting as interpreter, and live conversation or interview test. In the format of a role play test, several learners are informally tested at once, but the test is most effective when the number of learners is not more than ten. These learners carry out an impromptu conversation when specific roles are assigned to them. The rationale behind role playing test is to stimulate to produce spontaneous speech behaviour within given roles eliciting specific speech functions. In a role play test designed by Shohamy, *et al* (1986) the test-taker is given a card describing a situation and his or her role in it. The card is written in test-taker's mothertongue (Hebrew) so that the interference of reading comprehension in the foreign language could be avoided. The test-giver then engages the test-taker in stimulated conversation derived from the situation described on the card. The learner's performance is scored by the assessor who is not involved in the role play test. Test of acting as interpreter requires two testers for each learner. One tester speaks only the target language while the other speaks only the native language. The learner receives the message from the first tester in target language and interprets it in native language to the second tester. The message received from second tester in native language is interpreted by the learner in target language. The situation in this test usually develops as impromptu conversation. The reporting oral test is similar to the test of acting as interpreter. The rationale underlying this test is to stimulate the learner into a monologue in the foreign language, based on authentic input in Hebrew. In a reporting oral test designed by Shohamy, *et al* (1986), the learner is given a newspaper article in Hebrew. He or she is asked to read it silently and report its general content to the tester in his or her own words, in English. The learner is specifically asked not to translate the text, but rather to report freely, referring back to the text only if necessary.

"The most credible, or natural type of speaking test is a free conversation with the teacher or with another qualified speaker" (Valette, 1977: 155). Harris (1969) compares live conversation or interview test with composition test. "Roughly parallel to the composition as a measure of learner's written language is the scored interview as a device for assessing oral competence" (Harris, 1969: 6). In both of these tests, the learners are allowed to express their answers in their own words in a relatively unstructured testing situation. In interviews, the evaluation of learner's performance is generally made during the actual production of the responses. Usually, the examiner does not tape record the interview because, in most interview situations, the use of tapes has an undesirable effect on the learner. Therefore, the examiner has to concentrate on scoring the learner's performance during the actual interview. While commenting on the utility of interview test, Harris (1969) says, "Most teachers who use the interview test do so not out of any strong conviction that it is the best of all possible techniques, but simply because they have no better way of assessing the oral competence of their learners" (Harris, 1969:7).

Shohamy, *et al*, (1986) have found several deficiencies in the interview procedure used to test the oral communicative competence. The test consists of an informal, unstructured interview, and the topics of conversation between the tester and the learner vary freely from everyday matters to more sophisticated students, without any advance planning. The scores assigned to the test-taker as a result of this interview are impressionistic, based on the tester's subjective judgement, without the use of a rating scale.

An unstructured, informal interview procedure used to measure oral communicative competence usually represents a single speech style — an interview. It is, therefore, questionable whether it is a valid indication of the learners overall oral communicative competence. Such a test is not sensitive enough to reveal the existing individual differences because of its low variance and narrow distribution of scores. Finding an alternative to such a test constitutes a problem, since among the large number of tests available hardly any has been sufficiently explored further. According to Bachman and Palmer (1981), Shohamy (1982), Hinofotis (1976), Clifford (1977) that which has been researched extensively is the FSI (Foreign Service Institute) Oral Interview. However, the major shortcoming of this test is that it does not encompass variety of speech styles. Such a test cannot be valid measure for assessing all aspects of oral communicative competence. Shohamy, *et al* (1986) used four experimental tests as valid measures of overall oral communicative competence: Oral Interview, Role Play, Reporting Test and Group discussion. These represent the speech styles which the learners should master. It involves the use of socio-linguistic and pragmatic features in oral discourse. The rationale behind these is to focus on a variety of speech styles which are likely to be needed in various oral communicative situations.

The model of the Foreign Service Institute Oral Interview (Lowe, 1982) and the other tests which followed that model include the following four phases:

1. **Warm-up**: In this phase the test taker is put at ease and the test derives a preliminary indication of the test-taker's level of oral communicative competence and understanding.
2. **Level-Check**: In this phase, the tester checks the functions and content where the test-taker's performance is accurate.
3. **Probing**: In this phase the tester assesses the highest level at which the candidate can function.
4. **Wind-up**: In this phase the test-taker is returned to the levels at which he or she can function most comfortably, and thus is left with a feeling of accomplishment. The scoring of the test-taker's performance on the oral interview is done on the basis of the rating scale used for all the tests.

For improving the scored interview, Harris (1969) proposes the following seven suggestions:

1. Decide in advance on interview methods and rating standards.,
2. Conduct the interviews in some quiet place with suitable accostics.
3. Reserve sufficient time for each interview.
4. Use at least two raters for each candidate.
5. Rate the candidates without reference to other test scores.
6. Record the ratings after the interview.
7. Obtain each candidate's final score by pooling or

averaging the two (or more) ratings that have been given him or her. The interview is brought courteously to an end when the interviewer is satisfied that he can make an accurate appraisal of the candidate's English proficiency (Harris, 1969: 93).

Testing Reading Comprehension

When we come to the testing of reading comprehension, we are concerned with the abilities needed in reading the second language. Therefore, before considering efficient approaches to the testing of reading, it is essential to distinguish clearly two activities which go by the concept of reading comprehension. A learner may be considered reading when he pronounces series of sounds which are symbolized by printed or written marks. This he may do in a comprehensible, conventional and acceptable way, without drawing meaning from the sounds which he enunciates. But, this activity is not the final goal in second or foreign language teaching. The learner must be able to comprehend meaning of what he reads. "He must also be taught to derive meaning from the word combinations in the text and to do this in a consecutive fashion at a reasonable speed, without necessarily vocalizing what he is reading" (Rivers, 1968: 215). Thus, the abilities needed in reading comprehension can be grouped under two headings. (1) Graphic symbols and sound systems, (2) Ideas represented by the graphic symbols.

(1) *Graphic Symbols and Sound Systems*: Graphic symbols and associated sound system include the following abilities:

a. Ability to comprehend lexical items (word recognition).
b. Ability to understand the morphological and syntactic patterns.
c. Ability to understand graphic symbols of writing.
d. Ability of using correct intonation patterns and stress.
e. Ability to understand the tone of the writing (the

writer's attitude towards the subject and the reader).

f. Ability to understand stylistic devices and methods by which the writer conveys his thoughts and ideas.

(2) *Ideas Represented by the Graphic Symbols*: Ideas represented by the graphic symbols include the following abilities :

a. Ability to identify the objectives of reading.
b. Ability to identify the writer's purpose of writing the text.
c. Ability to understand the central idea.
d. Ability to understand the subordinate or supporting ideas.
e. Ability to draw correct conclusions.
f. Ability to draw valid inferences.

In testing learner's reading comprehension the tester is concerned with measuring learner's acquisition of these complex abilities.

In testing reading ability for communicative interactions, the tester pays little attention to the errors committed by the learner at syntactic and phonological levels. "When people read a sign, a newspaper or a letter, they want to understand the message that the writer intends to convey. They will tolerate typographical errors, misspellings, and clumsy constructions as long as these are not so frequent as to interfere with communication. In testing reading ability at this level, the teacher strives to ascertain whether communication has taken place" (Valette, 1977:201).

Reading comprehension can also be tested by the way of translation. Some test designers shy away from translation because of the fear that this testing technique will encourage the learners to speak their native language more than the target language. In this testing technique the learners give a native language equivalent of the entire passage in a target language. In a partial translation test, "One part of the page contains the target language text. The other part of the page contains segments of the native missing words, phrases and/or sentences." (Valette, 1977:209). This text is longer to prepare, but it is shorter to grade because the attention of the examiner is focused only on the problem areas and not on the entire text.

Testing Writing

Lado defines writing a foreign language as 'the ability to use the language and its graphic representation productively in ordinary writing situations' (Lado, 1961:248). He recognizes two major elements in writing a foreign language: the language elements and the graphic representation of the language. He has not considered the learner's achievements in written communication and has not dealt with testing learner's written communicative competence. In testing learner's ability in 'writing'. Harris (1969: 68) recognizes the following five general components:

1. ***Content***: The substance of the writing; the ideas expressed.
2. ***Form***: The organization of the content.
3. ***Grammar***: The employment of grammatical forms and syntactic patterns.
4. ***Style***: The choice of structures and lexical items to give a particular tone or flavour to the writing.
5. ***Mechanics***: The use of the graphic conventions of the language.

Referring to the above five general components of writing process, Harris agrees that the writing skill is a highly sophisticated skill combining a number of diverse elements only some of which are strictly linguistic. But, like Lado (1961), he too does not refer to the 'communicative' aspect of writing process and its evaluation.

In testing writing, the essay or composition testing is favoured by some test-designers for following reasons:

1. Essay-type tests are easy to design.
2. Essay-type tests can be prepared quickly.
3. The learners organize their answers in their own way.

4. The learners use their own style, choice of structures and vocabulary.
5. Essay-type tests compel the learners to improve their composition.

Those who favour objective tests of writing do not agree with essay-type tests for the following reasons.

1. Essay-type tests encourage rote memorization.
2. Essay-type tests do not allow comprehensive testing of syllabus-objective achievements in language courses.
3. Essay-type tests require more scoring time than objective tests.
4. Essay-type tests allow the learner to cover-up their weaknesses by avoiding problems.
5. Learner's performance on the same test differs at different occasions.
6. The scoring of essay-type tests is highly subjective. "Over the years various studies have shown that the answers to essay questions are scored differently by different teachers and that even the same teachers score the answers differently at different times. Such results hardly, foster confidence in the essay test" (Gronlund, *et al* 1990: 216).

In testing learner's written communicative competence through directed composition, the main concern is the intelligibility of the written message. The scoring of directed composition shows this concern for effective communication. 'Spelling mistakes and missing accent marks, for instance, usually do not hinder the native speaker who is reading the text. Errors in the choice of vocabulary and word-order, however, may make comprehension difficult' (Valette, 1977 : 249). According to Valette the criteria for testing directed composition is to see if a native speaker of the language can easily understand the text. If the native speaker easily understands the text, the learner is successful in communicating. In directed composition, the learner is provided with a rather detailed framework and it primarily tests the learner's ability to express himself in writing. In directed composition, the framework may be introduced with visual, oral and written cues. The visual cues, may include series of pictures, cartoon, silent movie, filmstrip etc. In oral cues the learner are asked to listen the interview and write as complete description of it as they can. The learners are asked to write the message which they receive orally. Sometimes, the teacher dictates a letter and learners are asked to write it appropriately. In some cases, the teacher reads a narrative or a paragraph and the learners are asked to write a summary. In written cues, the teacher asks his learners to write down a conversation which is built around the suggested cues. For example the learners produce written version of spoken discourse; the learners are asked to write personal and business letters to an imaginary receiver, or to write a letter responding to an advertisement in a local newspaper etc.

The tests of directed composition expect restricted response from the learners. In these tests, the nature, length or organization of the response is limited. Restricting the type of response not only reduces the difficulty of scoring but it makes efficient the measuring of the learners knowledge of factual material. Yet the carefully prescribed and highly structured task in directed composition makes it less effective as a measure of the ability to select, organize, and integrate ideas.

In free composition tests, on the other hand, the learners are given almost complete freedom in making their responses. These tests permit the learners to decide which facts are most relevant, to select their own method of organizing the answers and to write at any length to make their answers most comprehensive. Such a test reveals the learner's ability to evaluate, select, organize and integrate the ideas. To some extent, it also helps to find out the individual differences in creative ability, attitudes and values. 'Yet free composition tests, like English essay tests, have two drawbacks: scoring is time-consuming and grades tend to lack objectivity. Not only will different teachers assign different grades to the same paper, but a teacher reading a set of papers for a second time will rarely give them the same grades as he or she gave after the first readings' (Valette. 1977: 254). The evaluation of free composition can be formal or informal. For formal evaluation. the learner is given a test in which he writes a composition with specific conditions on specific topic. For informal evaluation, the learner is allowed to write about almost anything that interests him. Usually, the teacher determines the aspects of composition which are to be scored and announces them. For example, the rating scale is prepared on the aspects like organization, vocabulary, clarity of expression etc. The choice of a composition topic depends upon the objective of evaluation. For example in grammar-oriented composition, the use of specific structures is evaluated; in 'point of view' composition, learner's imagination and consistency of style is evaluated; in 'thought-provoking' essays learner's logical reasoning, organization sophistication or effectiveness of communication is evaluated; in vocabulary based composition the richness and appropriateness of learner's vocabulary is evaluated.

Evaluation System of Communicative Competence

1. Evaluation of Language Used for Vocational Purposes

There are two types of communicative competence tests according to Rea (1976). The first type includes those tests which are primarily concerned with the evaluation of language used for vocational purposes. For example, the language used for communicative purposes in business, industry, government, education and various professions where every work situation demands a wide variety of communicative abilities. People in management positions discover that most of what they do in their jobs is communication. Management requires the ability to organize, co-ordinate. delegate duties and responsibilities, and integrate the efforts of a team. All of these managerial tasks require the ability to communicate clearly and persuasively (Bormann, *et al* 1986). The MBAs, especially, need to acquire these communicative skills to help themselves to move through what is popularly called the maze of bureaucratic redtape whether they are trying to register for classes, get a computer error changed at a large corporate bank, or deal with government agencies at the city, district, state and national levels. Rea's (1976) first type of tests aim at assessing whether the learners have acquired these communicative skills and sufficiently adequate command of the target language to enable them to carry out a particular job or task in different contexts. Cartier (1968) has called these tests as criterion referenced language tests.

2. Criterion Referenced Tests

Criterion referenced test generally measures a learner's performance according to a particular standard or criterion which has been agreed upon. The learner is expected to reach this level of performance in order to pass the test. Therefore, a learner's score is interpreted with reference to the criterion score rather than to the scores of other learners (Richards, 1985).

The criterion referenced test shows whether the learner has achieved predetermined objectives of the course. It indicates whether he has mastered the rhythm and accent of the target language. It shows if he is able to rewrite a paragraph from the present tense into the past tense. The learner's performance is graded on a pass-fail basis and the opportunity for retesting is provided. It is based on the specific material and it is given at the end of the unit. "In broader terms the criterion-referenced test may be conceived as a placement or proficiency test. According to the learner's scores on the test, he or she is placed on a specific course or given a rating that indicates, for example, his or her speaking ability" (Valette, 1977: 11). According to Valette, formative test is a type of criterion-referenced test.

Benjamin Bloom (1971: 10) developed the concepts of formative and summation evaluation. The formative test is given during the course of instruction. Its purpose is to show which aspects of the chapter the learner has mastered and where the remedial work is necessary. In formative tests, learners' performance is graded on pass-fail basis. The learners who fail in the test, are given the opportunity to study and then take the test again.

3. Criterion-Referenced Tests Vs. Norm-Referenced Tests

The criterion referenced language tests may be contrasted with the norm reference tests. Norm referenced tests are designed to measure how the performance of a particular learner or a group of learners compares with the performance of another leaner or a group of learners whose scores are given as a norm. A learner's score is interpreted with reference to the scores of other learners or groups of learners, rather than to an agreed criterion score.

Gronlund, *et al* have defined criterion referenced test as "A test designed to provide a measure of performance that is interpretable in terms of a clearly defined and delimited domain of learning tasks." (Gronlund, *et al* 1990:14). They have defined norm-referenced test as a test designed to provide a measure of performance that is interpretable in terms of an individual's relative standing in some known group. They have pointed out certain common characteristics of criterion referenced tests and norm referenced tests as given below.

A. Common Characteristics of the Criterion-Referenced and Norm-Referenced Tests

1. Both require specification of the achievement domain to be measured.
2. Both require a relevant and representative sample of test items.
3. Both use the same types of test items.
4. Both use the same rules for item writing (except for item difficulty).
5. Both are judged by the same qualities of goodness (validity and reliability).
6. Both are useful in educational measurement.

B. *Differences Between Criterion-Referenced and Norm-Referenced Tests*

Cartier (1968) has pointed out eight points of differences between norm-referenced tests and criterion referenced tests.

1. NRT (Norm-Referenced Test) is designed to produce a normal distribution of learner score, but CRT (Criterion-Referenced Test) is not designed to produce even a range of scores as learner's scores are not compared with each other.
2. NRT usually only samples the course objectives; it is hoped that the learner knows more than he is tested on, but CRT tests every essential behaviour.
3. NRT is usually satisfied with indirect testing of the job requirements that is, his knowledge about the job is tested. CRT insofar as possible, requires the learner to demonstrate his ability to perform the job actually.
4. A learner can pass a NRT even though he misses a certain predetermined number of items. Sometimes the passing score is even determined after the test has been given. The number of items the learner can miss and still graduate is often as high as fifty percent. But on CRT each learner is expected to get all the items right, though for practical reasons he can miss some ten percent of the items.
5. In grading NRT one does not attempt to find out which items a learner missed, one only counts them. So, one never knows what misconceptions the graduate may take away with him. But, in CRT, each learner is given at least some remedial training on any item he missed even if he got the passing 90 per cent.
6. Test security is a constant problem with the sampling - type, competitive NRT. On the other hand, since CRT actually tests for on the job competence, the learner can be given full information about the nature of the test at the very beginning of the course. Indeed the ideal CRT constitutes a statement of the course objectives.

7. NRTs are easy to devise and administer but provides less reliable and less valid information about learner's ability. On the other hand, CRTs are much more difficult to devise and administer, but provide more reliable and valid information about learner ability.
8. If an item on NRT is missed by a great number of learners the item is revised. But, if a item on a CRT is missed by great number of learners the course is revised.

There remain certain notable differences between NRTs and CRTs which can be stated as under:

1. The NRTs are used primarily for 'survey' testing whereas CRTs are primarily used for testing learners' mastery.
2. In NRTs emphasis is given on the concept of 'discrimination' among learners in terms of relative level of learning. But CRTs emphasize description of what tasks the learners can and cannot perform.
3. In NRTs test designer typically omits easy items and favours items of average difficulty. In CRTs the test designer matches item difficulty to learning tasks. He neither alters item difficulty nor omits easy items.

The criterion referenced tests are particularly suitable for use in ESP programmes because of the fact that the tests in ESP programmes are specifically based on the inventory of language items or functions that have been learned through a specified programme of instruction. CRTs can also be used when "they are based on the language requirements which have been identified by an on-the-job analysis of the language requirements in a given communicative situation such as doctors working in a Casualty Department of a hospital and an air hostesses on duty in a plane" (Patil, 1984: 195).

EVALUATION OF COMMUNICATIVE COMPETENCE IN GENERAL ENGLISH

There are two types of communicative competence tests.

The first type of tests are concerned with the evaluation of language for vocational purposes — Cartier (1968) has called these tests Criterion-referenced language tests which we have already discussed. According to Rea (1976), the second type of communicative competence tests are designed for the general English teaching programme. "The latter type are, in a sense, more difficult to construct as the inventory of possible items for inclusion in such test can be considered as virtually infinite in number. Additionally, the contents of the English language teaching syllabuses vary, if not from school to school then from state to state and from country to country all of which contribute to the very difficult process of item selection and sampling" (Rea, 1976: 68). The designer of communicative competence tests has to consider certain more variables than the basic levels of phonology, syntax and lexis. He has to take into account the variables like the levels of meaning, context of situation and social nature of language. Hymes (1971), Cooper (1968), Widdowson (1971, 1975) and Jacobovits (1970) have drawn attention to an equally important factor of contextual appropriacy. Therefore, communicative competence testing must take into account rules of use and language features appropriate to the relevant social context. It follows that in measuring communicative competence which subsumes both linguistic and contextual competence, dealing with one component alone will not usually be valid.

Though the 'rules of use' must be taken into consideration by the test designer, we cannot have a complete and unambiguous inventory of all the behaviours involved in communication through language. The linguistic science is not yet sufficiently developed to provide us with such an unambiguous inventory. Patil states. "Whereas discrete point language tests give us some kind of measure of behaviour which may be called "surface" behaviour on the analogy of a floating icebergs, the criterion referenced language tests can be used in a very limited number of situations involved in actual jobs. What constitutes the bulk of communicative competence is the unidentified and unmeasured variables 'underneath the surface' behaviour" (Patil, 1984:196).

Carrol's Two-dimensional Specification Framework

Carrol's (1961) two dimensional specification framework could be theoretically used to indicate measures of learner's competence in communicative language skills like auditory comprehension, oral production, reading and writing. According to him, the kinds of performance that should be tested on the proposed external proficiency examination should be dictated by, and flow from the specifications of the performance abilities desired in the learner. Thus, one could theoretically get measures of ability in each cell of the following grid:

Skill	Language Aspect			
	Phonology or Ortho-graphy	Morphology	Syntax	Lexicon
Auditory Comprehension				
Oral Production				
Reading				
Writing				

FIG. 9.1 : Carroll Two-dimensional Specification Framework.

The sixteen cells representing sixteen categories of language ability could be measured rather only theoretically. In practice, however, it would be a difficult attempt to obtain these sixteen different measures, for this would be carrying the process of analysis too far. While measuring these separate aspects of language competence, Carroll does not recommend the 'discrete-point approach' which measures knowledge of individual language items. According to him, "The examinee is not concerned with specific structure points or lexicon, but with the total meaning of the sentences, however he is able to grasp it" (Carroll, 1961:370). He recommends the 'integrative approach', which requires a learner to use several language skills at the same time. According to Carroll, (1961) an integrative approach requires an integrated, facile performance on the part of the examinee. He argues, "If we limit ourselves to testing only one point at a time, more time is ordinarily allowed for reflection than would occur in a normal communication situation, no matter how rapidly the discrete items are presented. For this reason I recommend test in which there is less attention paid to specific structure points or lexicon than to the utterance" (Carroll, 1961:1969-70). While commenting on Carroll's grid in terms of sixteen theoretically possible cells. Cooper states, "Before items can be written, each of the skills and linguistic aspects must of course be specified further, the global skills in terms of more detailed, componential operations, and the linguistic aspects in terms of particular grammatical rules (in the case of phonology, marphology and syntax) or specific semantic fields and lexical frequencies (in the case of lexicon)" (Cooper, 1968:57). Carroll himself has pointed out that although each cell is logically distinct, the behaviours they represent are unlikely to be completely independent. Thus, the 4x4 grid provides a model of the theoretically possible kinds of behaviours from which the test designer can select those that he wishes to assess. Carrol recommends that beside testing the behaviour represented by a single cell, language tests should elicit integrated performances requiring knowledge of all four aspects of language combined and that such performances should be emphasized. However, the ability required for such integrated performances depends upon something more than knowledge of language. Cooper (1968: 58) points out that this ability depends upon the learner's knowledge of contextual constraints as well. Therefore, to the 4x4 grid described by Carroll, Cooper (1968) adds a fifth column which is called "Context".

Skill	Knowledge				
	Language Aspect				Context
	Phonology or Orthography	Morphology	Syntax	Lexicon	
Auditory Comprehension					
Oral Production					
Reading					
Writing					

FIG.9. 2 : Cooper's Fifth Column — 'Context'

Cooper's Fifth Column — 'Context'

The four additional cells would include items that test the learner's ability to comprehend and produce spoken and written utterances in connected discourse. It is to be noted that the heading for the fifth column is not subordinate to the heading "language aspect". It is coordinate to "language aspect" because this arrangement is meant to indicate that two different categories of knowledge are represented by the two sets of specifications— the knowledge of language and the knowledge of contextual restraints. Thus, Cooper has pointed out two inadequacies in Carroll's grid: (1) Carroll ignores knowledge of contextual constraints upon which depends the learner's integrated performance, and (2) Carroll looks upon the target language as a linguistically undifferentiated, single code. In order to remove the first inadequacy, Cooper combines Chomsky's (1965) notion of linguistic competence and Hymes's (1971) notion of communicative competence. He is of the opinion that effective communication is possible if the speaker knows not only how to produce any and all grammatical utterances of language but also how to use them appropriately. He says, "the speaker must know what to say, with whom, and when and where" (Cooper, 1968: 60).

Cooper's (1968) framework serves to distinguish between two kinds of inferences made from a learner's language test score. The first concerns his knowledge of language, and the other concerns his ability to communicate through that language in specific situations. This framework helps to measure the learner's two sets of competence: the knowledge of linguistic rules and the knowledge of contextual rules. The learner applies his knowledge of linguistic rules to produce any and all grammatical sentences comprising his language and, secondly, he applies his knowledge of contextual rules to his knowledge of linguistic rules to produce any and all utterances that are appropriate for the settings in which he speaks, and the social relationships and interactions in which he participates. Thus, according to him, communicative competence which consists of two sets of competencies are logically distinct and can be measured distinctively.

Both sets of competencies, linguistic and contextual, are presumably acquired together in the first language learning. But, in second language learning, they may be acquired distinctively. Both of these components are necessary contributing factors for communicative competence of the learner, since "both components are necessary conditions for communicative competence, and since neither is a sufficient condition, we should not assume that we can assess a person's ability to communicate effectively by measuring one component alone" (Cooper, 1968: 61).

Cooper (1968) draws upon Labov (1966) and Gumperz (1964) for removing the second inadequacy as a linguistically undifferentiated, single code. Labov (1966) has found in his Study of *New York City* Speech that certain speech variants vary as a function both of social class and the elicitation procedure (Where the procedures are designed to elicit speech of varying degrees of casualness). According to Labov (1966) if codes can be identified by clusters of covariants which shift in response to changes in the social context, the speakers who are usually thought of as monolingual may possess not a single code but several. Ferguson (1959), Rubin (1961), and Fishman (1965) have also found that a single speaker controls more than a single code. It is more obvious in situations of stable, within group bilingualism, where linguistic systems which traditionally are considered separate are functionally distinct and separate. According to Gumperz (1964, 1966, 1967) a speaker possesses linguistic repertoire. By linguistic repertoire is meant the total linguistic resources controlled by the speaker, whether these resources are traditionally viewed as different "languages", "dialects", or "styles". From his linguistic repertoire, the speaker selects those varieties which are appropriate for the different social situations in which he participates. He selects different varieties for the different combinations of settings, time and role relationship that constitute the social context for speech.

Cooper's Three-dim nsional Framework

According to Cooper (1968) a single code framework would provide an inadequate model for the assessment of the learner's communicative competence in different settings. He says, "If the target language is thought of not as a single code but as a set of varieties which shift as a function of social context, we cannot employ a single code framework to assess a person's communicative competence unless the social situations which he is to enter require the use of a single variety only" (Cooper, 1968: 62). However, it might be argued that in settings where the components of a linguistic repertoire have fewer apparent linguistic differences, a single-code framework would suffice. For example, it might be said, although it remains to be verified, that the varieties required to communicate effectively in an American University have fewer and less important linguistic differences among them than the varieties required in an Indian University. Cooper proposes to improve the validity of his test model. For doing this, he poses three questions which one must attempt to answer. The questions are: (1) What is the linguistic repertoire needed to communicate effectively? (2) What are the social situations in which the varieties comprising the repertoire will be employed? and, (3) What are the selection rules for variety use ? (i.e. what varieties are used in what situations?) Cooper extends his

5x4 test blueprint to represent the three language varieties by means of an added, third dimension as shown in Figure 9.3.

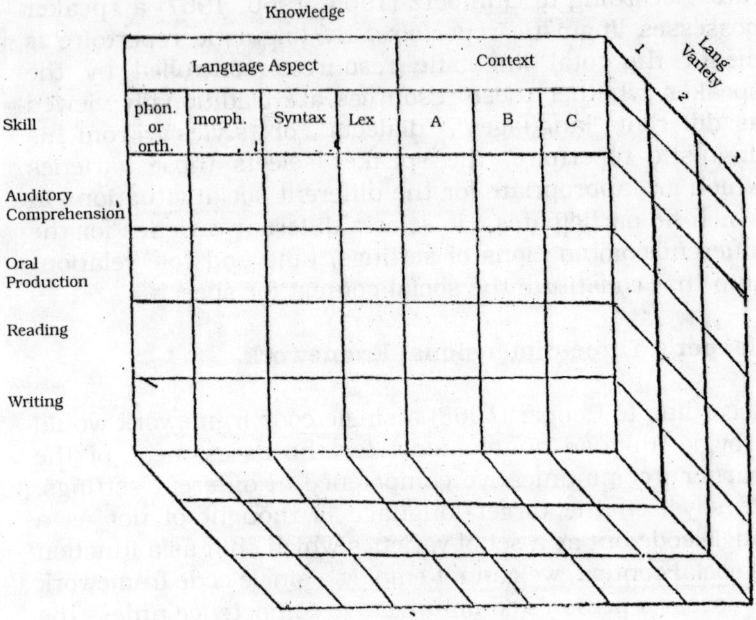

FIG. 9.3 : Cooper's Three Dimensional Language Testing Specification Model.

This dimension represents not the "target language" but the "target repertoire". Cooper says, "We can represent the three types of social situations by dividing the 'context' portion of the blueprint into three sections. That part of the text, in other words, that assesses integrated performance could be specified in terms of particular kinds of social situation, with each section representing items requiring, in addition to linguistic competence, knowledge of appropriate language use for that social context" (Cooper, 1968: 63-64).

Thus, having surveyed the trends in modern language testing, the testing devices of linguistic and communicative competence, the testing devices of communicative skills, and the evaluation systems of communicative competence in general English in the present chapter, we shall be able to evolve a most comprehensive and scientific way of evaluating the students' communicative competence in communicative syllabus in the following two chapters.

References

Allen, E.D., 1975: Communicative Competence. In *Eric Clearing house On Language and Linguistics*; Arlington, Virginia: Centre for Applied Linguistics.

Alderson, J. 1979: The Cloze Procedure And Proficiency In English as a Foreign Language. In *TESOL Quarterly*, 13,219-227.

Bachman, L. (1982). The Trait Structure of Close Test Scores. In *TESOL Quarterly*, 16, 61-70.

Bachman, L. 1985: Performance On Cloze Tests With Fixed - ration and Rational Deletions. In *TESOL Quarterly*, 19, 535-556.

Bachman, and Palmer, 1981: In - Shohamy, E., T. Reves, and Y. Bejarano, 1986: Introducing A New Comprehensive Test of Proficiency. In *ELT Journal*, Vol. 40/3 1986. Oxford University Press.

Bartz, W.H., 1974: *A Study of the Relationship of Certain Learner Factors with the Ability to Communicate in a Second Language for the Development of Measures of Communicative Competence*, Ph.D. Diss., Chio State University.

Benson, M.J., 1987: The Construction of Curriculums in ECL and EFL, Artful Tasks In *FORUM* Vol. XXV/1 Jan.

Bloom, B.B., J.T. Hastings, G.F. Madans, (Eds.), 1971: *Handbook on Formative and Summative Evaluation of Learner Learning.* New York: McGraw Hill.

Boomer, D.S. and Laver, J. (1968) Slips of The Tongue, *Brits. J. Dist. Comm.*, No. 3, pp. 2-12.

Bormann, E.G. and N.C. Bormann, 1986: *Speech Communication. A Basic Approach.* New York: Harper & Row, Publishers.

Brown, J. 1983: A Closer Look At Cloze'. Validity and Reliability. In J. Oller, Jr. Ed., *Issues in Language Testing Research* (pp.237-250). Rowley, Mass; Newburg House Publishers.

Brown, J. 1988: Tailored Cloze : Improved With Classical Item Analysis Techniques. In *Language Testing*, 5,19-31.

Brown, J. 1989: Cloze Item Difficulty. In *JALT Journal*,11,46-67.

Campbell, R. and R. Wales, 1970: The Study Of Language Acquisition. In Lyons, John, (ed.) *New Horizons in Linguistics*, Penguin.

Carroll, J.B., 1961: Fundamental Considerations in Testing For English Language Proficiency For Foreign Learners. In J.E. Alatis (Ed.), *Testing The English Proficiency of Forcign Learners.* Washington D.C.: Centre for Applied Linguistic, 31-40.

Carroll, B.S., 1982: Language Testing — Is There Another Way? In J.B. Heaton (Ed.) 1982. *Language Testing*, Hays: Modern English Publications.

Carroll, B.S., 1983: Psychometric Theory and Language Testing In J.W. Oller (Ed.) 1983, *Issues in Language Testing Research.* Massachusetts: Newsburg House.

Cartier, F.A., 1968: Criterion-Referenced Testing of Language Skills. In *TESOL Quarterly*, 2,27-32.

Chavez, Oller, M., Chihara, T.Weaver, K. & J. Oller, 1985: When Are Cloze Items Sensitive to Constraints Across Sentences? In *Language Learning*, 35,181-203.

Chomsky, N., 1965: *Aspects of The Theory of Syntax.* Cambridge Mass: M.I.T. Press.

Clifford, 1977: In Shohamy, E., T. Reves, and Y. Bejarano, 1986: Introducing A New Comprehensive Test of Proficiency. In *ELT Journal*, Vol. 40/3 1986. Oxford University Press.

Cooper, R.L., 1968: An Elaborated Testing Model. In J.A. Upshur and Julia Fata (Eds.) *Problems in Foreign Language Testing*; *Language Learning* Spl. Issue No. 3, 57, 72.

Corder, S. Pit, (1973): *Introducing Applied Linguistics*, Penguin, U.K.

Cziko, G.A., 1982: Improving The Psychometric, Criterion Refers Need and Practical Qualities of Integrative Language Tests. In *TESOL Quarterly* Vol. 16/3, Sept. 1982.

Cziko, G.A.& N.J. Lin, 1984: The Construction and Analysis of The Short Scales of Language Proficiency. Classical Psychometric, Latent Trait and Nonparasitic Approaches. In *TESOL Quarterly* 18:4, 627-647.

Eisher, E.W., 1967: Educational Objectives: Help or Hindrance?, In *School Review*, 75.

Farhady, H. 1979. The Disjunctive Fallacy Between Discreet Point And Integrative Tests. In *TESOL Quarterly* 13,347-357.

Ferguson, C.A., 1959: Diglossia, In Giglioli (Ed.) *Language and Social Context*, Pengnin, 1972 (Reprinted from *Word*, Vol. 15).

Fishman, J.A., 1965: Who Speaks What Language To Whom

And When? In *La Linguistique*, 67,88.

Fotos, S.S. 1991: The Cloze Test As An Integrative Measure Of EFL Proficiency A Substitute For Essays On College Entrance Examination?. In *Language Learning* 41:3, 313-336.

Gronlund, N.E., and R.L. Linn, 1990: *Measurement and Evaluation In Teaching*, New York: Macmillan Publishing Co.

Groot, P.J.M., 1975: Validation Of Language Tests. In Leslie Palmer and Bernard Spolsky (Eds). *Papers On Language Testing* 1967-1974. Washington, D.C. *TESOL Quarterly*.

Gumperz, J.J., 1964: Linguistic And Social Interaction In Two Communities. In J.J. Gumperz and Dell Hymes (Eds). *The Ethnology of Communication*. American Anthropologist, Vol. 66, Part-2, 137-53. Menasha Wisc. American Anthropological Association.

Gumperz, J.J., 1966: On The Ethnology Of Linguistic Change. In William Bright (Ed.), *Sociolinguistics*. Hague: Mouton, 1966, 27-49.

Gumperz, J.J. 1967: On The Linguistic Markers Of Bilingual Communication. In John Macnamara (Ed.) *Problems of Bilingualism; Journal of Social Issues*, 1967, 23,8-28.

Halliday, M.A.K. 1971: Language in a Social Perspective. In *Explorations In·The Functions of Language*. Edward Arnold 1973.

Halliday, M.A.K. 1972: Towards a Sociological Semantics. In *Explorations In The Functions of Language*. Edward Arnold, 1973.

Hanania, E. & M. Shikhani, 1986: Interrelationship Among Three Tests of Language Proficiency: Standardized ESL Cloze and Writing. In *TESOL Quarterly* 20, 97-109.

Harris, D., 1969: *Testing English As A Second Language*. McGraw-Hill Inc.

Heaton, J.B., 1975: *Writing English Language Tests*. London: Longman.

Heilenman, L. 1983: The Use of A Cloze Procedure in Foreign Language Placement. In *Modern Language Journal*, 67, 121-126.

Hinofotis, F. 1976: In - Shohamy, E., T. Reves, and Y. Bejarano, 1986: Introducing A New Comprehensive Test of Proficiency. In *ELT Journal*, Vol. 40/3 1986. Oxford University Press.

Hinofotis, F. 1987: Cloze Testing: An Overview In M. Long & J Richards (Eds) *Methodology In TESOL*. Rowley Mass, Newburg House.

Hymes, D., 1971: On Communicative Competence. In J.B. Pride and J. Holmes (Eds.) (1972), *Sociolinguistics*. Penguin.

Jakobovits, L.A., 1970: *Foreign Language Learning: A Psycholin guistic Analysis of the Issues*. Rowly, Mass: Newburg House.

Jacobovitz, L.A., Gordon, Barbara, 1974: *The Context of Foreign Language Teaching* - Rowley, Mass. Newburg House.

Klein-Braley, C. 1983: A Cloze Is A Question. In J. Oller Jr. (Ed.) *Issues in language testing research*, (pp. 281- 328). Rowley Mass, Newburg House.

Labov, W., 1966: The Social Stratification of English, In *New York City*. Washington D.C.: Centre for Applied Linguistics.

Lado, R., 1961: *Language Testing: The Construction And Use Of Foreign Language Tests*. London: Longman.

Laech, K & A. Van Kleeck, 1987: The Cloze Test As an Alternative Measure of Language Proficiency of Children Considered For Exit Bilingual Education Programs. In *Language Learning*, 37, 171-189.

Logan, G.E., 1973: *German Conversational Practice*. Rowley, Mass: Newberg House.

Logan, G.E., Bals, Hilda, 1976: *Spanish Conversational Practice*. Rowley, Mass.: Newburg House.

Maclean, M. 1984: Using Rational Cloze for Diagnostic Testing In L1 and L2 Reading. In *TESL Canada Journal* 2,53-63.

Manning, W. 1986: Using Technology To Assess Second Language Proficiency Through Cloze-Elide Tests. In C. Stansfield (Ed.) *Technology and Language Testing*. Washington D.C. TESOL.

Mathews Margaret, 1990: The Measurement Of Productive Skills: Doubts Concerning The Assessment Criteria of Certain Public Examinations. In *ELT Journal* Vol 44/2, 1990. Oxford University Press.

Moller, A., 1975: *Validity In Proficiency Testing*. In *ELT Documents* (75/3). London: English Teaching Information Centre. The British Council.

Munby, J., 1978: *Communicative Syllabus Design*. Cambridge University Press.

Oller, J. Jr., 1973: Pragmatic Language Testing. In *Language Sciences*, 28, 7-12.

Oller, J. Jr., 1973: Cloze Tests of Second Language Proficiency and What They Measure. In *Language Learning* 23, 105-118.

Oller, J. Jr., 1979: *Language Tests at School*. London: Longman.

Oller, J. Jr., 1988: *Pragmatic Language Teaching and Testing*. Lecture Presented at Temple University Japan Distinguished Lecturer's Series, Tokyo, Japan.

Patil, D.K., 1984: *English Language Achievements of Shivaji University Arts Graduates*, Kolhapur: Shivaji University.

Rea, P.M., 1976: Linguistic Theory, Linguistic Description and

Language Testing. The Dissertation for M.A. The University of Lancaster.

Richards, J., J. Platt, H. Weber, 1985: *Longman Dictionary of Applied Linguistics*, Longman.

Rivers, W., 1968: *Teaching Foreign Language Skills* University of Chicago Press.

Rubin, J., 1962: Bilingualism In Paraguay. In *Anthropological Linguistics*, 1962, 4, 52-58.

Shohamy, E. 1982: In - Shohamy, E., T. Reves, and Y. Bejarano, 1986: Introducing A New Comprehensive Test of Proficiency. In *ELT Journal*, Vol. 40/3 1986. Oxford University Press.

Shohamy, E., T. Reves, and Y. Bejarano, 1986: Introducing A New Comprehensive Test of Proficiency. In *ELT Journal*, Vol. 40/3 1986. Oxford University Press.

Sinclair, J. M., I.J. Forsyth, R. M. Coulthard and M. Ashby, 1972: *The English Used by Teachers and Pupils: Final Report to SSRC*, Dept of English Language and Literature, Birmingham University.

Stubbs, J. & G. Tucker, 1974: The Cloze Test as a Measure of English Proficiency. In *Modern Language Journal*, 58, 239-241.

Taylor, W., 1983: Cloze Procedure: A New Tool for Measuring Readability. In *Journalism Quarterly*, 30, 414-438.

Underhill, N., 1987: *Testing Spoken Language*. Cambridge: Cambridge University Press.

Upshur, J.A., 1983: Measurement of Individual Differences and Explanation in The Language Sciences. In *Language Learning* 33(5), 99-140.

Valdman, A., 1975: Learner Systems and Error Analysis. In Gillbert A. Jarvis, ed., *Perspective: A New Freedom, The ACTFL Review of Foreign Language Education*, Vol. 7, National Textbook Company.

Valette, R.M., 1977: *Modern Language Testing*. Harcourt, Brace, Jovanovich, Inc.

Widdowson, H.G., 1971: The Teaching of Rhetoric to Learners of Science and Technology. In *Science and Technology*. In a Second Language. Centre for Information on Language Teaching and Research.

Widdowson, H.G., 1975: *EST in Theory and Practice*. In English for academic study. British Council English Teaching Information centre.

Wilkins, D.A., 1972: *The Linguistic and Situational Content of the Common Core In a Unit/Credit System*. In Systems Development in Adult Language Learning. Strasbourg, Council of Europe,1973.

PART - III

COMMUNICATIVE SYLLABUSES

10

COMMUNICATIVE SYLLABUSES

"Man's main task in life is to give birth to himself, to become what he potentially is. The most important product of his effort is his personality."

— Erich Fromm

THE NOTION OF SYLLABUSES

A syllabus has often been described as an outline of a 'course of study'. According to Biswas and Agarwal (1971), it is an official guide for the use of supervisors, teachers and students of a particular school or school system to help teaching in a subject for a certain grade or class. The course of study includes the general and specific objectives of the course, the expected goals and suggestions regarding supplementary reading, audio-visual aids, related activities and special teaching methods. The syllabus is "expected to statc both, the immediate pedagogical objectives and the ultimate social ones" (Shastri, 1972: 172). In English language teaching, it aims at specific form of terminal behaviour e.g. to speak the language like a native, or to be able to use it in business correspondence, report writing etc. The syllabus designer or the pedagogic decides how and in what order processes are to be chosen to arrive most efficiently at the stated goals of the operation.

According to Richards, *et al* (1985), a language teaching syllabus design includes:

a. The study of the purposes for which a learner needs a language (needs analysis);
b. The setting of objectives and the development of

teaching material and methods; and,

c. The evaluation of the effects of these procedures on the learner's language ability.

Thus, the syllabus design includes the educational purpose of the programme (the ends); the content, the teaching procedures and learning experiences which will be necessary to achieve this purpose (the means); and, some means for assessing whether or not the educational ends have been achieved.

THE TYPES OF SYLLABUSES

The Structural, Situational and Notional Syllabuses

Language teaching syllabuses are of three types:

A. Structural Syllabuses
B. Situational Syllabuses
C. Notional Syllabuses

A. Structural Syllabuses

The structural syllabus is a syllabus for the teaching of language, which is based on a selection of the grammatical items and structures (e.g. tenses, grammatical rules, sentence patterns) which occur in a language and the arrangement of them into an order suitable for teaching. According to Richards, *et al*, (1985), the order of introducing grammatical items and structures in a structural syllabus may be based on such factors as frequency, difficulty, usefulness or a combination of these.

B. Situational Syllabuses

The situational syllabus is a type of syllabus for the teaching of language, which is based on the language needed for different type of situations. Situational method of language teaching refers to a programme or method in which the selection, organization and presentation of language items is based on situations (e.g. at the bank, supermarket home etc). A syllabus for such a language course or text book is referred to as situational syllabus. Many methods of language teaching make use of simulated situations a way of practicing language item, but use other criteria for selecting and organizing the content of the course.

C. Notional Syllabuses

The Notional Syllabus deals with the meanings and communicative functions which the learner needs to express in the target language. In language teaching, notional syllabus is a syllabus in which the language content is arranged according to the meanings the learner needs to express through language, and the functions the learner will use the language for. The term 'Notional' is taken from 'Notional Grammar'. A notional syllabus is contrasted with a grammatical syllabus or structural syllabus (one which consists of a sequence of graded language items) or a situational syllabus (one which consists of situations and the relevant language items). A notional syllabus contains:

a. The meanings and concepts the learner needs in order to communicate — (e.g. time, quantity, duration, location etc.) and the language needed to express them. These concepts and meanings are called notions.
b. The language needed to express different functions or speech acts — (e.g. requesting, suggesting, promising, describing etc.).

These notions and functions are then used to develop learning/teaching units in a language course.

THE SYNTHETIC AND ANALYTIC SYLLABUSES

According to Wilkins, syllabus types can be divided into two classes — synthetic and analytic (Wilkins, 1974, 1976).

A. Synthetic Syllabuses

The synthetic syllabuses segment the target language into

discrete linguistic items. "Different parts of language are taught separately and step by step so that acquisition is a process of gradual accumulation of parts until the whole structure of language has been built up" (Wilkins, 1976:2). The learner has to resynthesize the target language that has been broken down into discrete linguistic items with the purpose of making his learning task easier. 'The synthetic syllabus relies on learners' assumed ability to learn a language in parts (e.g. structures and functions) which are independent of one another and also to integrate or synthesize the pieces when the time comes to use them for communicative purposes (Long, 1992: 28). Thus, lexical, structural, notional and functional syllabuses are synthetic.

Syllabus designers who choose the linguistic elements—word, structure, function — to organize lessons and teaching materials commit themselves to a synthetic, type of syllabus (White, 1988). Synthetic syllabuses present linguistic forms separately and attempt to elicit immediate target like mastery of those forms. In the context of syntax, research has demonstrated that learners rarely move from zero to target like mastery of new items in one step. (Huebner, 1983; Johnston, 1985; Ellis, 1985; Sato, 1990; Meisel, Clahsen and Pieneman, 1981, Larsen-Freeman and Long, 1991).

B. Analytic Syllabuses

The Analytic Syllabuses offer the target language samples to the learner. These samples are not modified or controlled for structure or lexis in the traditional manner. In this context the term 'analytic' does not refer to what the syllabus designer does but to the analytic operations required of the learner. Wilkins (1976) writes, "since we are inviting the learner, directly or indirectly, to recognize the linguistic components of the language behaviour he is acquiring, we are in effect basing our approach on the learner's analytic capabilities" (Wilkins, 1976:14). Long and Crookes have updated Wilkins' definition a little as they write, "Analytic syllabuses are those which present the target language whole chunks at a time, without linguistic interference or control" (Long, 1992:29). Procedural, process and task syllabuses are all examples of the analytic syllabuses.

WHITE'S TYPE-A AND TYPE-B SYLLABUSES

Wilkins' synthetic - analytic distinction is partially reflected in R.V. White's (1988) Type-A and Type-B syllabuses. Type-A syllabuses are interventionist. They focus on 'what' is to be learned by the learner rather than on 'how' the language is to be learned. In such syllabuses, someone preselects and predigests the language to be taught and segments it into small pieces. The learning objectives are determined in advance. White (1988) points out that Type-A syllabuses are external to the learner, determined by authority, treat the subject-matter of instructions as important, set the teacher as decision-maker, and finally, assess success and failure in terms of achievement or mastery. On the other hand, Type-B syllabuses are non-interventionist. They focus on 'how' the language is to be learned — rather than 'what' is to be learned. They do not involve artificial preselection or prearrangement of the language items to be taught. The objectives are determined by the process of negotiation between the teacher and learners after they meet. Thus, Type-B syllabuses are internal to the learners, the teacher and learners are joint decision-makers and assess accomplishment in relationship to learners' criteria for success. The precursors of task-based, analytic, Type B syllabuses (Macnamara, 1973, Newmark, 1964, 1966; Newmark and Reibel, 1968; Reibel, 1969) had little institutional backing, but recently the Type-B syllabuses are getting larger institutional support (Kementarian Pelajaran Malaysia, 1975; Rodgers, 1984; Samah, 1984; Bangalore/Madras Communicational Teaching project 1979-1984; Prabhu, 1980, 1984, 1987) Procedural syllabus (analytic, Type-B syllabus) is associated with the work of Prabhu, Ramani and others on the Bangalore/Madras Communicational Teaching project (1981-84). The second task-based approach to syllabus design is the process syllabus (Breen, 1984, 1987; Breen and Candlin, 1989;

Candlin, 1984, 1987; Candlin and Murphy, 1987). Procedural and task syllabuses have one characteristic in common — they make an initial specification in substantive terms of the kinds of tasks the learners will work on before teacher and students meet. They specify the target tasks and allow the pedagogic tasks to be negotiated. But process syllabuses are Type-B thoroughbreds. 'They allow negotiation of language and constraints on the tasks chosen' (Long, 1992:30).

Note : Please see References of this chapter at the end of Chapter 11.

11

SYLLABUS EVALUATION

"Judge not, that you be not judged."

— Mathew 7:1

SYLLABUS DESIGNING

Ghosh, *et al,* (1977) propose four important requirements for syllabus designing:

1. Control
2. Co-ordination
3. Consolidation
4. Correlation

Control

The first requirement, 'control' implies that syllabus designing must be subjected to controls like: Linguistic, cultural, psychological and so on. The course limits are the predetermined entry level and the terminal level. For example, the entry level for the MBA course is the terminal level of the college course. And the terminal level for the MBA course in WAC is the communicative competence level which the student is expected to attain by the end of the first year MBA course. The terminal level is expected to be specified by the syllabus designers in terms of the precise nature and extent of the skills expected from the learners.

Co-ordination

The second requirement, 'Co-ordination' implies that, "each

stage of a language programme must be visualized in relation to the total programme, and not in isolation from the other stages" (Patil, 1984:45). Such co-ordination is also known as the 'vertical integration' of a course.

Consolidation

The third requirement, 'consolidation' implies that the language skills learnt at the previous stage must be consolidated with the new items. The syllabus designer of a language course has to consider how much of the 'old' is to be revised in conjunction with the 'new'.

Correlation

Lastly, the fourth requirement, 'correlation' implies the 'multi-skill' approach to language teaching. "Language is a network, a highly complex system of inter-locking systems of phonology', syntax and semantics" (Patil, 1984:45). For language teaching, these inter-locking systems and their sub-systems are to be taken up together at some given stage in the language programme. The syllabus designer has to provide for this correlation or horizontal integration.

EVALUATION OF A COMMUNICATIVE SYLLABUS

The Absence of Operationally Stated Syllabus Objectives

It has been found that communicative competence evaluation of the students in the paper 'Written Analysis and Communication' through University examination system presents a host of difficulties. The evaluative design is incompatible with the teaching goals and procedures. Another serious methodological problem in this area is related to the criteria of success as these are related to the syllabus objectives. The problem is to decide what constitutes an acceptable set of criteria in evaluating outcomes of the curricular programme in this subject. The problem arises due to the variety of such outcomes and their varying importance according to communicative situations. The changes in students' communicative performance must be reflected in the final outcome of the programme. But, these outcomes are not specified by the syllabus designers. In the planning phase, the syllabus of 'Written Analysis and Communication' does not indicate that the syllabus designer has identified the communicative needs of the MBAS, especially in the view of their future on-the-job performance requirements. The depth and breadth of theoretical knowledge and practical skills necessary for specific communicative activities are to be defined on the basis of the objectives of curriculum and other operating facilities available. The stated objectives of any syllabus design should provide the likely outcomes of the curricular activities. However, the official 'MBA-I, Written Analysis and Communication' syllabus document of the selected University, as a rule, does not contain the clear statements of the specific objectives nor does it give specifications of the students' acquisition of the communicative abilities which are to be tested by the University examination at the end of the academic year. There has been an increasing awareness that in the absence of clearly defined instructional objectives neither teaching nor testing can be effective. Though there is an extensive discussion of 'learner-based objectives', 'behavioural objectives', and 'performance objectives' in educational books and journals, the syllabus designers and the University authorities do not seem to have taken much cognisance of it. The operationally stated objectives point to the behavioural part of the pupil. Specification of such objectives greatly facilitate identification of the target behaviours or outcomes. When the objectives are not clearly specified there may be discrepancies between what the curriculum designer intends, what the teachers and learners do and what the tester looks for.

ANALYSIS OF THE QUESTION PAPER OF COMMUNICATION (WAC)

The Question Paper of 'Written Analysis And Communication' (WAC) — Paper VIth, MBA Part-I Examination, (See

Appendix III), was of total 70 marks; and the maximum time allotted to examinees was 3 hours i.e. 11.00 a.m. to 2.00 p.m. All questions were compulsory.

The First Section consisted of two questions. The First Question consisted of two cases requiring the candidate to apply the knowledge of concepts, tools and techniques acquired. The candidates had to attempt any one case. The first question carried 25 marks.

The Second Question consisted of 4 short-notes. The candidates had to write only one of the four short-notes. The second question carried 5 marks.

The Second Section consisted of three questions. There were two essay-type questions in the Third Question. The candidates had to attempt any one of the two essay-type questions. The third question carried 15 marks.

There were two essay-type questions in the Forth Question. The candidates had to attempt any one of them. The fourth question carried 15 marks.

Finally, the Fifth Question consisted of 4 shortnotes. The candidates had to write short notes on any two of them.

The first case in Question-1 was concerned with the problem of the lack of downward communication in a business house. Due to lack of downward communication, a strike developed, and this generated tension and fear among the executives. Several Engineers and Executives left the job. The candidates were expected to analyze the problem, to understand its different aspects and finally to suggest a solution.

The questions given below the case were :

1. Give a brief analysis of the case.
2. Why did the Executives leave the job?
3. Explain the reasons for fear and tension.
4. Suggest solution for the problem.

The first question carried 7 marks and the remaining three questions carried 6 marks each. The question given below the case-passage certainly tests the candidate's comprehension of the problem and its background. The first question asks to analyze the case, to segment background of the problem and the problem itself into parts in order to clarify how the problem originates, develops and poses threat to the smooth working of the organization. The candidate is expected to consider only the problem of communication. The second and third question test the candidates' comprehension of the problem; and the last question tests the candidates' ability of deciding a suitable solution.

Thus the first case is primarily concerned with the downward channel of communication and with the psychological barrier to communication i.e., fear. The case dose not test the candidates' knowledge and skills in other formal and informal channels of communication.

The second case in Question-1 is concerned with the problem of excessive cost of production. Yet, the candidates are expected to deal only with the problem of communication. The communication problem arises from the Production Manager's closed-mindedness and inability of using the communicative skills. In order to tackle the problem of excessive cost of production, he decides to consult the experts, but actually he never consults any expert. Next, he convenes a meeting of the foremen, but never allows them to speak and reflect over the new system of production which he introduces in the meeting. He imposes the new system on them and insists that everyone of them should ensure the success of it. A senior foreman replied after consulting the other foremen that they had a list of 12 changes to be made in the new system, otherwise it would not work effectively. The Production Manager got annoyed and told the foreman that either he did as he was asked to do or he will have to leave the job. The Production Manager is not ready to listen to any arguments. The communication problem arises from the closed-mindedness of the Production Manager. He is not a good listener. He does not understand the very purpose of the meeting, i.e. to exchange thoughts feelings, ideas, views, opinions and experiences with the participants. He is not a good conversationalist. He shouts in the meeting that the system had worked in other plants and it must work in this company too. The Production Manager's closed-mindedness, inattentiveness, emotional state of mind and bad-listening become barriers to communication. Thus the case was mainly concerned with the communication barriers like closed-mindedness, bad-listening, inattentiveness, and emotional state of mind.

The questions given below the case are :

(1) Give a brief analysis of the case.
(2) Do you feel that the Production Manager did not use the skill of communication effectively? If yes, comment on it.
(3) Explain the problem.
(4) Suggest a proper solution.

The first two questions carried 6 marks each. The third question carried 7 marks; and the last question carried 6 marks. The questions given below the case-passage tested the candidates' comprehension of the communication problem and its background. The first question asked to analyze the case, to segment background of the problem and the problem itself into parts in order to clarify how the problem originates, develops and poses threat to the smooth working of the organization. The candidates was expected to consider only the communication problem in the case. The second question tested the candidates' comprehension of the problem in the case by asking 'Do you feel that the Production Manager did to use the skill of communication effectively?' The problem lies in the fact that the Production Manager is unable to use the communication skills effectively. The third question 'Explain the problem' is a direct question that tests the candidates' comprehension of the problem. Yet both the questions (2nd and 3rd) tested the candidates' comprehension of the same problem, and it seems that any one of these could have been dropped. The last question tested the candidates' ability of finding a suitable solution.

Thus, the second case was primarily concerned with the Production Manager's inability of using communication skills due to certain communication barriers. Therefore, it can be said that the case tested the candidates' knowledge of a few communication barriers.

The Second Question consisted of four shortnotes. The first short-note, 'Objectives of Communication' was not a suitable topic for a short note. There are several objectives of communication. Each one of them can become a suitable topic for short note. The Paper-setter has given a proof of his unseriousness by giving one of the objectives of communication as a topic for third short note in the same question. The third short note 'Persuasion and Propaganda' was concerned with one of the important objectives of business communication—'Persuasion'. Persuasion or the persuasive appeals are used in propaganda. The second short note 'Signs and Signals' was intended to test the candidates' knowledge of the conventional use of arbitrary symbol systems for imparting meaning of the messages. The forth short note 'Open Door Policies' was wrong in itself. It should have been 'Open Door Policy'. An open door policy is a method used for receiving 'suggestions'. Suggestion is an objective of business communication. It seems rather odd firstly because out of four short-notes one short-note is on all the objectives of communication. And secondly because it is wrong to include the test-items to test repetitively the same content areas of the syllabus when there remained large syllabus contents areas untouched.

In Second Section, the Third Question consisted of two essay-type questions. The candidates had to attempt any one of them. These two questions were not numbered. They should have been numbered for referential purpose. The question, "Describe the role of Audio-visuals in communication, its advantages and disadvantages" tested the candidates' knowledge of the advantages and disadvantages of the audio-visual aids like television and films. Another alternative question, "How can sales letters help in building up goodwill?" tested the candidates' knowledge of the goodwill function of the sales letters.

The Fourth Question consisted of two essay-type questions. The candidates had to attempt any one of them. These two questions are also not numbered. They should have been numbered for referential purpose. The question, "Prepare a speech on the prospects of the Electronic Industry in India", tested the candidates' ability of writing a speech on the given topic. Another alternative question, "Draft the minutes of the Annual General Meeting of Bharat Chemicals Ltd.," expected the candidates to draft the meeting minutes of the Annual General Meeting. The agenda or the topics to be discussed in this meeting were not specified. The fourth question carried 15 marks.

In the Fifth Question, there were four short-notes. The candidates had to attempt any two of these short notes. The first short note "Use of micro-phone in public speaking" expected the candidates to know the use of microphone in public speech. This short-note appears to be rather irrelevant because the syllabus expects the candidates to know about - understanding of the audience; planning and preparation of public speech; deciding purpose and objectives; acquiring adequate knowledge of the subject; selecting suitable pattern like — topical, chronological, spatial, causal etc; determining supporting material like analogies, quotations, statistical data, examples etc; the language features of public speech; modes of speech delivery like impromptu, extemporaneous memorized, manuscript etc. use of visual and vocal cause like eye contact, facial expressions postures and other body movements, articulation of sounds, pronunciation etc. Considering what the syllabus expects the students to know about the 'public speech', the first shortnote 'Use of microphone' appears to be irrelevant though microphone is sometimes an essential mechanical device that increases the volume of sound.

The second short-note in the fifth question, "Language of communication" was vague and it was not clear whether the candidates were expected to write on the need of using common language in communication or on the language of communication in written media and/or the oral media and/or the non-verbal and other media of communication, or on the structural and/or semantic and other aspects of the language of communication.

The third short-note, "Salutation in letter writing", represented as a test item on the syllabus content area 'Structure of Business Letters'. Yet there was not any test-item to represent the syllabus areas like significance of business correspondence, essentials of effective layout, functions of business correspondence, types of business letter etc.

The last short-note in the fifth question, "Physical barrier" referred to the physical barriers to communication like (i) Noise (ii) Time (iii) Distance (iv) Age (v) Sex. Therefore the short note "Physical barrier" should have been "Physical barriers to communication".

It is necessary to point out that the representative test items on the following syllabus content areas were not found in the question paper:

1. Definitions of Communication.
2. The process of communication; model of communication cycle; components of communication situation.
3. Significance of communication in business.
4. Horizontal channel of communication; Grapevine; consensus.
5. Oral media: meaning, essentials of effectiveness, advantages and disadvantages.
6. Written media: nature, need, advantages and disadvantages.
7. Nonverbal media; meaning, importance, kinesic, proxemics, chronemics paralanguage artifacts.
8. Barriers to communication; Language and semantic barriers; organizational barriers.
9. Principles of effective business communication.
10. Group communication: characteristics; committees—types, advantages, disadvantages, factors responsible for the failure of committee meetings, essentials of effective committee meetings; conference—characteristics, significance, committees and conferences, conference leadership, essentials of effective conference meeting.
11. Journalistic style: essential aspects of press reports; organization of press reports.
12. Business Report writing: meaning, significance,

organization of business reports, constituents parts of business reports, types of business reports.

Thus, the question paper of WAC, MBA-I is neither comprehensive nor adequately representative testing instrument.

LACUNAE OF THE COMMUNICATIVE SYLLABUS AND TESTING DESIGN

The annual examination of all papers of MBA-I including Written Analysis and Communication (WAC) is the written examination that involves considerable amount of writing. But this written test, especially of communicative skills, does not guarantee the students' communicative competence in oral expressions. The question paper of Written Analysis and Communication demands the paragraph answers and essay type of answers which mostly require reproduction from the memory of the stock answers to the stock questions. Though suitability of items or item types for testing students' communicative competence in written expressions is borne in mind to some extent by those who set the question papers for students' final evaluation at the end of the year, the items for testing the students' competence of oral expressions in communicative situations is completely ignored. The following conclusions were derived from the statement of syllabus of WAC and the analysis of the sample question paper of WAC:

(1) The syllabus of 'written Analysis and Communication' (WAC) does not prove that the syllabus designer has identified the communicative needs of the MBAs, especially, in the view of their future on-the-job performance requirements.

(2) The syllabus of WAC does not contain the clear statements of specific objectives as learning outcomes. The operationally stated syllabus objectives are absent.

(3) The syllabus of WAC does not give specifications

of the students' achievement of the instructional objectives which are to be discovered through the achievement test at the end of the academic year.

(4) The annual University examination system of WAC is inadequate and faulty because if fails to evaluate the students' achievement of the instructional objectives in a comprehensive manner.

(5) The annual University examination of WAC is incompatible with the teaching goals and procedures. The question paper does not allow the inclusion of sufficient number of test- items to give coverage to the comprehensive testing of the students' achievement of all the syllabus objectives.

(6) The annual University examination of WAC involves paragraph or essay-type of answers which do not measure the students' communicative competence in oral expressions. The examination does not include tasks for testing oral performance of the students in order to discover their achievements in oral communication.

(7) The annual University examination of WAC does not test all the aspects of students' written communicative competence, though this examination tests the students' written performance only.

(8) The annual University examination of WAC is neither comprehensive nor adequately representative.

(9) Though annual University examination of WAC is administered according to the standardized procedure, the assessment of the students' essay-type of responses is subjective and its reliability is limited.

(10) The examiner's assessment of the students' performance is quantitative. The responses of the students are not qualitatively assessed.

Evaluation of Communicative Syllabus as per Ghosh, *et al.*, Checklist

This checklist enables the teacher to evaluate the communicative syllabus and to make the classroom teaching and later, achievement testing more successful by presenting a criterion to evaluate the syllabus design. Let us try to evaluate the syllabus of WAC with reference to the Ghosh, *et al*, checklist.

1. *Stage of Language Learning*

Post Graduates (after the 10+2+3 structure)

2. *Entry Behaviour*

a) Years of English the learner had: 11 years
b) Hours of Instruction the learner had:
   i) About 960 hours upto XII standard
   ii) About 360 hours from F.Y.B.A. to T.Y.B.A.
   iii) About 240 hours from F.Y.B.Com. to T.Y.B.Com.
   iv) About 120 hours from F.Y.B.Sc. to T.Y.B.Sc.
   Arts Graduates : about 960+360 hrs. in all
   Commerce Graduates : about 960+240 hrs. in all
   Science Graduates : about 960+120 hrs. in all
c) State of English at the earlier stages. Third language for six years and second language for five years.
d) The attitudes of English
   i) *The Teachers*: Teachers of English seem to consider it important only from the point of view of examination. At the High School, Jr. College and Sr. Collage levels the teachers of other subjects seem to be indifferent towards it.
   ii) *Students*: The students consider it partly as an examination subject for scoring at high school level, and passing at Higher Secondary and Undergraduate level. Hardly anyone seems to value English as a language for communication.
e) Kind of Teachers: Mostly wrongly trained at the High School (Shastri, 1972) and Higher Secondary level. The teachers at Under-Graduate level are often unsure of their own language abilities especially while using English for communicative purposes.
f) Objectives, language skills etc: Specified objectively at the High School level, 2500 vocabulary and 250 structures and the four skills (Patil, 1984). At the

Higher Secondary and Undergraduate levels unspecified but switch over to uncontrolled language.

g) E.B. and D.T.B. : Specified in terms of skills and linguistic items upto High School, but not at Higher Secondary and Undergraduate level.

h) Learning Experience: Examination oriented rote memorization.

i) Kinds of teaching materials: Controlled, tailor-made texts are used as teaching material along with supplementary Readers (not for examination) upto High School level. Uncontrolled text-material is used at the Higher Secondary and Undergraduate level.

j) Assessment of Learning: Set pattern of external examination partly objective but heavily text-oriented and encouraging rote memory.

3. *Objectives of the Present Syllabus*

The main objective of the syllabus of WAC is to enable the learner to understand how to use written and spoken English effectively with increased confidence in every area of business where communication is important. The content analysis of the syllabus, general objectives and over-all specific objective of the syllabus are given below:

a) Content analysis of the syllabus of Written Analysis and Communication.

b) Over-all objectives of the syllabus of Written Analysis and Communication.

4. *Co-ordination with the Earlier Stage*

Transition after the graduation from the faculties of Arts, Commerce, Engineering, Science, Social Sciences and Agricultural Science to MBA-I is not smooth. Their learning experience at the earlier stages was limited to examination oriented rote memorization, study of the controlled tailormade texts upto High School level, study of uncontrolled text-material at Higher Secondary and undergraduate level with supplementary grammars and composition. The objectives of language skills and enlargement of vocabulary were desirable but not wholly feasible. For example, listening and speaking was not testable therefore neglected. The skills of reading and writing were again controlled by the system of examination — partly traditional essay type, heavily text-book content oriented, encouraging rote memory. In the syllabus of WAC, emphasis is given on the communicative skills, especially on oral communication and written communication.

References

Adelstein, Michael, E, 1971: *Contemporary Business Writing*, New York: Random House.

Bapat, S.G. & S.G. Datar, 1973: *A Textbook of Business Correspondence*, Poona: Anmol Prakashan.

Biswas, A. and J.C. Agarwal, 1971: *Encyclopedic Dictionary and Directory of Education*, Vol-1. Karol Bagh New Delhi-5: The Academic Publishers (Indian).

Breen, M.P., 1984: Process Syllabuses of the Language Classroom. In C.J. Brumfit (Ed.), *General English Syllabus Design* (*ELT Documents* No. 118, pp. 47-60). London: Pergamon Press and British Council.

Breen, M.P., 1987: Learner's Contributions to Task Design. In C.N. Candlin and D. Murphy (Eds.) *Lancaster Practical Papers in English Language Education* : Vol. 7. Engle wood Cliff, N.J.: *Language Learning Tasks* (pp. 23-46) Prentice Hall.

Breen, M.P. and C. Candlin, 1980: The Essentials of a Communica tive Curriculum in Language Teaching. In *Applied Linguistics*, 1(2), 89-112.

Candlin, C.N., 1984: Syllabus Design as a Critical Process. In *ELT Documents* (No. 118, pp. 29-46). London: Pergamon Press and the British Council.

Candlin, C.N., 1987: Towards Task-Based Language Learning. In C.N. Candlin & D. Murphy (Eds.), *Lancaster Practical Papers in English Language Education*. Englewood Cliffs, N.J.: Vol. 7. *Language Learning Tasks* (pp. 5-22). Prentice Hall.

Candlin, C.N., & D, Murphy, 1987: *Language Practical Papers in English Language Education*, Englewood Cliff, N.J.: Vol. 7. *Language Learning Tasks*. Prentice Hall.

Ellis, R., 1985: *Understanding Second Language Acquisition*. Oxford: Oxford University Press.

Ghosh, R.N., Shastri, H.N.L. and B.K. Das, 1977: *Introductions to English Language Teaching*, Vol.3 Methods at The College Level. Hyderabad : Central Institute of English and Foreign language.

Goud, L.M. and K.R. Dixit. 1976: *Advanced Commercial Correspondence*, Kolhapur: Universal Publications, Kolhapur.

Gurky, Jean M., (Ed.): *A Reader in Human Communication* Random House, New York.

Huebrier, T., 1983: Linguistic Systems and Linguistic Change in an Inter Language. In *Studies in Second Language Acquisition*, 6(1), 33.53.

Johnston, M., 1985: *Syntactic and Morphological Progressions in Learner English*. Canberra, Australia: Department of Immigration and Ethnic Affairs, Canberra.

Kementerian Pelajaran Malaysia [Malaysian Ministry of Education], 1975: *English Language Syllabus in Malaysian Schools Tingatan* [Level] IV-V *Kementerian Pelajaran*, Kuala Lumpur.

Koontz, Harold and Cyril O'Donnell, 1971: *Essentials of Management*, New Delhi: Tata McGraw-Hill Pub. Co. Ltd.

Koontz, Harold & Cyril O'Donnell, 1976: *Management International Student's Edn.* McGraw-Hill Koga-Kusha Ltd.

Larsen, Freeman, D. & M.H. Long, 1991: *An Introduction to Second Language Acquisition Research*. London: Longman.

Long, Michael H. & Graham Crookes, 1992: Three Approaches to Task-Based Syllabus Design. In *TESOL Quarterly*, Vol. 26, No.1 Spring 1992.

Macnamara, J., 1973: Nurseries, Streets and Classrooms: Some Comparisons and Deductions. In *Modern Language Journal*, 57, 250-254.

Marting, et al (Ed.), 1977: *Effective Communication on the Job*, Bombay: Taraporwala Publishing Ind. Pvt. Ltd.

Massie, Joseph, L. 1987: *Essentials of Management*, New Delhi: Prentice-Hall of India Pvt. Ltd.

Meisel, H., Clahsen, H., & M. Pieneman, 1981: On Determining Developmental Stages in Second Language Acquisition, In Studies in Second Language Acquisition, 3(2), 109-135.

Mugali, V.N., 1975: *Business English*, Hubli: Book Centre.

Newmark, L., 1964: Grammatical Theory and the Teaching of English as a Foreign Language, In D.P. Harris (Ed.), *The 1963 Conference papers of the English language section of The National Association for Foreign Student Affairs* (pp. 5-8) New York.

Newmark, L., 1966: How not to Interfere With Language Learning. In International Journal of American Linguistics. 32(1), 77-83.

Newmark, L. and D.A. Reibel, 1968: Necessity and Sufficiency in

Language Learning. In *International Review of Applied Linguistics*, 6, 145-164.

Patil, D.K., 1984: The English Language Achievements of Shivaji University Arts Graduates, An Unpublished Ph.D. Thesis. Kolhapur: Shivaji University.

Prabhu, N.S., 1980: Reaction and Predictions [Special Issue]. *Bulletin* 4(1). Regional Institute of English, Bangalore.

Prabhu, N.S., 1984: Procedural Syllabus. In T.E. Read (Ed.) *Trends in Language Syllabus Design* (pp. 272-280). Singapore: Singapore University Press.

Prabhu, N.S., 1987: *Second Language Pedagogy*. Oxford Cliffs, N.J.: Oxford University Press.

Richards, J., Platt, J. and H. Weber, 1985: *Longman Dictionary of Applied Linguistics*, London: Longman.

Reibel, D.A., 1969: Language Learning Analysis. In *International Review of Applied Linguistics*, 7(4), 283-294.

Rodgers, T.S., 1984: Communicative Syllabus Design and Implementation, Reflections on a decade of experience. In J.A.S. Read (Ed.), *Trends in Syllabus Design* (pp. 28- 51), Singapore: Singapore University Press.

Samah, A.A., 1984: The English Language (Communicational) Curriculum for Upper Secondary Schools in Malaysia, Rationale design and implementation. In J.A.S. Read (Ed.) *Trends in Language Syllabus Design* (pp. 193-214). Singapore: Singapore University Press.

Sato, C.J., 1990: *The Syntax of Conversation in Inter Language Development*, Gunter Narr, Tubingen, Germany.

Shastri, S.V. 1972: The Teaching of English as a Foreign Language in Bombay, An Unpublished Ph.D. Thesis, Bombay: University of Bombay.

White, R.V., 1988: *The ELT Curriculum - Design, Innovation and Management*. Oxford: Basil Blackwell.

Wilkins, D.A., 1974: National Syllabuses and The Concept of a Minimum Adequate Grammar, In S.P. Corder & E. Roulet (Eds.), *Linguistic Insights in Applied Linguistics* (pp. 119-128) AIMAV, Brussels.

Wilkins, D.A., 1976: *Notional Syllabuses*, Oxford: Oxford University Press.

Wright, Charles R., 1974: *Mass Communication, a Sociological Perspective*, New York: Random House.

Zatter, Robert And W. George Gronch, 1961: *Successful Communication in Science and Industry*, McGraw-Hill Co. Inc.

PART - IV

COMMUNICATIVE COMPETENCE TESTING

12

PREPARING A COMPREHENSIVE TESTING DESIGN

"For by wise counsel you will wage your own war,
And in a multitude of counselors there is safty."
— Proverbs 24-6

As a sequel to the previous chapter, this chapter aims at developing testing design to test the communicative competence of the students who have completed the course of WAC, Paper-VI, MBA-I. It has been hypothesized that the university examination tests the students' communicative competence in WAC representatively. The testing design that is going to be developed in this chapter is meant to test communicative competence comprehensively.

First, the stages of preparing comprehensive testing design for Written Analysis and Communication are presented. Secondly, the section on 'Relating the Established Syllabus Objectives to Evaluative Procedures' describes the plan of: (a) analyzing the syllabus contents of WAC, (b) identifying general and specific objectives of WAC, and finally, (c) identifying the components of specific objectives on which the test items of Comprehensive Communicative Competence Test (CCCT) are based. Thirdly, the section on 'Preparing a Comprehensive Testing Design' describes how the analysis of the syllabus contents of WAC and the identification of specific syllabus objectives paves the way for preparing a comprehensive testing design to evaluate communicative competence of the students in WAC. In the section, 'Analysis of The Syllabus Contents and Specification of Objectives', all the contents of the syllabus of WAC are analyzed and the syllabus objectives are specified. Finally, the section, 'Coverage of the CCCT items' gives the details of the syllabus contents covered by the CCCT items. It confirms that all the learning points of the syllabus contents of WAC are adequately covered by the test items. Thus, it confirms the content validity of CCCT.

THE STAGES OF PREPARING A COMPREHENSIVE TESTING DESIGN

Bearing in mind the lacunae of the syllabus and examination system of WAC, MBA-I, it was decided to work on the following :

1. To analyze the syllabus of WAC.
2. To identify the communicative needs of the MBAs.
3. To identify the general and the specific objectives of the syllabus.
4. To identify the components of specific objectives on which the test-items of comprehensive test are to be based.
5. To prepare a comprehensive testing design to evaluate communicative competence of the MBAs in WAC.

The stages of preparing the comprehensive testing design for evaluating communicative competence of the students in Written Analysis and Communication are given below —

STAGE-1 : Analysis of the Syllabus Contents of WAC

STAGE-2 : Identification of the Communicative Needs of MBAs with Reference to the Syllabus of WAC

STAGE-3 : Identification of the General and Specific Syllabus Objectives of WAC

STAGE-4 : Preparing Test-Items Based on the Components of Specific Syllabus Objectives of WAC

STAGE-5 : Verifying the Reliability, Validity and Comprehensiveness of the Testing Design

STAGE-6 : Preparing and administering the Pilot Tests of the Comprehensive Communicative Competence Test

STAGE-7 : Analysis of the Pilot-Tests' Results and Effecting Necessary Changes in the Test-Items

STAGE-8 : Administration of the Final Comprehensive Communicative Competence Test

STAGE-9 : Analysis of the Final Comprehensive Communicative Competence Test Results

SYLLABUS OBJECTIVES AND EVALUATIVE PROCEDURES

The communicative needs of the students are based on the syllabus of a WAC course, therefore, it was necessary to analyse the syllabus of WAC. This syllabus analysis not only helped to know the communicative needs of the MBAs, but also paved the way for identifying the syllabus objectives. The components of specific syllabus objectives were identified through syllabus analysis. The syllabus objectives are stated in terms of what the curriculum expects the students to do at the end of the instruction. These statements direct attention to the students' communicative competence and to the types of performance they are expected to exhibit as a result of it. The focus given on the learning outcomes makes clear the types of performance of the students which will be acceptable as evidence that the instruction has been successful. In identifying syllabus objectives, it was easy to become confused by the seemingly endless array of learning outcomes and by the lack of authoritative information concerning the objectives of the course. Therefore, in preparing a list of syllabus objectives, the criteria for selecting objectives were decided. They are as follows:

1. The objectives must include all important outcomes of the course.
2. The objectives must be in harmony with the general goals of the course.
3. The objectives must be consistent with the sound principles of learning.
4. The objectives must be realistic in terms of the abilities of the students and the time and facilities available to them.

The above given four criteria are based on Gronlund and Linn's 'Criteria For Selecting Appropriate Objectives.' (Gronlund, 1990: 33-36).

In preparing a list of syllabus objectives, all the outcomes of the instruction in 'Written Analysis and Communication' are covered as these are based on the analysis of the syllabus. Secondly, these objectives are consistent with the general goals of the MBA syllabus of the selected University. Thirdly, these objectives are consistent with the sound principles of learning like the 'Principle of readiness' (the objectives must be appropriate to the age level and experiential background of the students)' the 'Principle of motivation' (the objectives must be related to the needs and interests of the students)' the 'Principle of retention' (the objectives must reflect those learning outcomes which are most permanent)' the 'Principle of transfer' (the objectives must refer to the learning outcomes that are most generally applicable to various specific situations). Finally, the objectives are reviewed in the light of the abilities of the students, the time available for achieving the objectives and the adequacy of the facilities available.

PREPARING A COMPREHENSIVE TESTING DESIGN

The objective of the present research is to measure the extent of the selected University MBA-I students' achievement of the instructional goals of the syllabus of Written Analysis and Communication. The identification of the communicative needs of the MBAs, the syllabus analysis, and finally, the analysis of syllabus objectives paves the way for preparing a comprehensive testing design to evaluate communicative competence of the students in WAC.

The choice of the evaluation criteria depends on the objectives of curriculum. Bloom and Krathwohl's, (1956) 'Taxonomy of Educational Objectives' illustrates well the relationship which should hold between the course objectives and the test items.

According to Richard Lindeman (1967), "The teacher should attempt to obtain the closest possible relationship between the aims or purposes of a given instructional sequence and the test he constructs to measure the achievement of those aims", (Lindeman, 1967:56). Anastasi, A. (1988), Mehrens, W.A. and Lehmann, I.J. (1987), Salvia, J. and Ysseldyke, J. (1988) have all supported the view of relating evaluation procedures to syllabus objectives.

The final examination which grades the students' success in the communicative performances is intimately connected with the communicative needs of the students and the establishment of syllabus objectives. If these objectives are precisely defined and established, it is possible to evaluate the students' communicative competence at the every expected achievement level. "Before determining a testing programme for a specific course — indeed, before setting out to teach a course — the teacher should clearly envision the course objectives. By so doing he or she will be sure that the teaching will be nationally oriented and that the tests will indicate how close each student has come to attaining the objectives" (Valette, 1967:17).

The more precise the objectives, the more precise is the evaluation of the students' communicative competence. The data of such evaluation can either be quantified (measured systematically, numerically) or unquantified (verbal, descriptive, unsystematic). The evaluation data of these two types have complementary advantages.

"Once the objectives of the course have been determined, the general parameters of the testing programme become evident. Test construction consists of translating these general statements into specific tests and quizzes" (Valette, 1967:23). To serve its purpose the achievement test is required to be designed to indicate individual and group progress towards the instructional objectives of the syllabus. "Instructional objectives encompass a variety of learning outcomes, and evaluation includes a variety of procedures. The key to effective evaluation of pupil learning is to relate the evaluation procedures as directly as possible to the intended learning outcomes" (Gronlund, 1990:512). Preparing test items which are relevant to the syllabus objectives requires matching the performance measured by the test items to the types of performance intended by the syllabus objectives. In preparing the comprehensive achievement testing design for the selected University MBA-I students in 'Written Analysis and Communication', it was decided to base the test objectives directly on the syllabus objectives. "In the preparation of an achievement test, one may base the test objectives directly on the objectives of the course." (Harris, 1969:95).

Note : Please see the References of this Chapter at the end of Chapter 13.

13

SYLLABUS ANALYSIS AND SPECIFICATION OF OBJECTIVES

"My analysis . . . led me to formulate 'The Peter Principle': In a Hierarchy Every Employee Tends to Rise to his level of Incompetence."

— Laurence Peter & Raymond Hull

While selecting every test-item, the syllabus objectives which were defined before the item selection are strictly borne in mind. Only those items are selected which provide the most direct measure of the performance task described in the intended instructional outcome. Every item confines itself to test whether the specific objective of the syllabus is achieved or not. The specified syllabus objectives which have been identified from the syllabus-content analysis, have proved extremely useful base for constructing the test-items. The general objectives of the syllabus of Written Analysis and Communication are derived from the analysis of the syllabus content. The general instructional objectives are stated in general terms to encompass a set of specific learning outcomes. When major objectives are stated in more general terms, they provide for the integration of specific facts and skills into more complex response patterns. The verbs of the beginning of each statement of objective is general enough to encompass a range of more complex specific learning outcomes. The degree of generality may vary somewhat with the period of instruction for which the list is being prepared. The objectives for a comparatively brief unit of instruction are likely to be more specific than those for an entire course of study. These general course objectives are broad in nature. It was necessary to break them down into their specific components.

Considering specific components of the general objectives, the general objectives were further sub-divided into specific objectives. Statements of specific learning outcomes specify the types of pupil performance acceptable as evidence that the general instructional objective has been achieved. The analysis of these objectives has provided a concrete basis to write and select the test-items.

The syllabus of "Written Analysis and Communication"— unit course-6, MBA-I, the selected University, is divided into two sections — Section I and Section II. Each of these sections are divided into three divisions. Thus, the contents of the syllabus are grouped into six divisions.

Given below is the analysis of the syllabus contents.

SECTION - I

1. Communication in Organization — Nature, Function, Scope and Limitations — Management Communication:

For effective management communication in business organizations, the students are expected to learn about — A) Nature, B) Functions, C) Scope, D) Limitations of business communication.

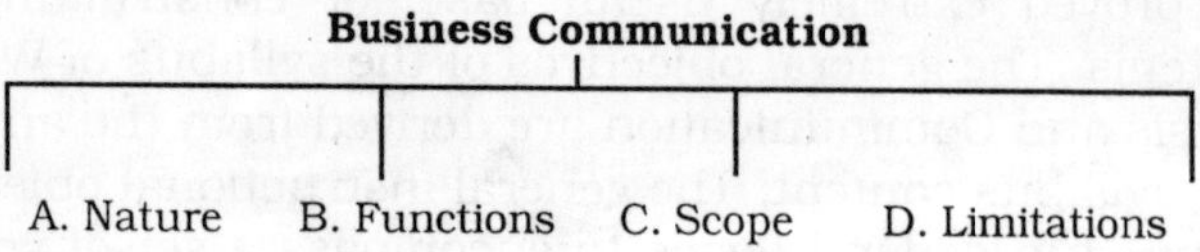

A. ***Nature***: The students have to learn about —

i. The meaning of communication
ii. The components of communication situation
iii. The cycle of communication

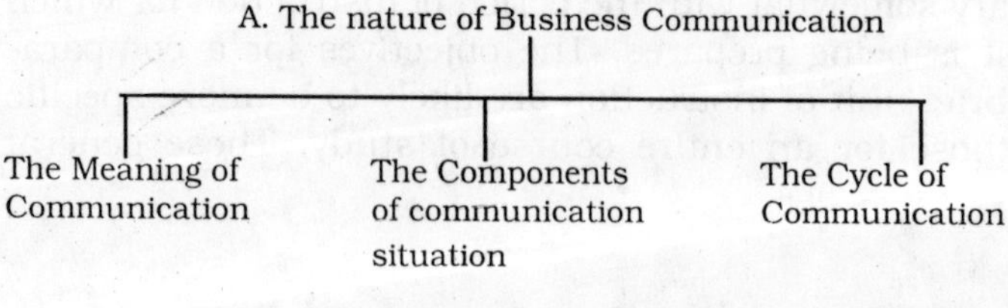

The students have to learn the meaning and definitions of communication, the components of communication situation, and the cycle or process of communication. The general and specific objectives of this part of the syllabus are —

GO-1: (General Objective) — To know the meaning and process of business communication.

SO-1: (Specific Objective) — To know the meaning of business communication.

SO-2: To know the components of communication situation.

SO-3: To know the cycle of communication.

B. ***Functions*** : The students have to learn about the functions of business communication like Information, Advice, Order, Suggestion, Persuasion, Education, Instruction, Warning, Raising Morale, Motivation.

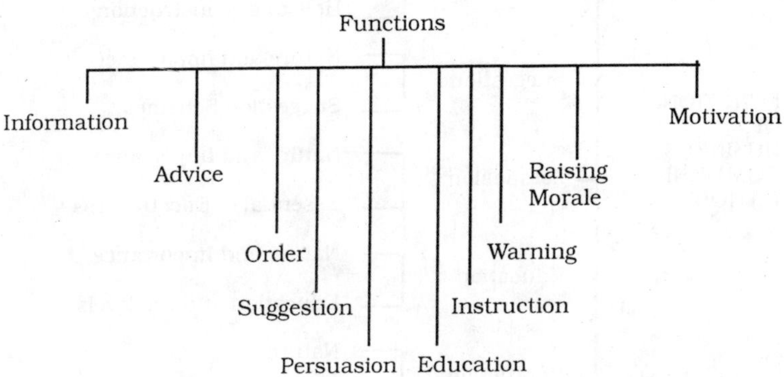

(i) *Information* : Need and types ; The sources of information; Reliability of information

(ii) *Advice:* Meaning and importance; Essentials of effectiveness; Difference between advice and counselling.

(iii) *Order:* Nature and importance; Types; How to issue orders.

(iv) *Suggestion:* Nature and importance; Suggestion schemes.

(v) *Persuasion:* Nature and importance; essentials of effectiveness

(vi) *Education*: Nature and importance of education at three levels in business

(vii) *Instruction*: Nature; How to give instructions

(viii) *Warning:* Nature and importance; Essentials of effectiveness.

(ix) *Raising Morale*: Nature and importance; Factors conducive to morale raising

(x) *Motivation*: Meaning and importance; Factors conducive to motivation

FUNCTIONS OF BUSINESS COMMUNICATION

- Information
  - Need and Types
  - Sources of Information
  - Reliability of Information
- Advice
  - Meaning and Importance
  - Essentials of Effectiveness
  - Advice and Counselling
- Order
  - Nature and Importance
  - Types
  - How to give instructions
- Suggestion
  - Nature and Importance
  - Suggestion Schemes
- Persuasion
  - Nature and Importance
  - Essential of Effectiveness
- Education
  - Nature and Importance
  - Education at three levels
- Instruction
  - Nature
  - How to give Instructions
- Warning
  - Nature and Importance
  - Essential of Effectiveness
- Raising Morale
  - Nature and Importance
  - Factors Conducive to Morale Raising
- Motivation
  - Meaning and Importance
  - Factors Conducive to Motivation

The students have to learn about the above given functions of business communication. The general and specific objectives of this part of the syllabus are -

GO-2 : To know the functions of business communication.

SO-4 : To know about the need and types of information.

SO-5 : To know about the sources of information.

SO-6 : To know about the reliability of information.

SO-7 : To know the meaning and importance of advice.

SO-8 : To know the essentials of effective advice.

SO-9 : To know the difference between advice and counselling.

SO-10: To know the nature and importance of order.

SO-11: To know the types of order.

SO-12: To know how to issue orders.

SO-13: To know the nature and importance of suggestions.

SO-14: To know about the suggestion schemes.

SO-15: To know the nature and importance of persuasion.

SO-16: To know the essentials of effective persuasion.

SO-17: To know the importance of education and training at three levels in business- (i) Management, (ii) Employees, (iii) Outside public.

SO-18: To know the nature of instructions.

SO-19: To know how to give instructions.

SO-20: To know the nature and importance of warning.

SO-21: To know the essentials of effective warning.

SO-22: To know the nature and importance of high morale.

SO-23: To know the factors conducive to morale raising.

SO-24: To know the meaning and importance of motivation.

SO-25: To know the factors conducive to motivation.

C. ***Scope:*** The students have to learn about the significance of oral and written media used for variety of purposes in business communication. The general and specific objectives of this part of the syllabus are-

GO-3: To enable the students to understand how the managerial communication plays an important role in the complex world of business.

SO-26: To know the significance of communication in business interactions.

D. Limitations: The students have to learn about the limitations of managerial communication. In business transactions and interpersonal activities, communication is limited to the specified communicative functions discussed earlier in —

Channels of Business Communication

Downward communication-Upward communication-Horizontal communication-Purpose, Kinds, and Methods, constraints and Limitations-Psychological variables, personal variables, structural variables-Effectiveness of communication:

A. Downward, Upward and Horizontal Communication— The students have to learn about the Nature, Purpose, Methods, Constraints and limitations of the formal as well as informal communication channels.

B. The Constraints and Limitations - Under 'constraints and Limitations' of the above channels, the students are expected to learn about the psychological, structural and personal barriers to effective business communication.

C. Effectiveness of Communication — The students have to learn about all the essentials of effective communications business organization.

[A] The Downward, Upward and Horizontal Communication — The general and specific objectives of this part of the syllabus are:

CHANNELS OF COMMUNICATION

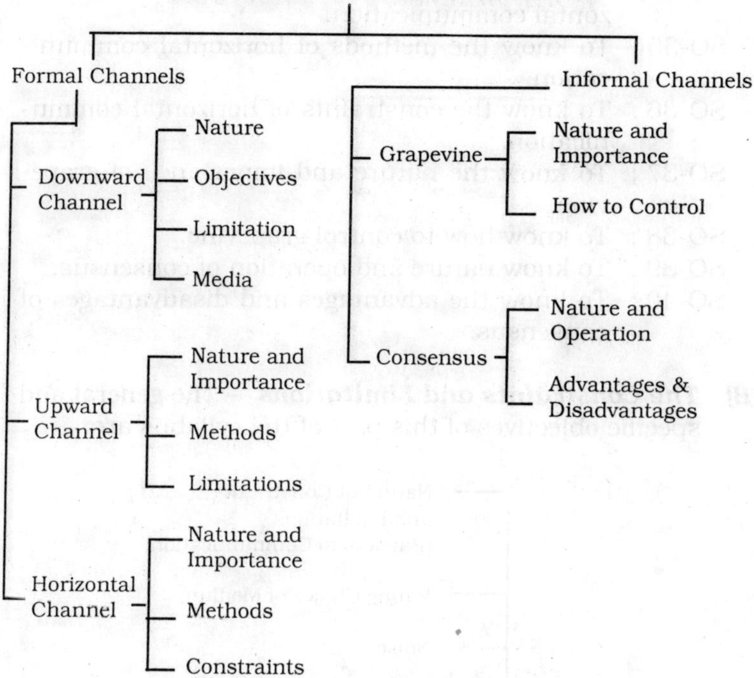

GO-4 : To know the nature,purpose, methods and limitations of the formal and informal channels of communication.

SO-27 : To know the nature of downward communication.

SO-28 : To know the objectives of downward communication.

SO-29 : To know the media used in downward communication.

SO-30 : To know the limitations of downward communication.

SO-31 : To know the nature and importance of upward communication

SO-32 : To know the methods of upward communication.

SO-33 : To know the limitations of upward communication.

SO-34 : To know the nature and importance of horizontal communication.

SO-35 : To know the methods of horizontal communication.

SO-36 : To know the constraints of horizontal communication.

SO-37 : To know the nature and importance of grapevine.

SO-38 : To know how to control grapevine.

SO-39 : To know nature and operation of consensus.

SO-40 : To know the advantages and disadvantages of consensus.

[B] ***The Constraints and Limitations*** — The general and specific objectives of this part of the syllabus are:

CONSTRAINTS AND LIMITATIONS TO EFFECTIVE COMMUNICATION

- Nature of Constraints and Limitations (Barriers to Communication)
- Wrong Choice of Medium
- Noise
- Time
- Abstracting
- Slanting
- Attitudes and Opinions
- Semantic Barriers
- Emotions
- Closed Mind
- Status Consciousness
- Inattentiveness
- Inference
- Distortion
- Allness

GO-5 : To know the 'constraints and limitations' or barriers to effective communication in business.

SO-41 : To know the nature of barriers to business communication.

SO-42 : To know the barrier 'Wrong choice of medium.'

SO-43 : To know the barrier 'Noise.'

SO-44 : To know the barrier 'Time.'

SO-45 : To know the barrier 'Abstracting.'

SO-46 : To know the barrier 'Slanting.'

SO-47 : To know the barrier 'Attitudes and opinions.'

SO-48 : To know the 'Semantic' barriers.

SO-49 : To know the barrier 'Emotions.'

SO-50 : To know the barrier 'Closed mind.'

SO-51 : To know the barrier 'Status consciousness.'

SO-52 : To know the barrier 'In attentiveness.'

SO-53 : To know the barrier 'Inference.'

SO-54 : To know the barrier 'Distortion.'

SO-55 : To know the barrier 'Allness.'

[C] The Effectiveness of Communication — The general and specific objectives of this part of the syllabus are:

ESSENTIALS OF EFFECTIVE BUSINESS COMMUNICATION

- Clarity of Thought and Expression
- Brevity and Conciseness
- Completeness
- Correctness
- Attentiveness
- Objectivity
- Adaptability
- You' Attitude
- Courtesy
- Knowledge of the Subject

GO-6 : To know the essentials of effective Business communication.

SO-56 : To know about 'clarify of thought and expression.'

SO-57 : To know about 'brevity and conciseness.'

SO-58 : To know about 'completeness.'

SO-59 : To know about 'correctness.'

SO-60 : To know about 'attentiveness.'

SO-61 : To know about 'appropriateness.'

SO-62 : To know about 'objectivity.'

SO-63 : To know about 'adaptability.'

SO-64 : To know about "You"-attitude.

SO-65 : To know about 'courtesy.'

SO-66 : To know about 'knowledge of the subject.'

Media of Communication

Communication skills-written media-advantages and usefulness oral media-advantages and usefulness-Aids to communication:

a. *Written media-advantages and usefulness*: The students have to learn about the advantages, limitations, aids and essentials of effectiveness of the written media.

b. *Oral media-advantages and usefulness*: The students have to learn about the advantages, limitations aids and essentials of effectiveness of the oral media.

c. *Aids to communication*: The students have to acquaint themselves with the various technical aids available in the oral, written and nonverbal media.

GO-7 : To know the advantages, limitations, aids, and essentials of effective written and oral communication.

SO-67 : To know the merits of written media.

SO-68 : To know the limitations of written media.

SO-69 : To know the essentials of effective written communication.

SO-70 : To know the advantages of oral communication.

SO-71 : To know the limitations of oral communication.

MEDIA OF COMMUNICATION

- Written Media
  - Aids
    - Letters
    - Reports
    - Minutes
    - Journalistic Writing
  - Merits of Written Media
  - Essentials of Effective Written Communication
  - Limitations of Written Media
- Oral Media
  - Aids
    - Public Speaking
    - Group Communication
  - Merits of Oral Media
  - Essentials of Effective Oral Communication
  - Limitations of Oral Media

SO-72 : To know the essentials of effective oral communication.

The specific objectives on 'Aids to Written and Oral Communication' are given in Section-II: 4 Foundations of Effective Writing — Aids; Section-II -5: Verbal Massages - Nonverbal Massages; and in Section-II-6 : Public speaking.

SECTION - II

Foundations of Effective Writing

AIDS :

a. Letters — how to write — Types of letter.
b. Reports — format of a report — steps in writing the report — Different types of reports.
c. Meetings and conferences.
d. Journalistic Style — writing procedures — General knowledge - organizing the writing - Specialization in style.

a. *Letters* — The students have to learn about how to write the business letters and the types of business letters. In order to know how to write the business letters, the students must know the structure of business letter and the essentials of effectiveness.

BUSINESS LETTERS

- Structure of Business Letters
  - Heading
  - Inside Address
  - Salutation
  - Body of the Letter
  - Complimentary Close
  - Signature
  - Enclosures
  - Postscript
- Essentials of Effective Written Communication
- Types of Business Letters
  - Enquiries and Replies
  - Orders and Execution
  - Credit and Status Enquiries
  - Complaints and Adjustments
  - Collection Letters
  - Circular Letters
  - Sales Letters
  - Agency Letters

Letters : The general and specific objectives of this part of the syllabus are —

GO-8 : To know how to write business letters and the types of business letters

SO-73 : To know the structure of business letters

SO-74 : To know the types of business letters.

The essentials of effective written communication are given in Section-I, Part-3, (a) Written Media

b. *Reports* — The students have to learn about the formats and types of business reports, in order to know how to write reports, the subject must know the formats of business reports, steps of report writing and the essentials of effectiveness.

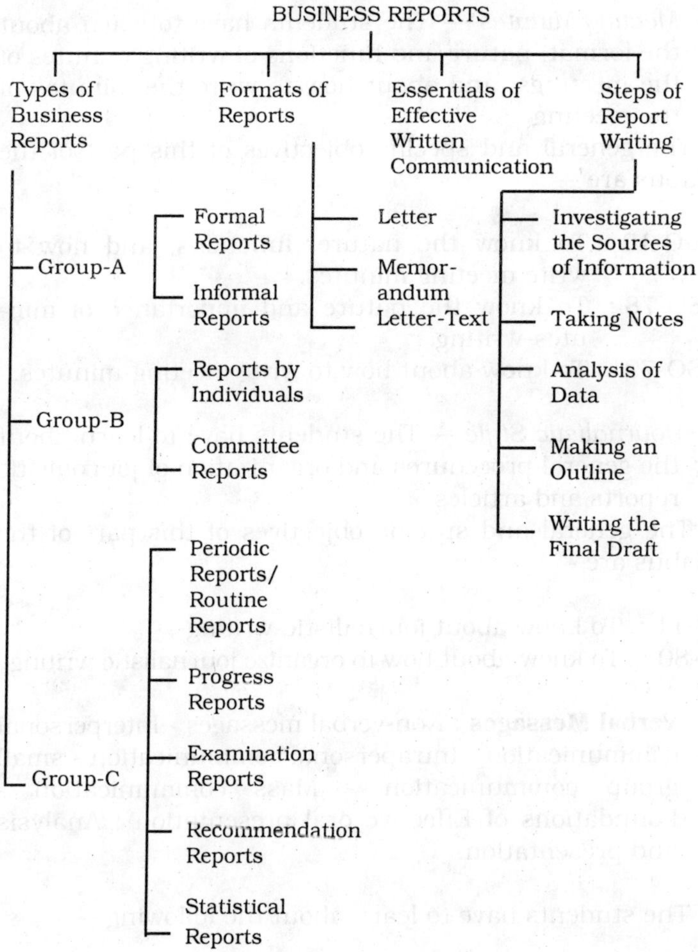

Reports: The general and specific objectives of this part of the syllabus are -

GO-9 : To know the formats, types, essentials of effectiveness, and steps of report writing.
SO-75 : To know the nature and types of business reports.
SO-76 : To know the steps of business report writing.
SO-77 : To know the formats of business reports.

c. *Meeting-Minutes* — The students have to learn about the format, nature and functions of writing minutes of the meetings, and about how to write the minutes of the meeting.

The general and specific objectives of this part of the syllabus are —

GO-10 : To know the nature, functions, and how to write meeting minutes.
SO-78 : To know the nature and importance of minutes-writing.
SO-79 : To know about how to write meeting-minutes.

d. *Journalistic Style* — The students have to learn about the general procedures and organization of journalistic reports and articles.

The general and specific objectives of this part of the syllabus are -

GO-11 : To know about journalistic-writing
SO-80 : To know about how to organize journalistic writing.

5. **Verbal Messages** : Non-verbal messages - Interpersonal communication - Intrapersonal communication - small group communication - Mass communication - Foundations of Effective oral presentation : Analysis and presentation.

The students have to learn about the following —

A. Verbal and Non-verbal messages — the difference.
B. Interpersonal and Intrapersonal communication — the difference
C. Small group communication and mass communication — the difference.
D. Foundations of effective oral presentation, Analysis and presentation — for effective oral presentation, the students have to collect the data, analye the data and organize the speech before speech delivery.

A. VERBAL AND NON-VERBAL MESSAGES

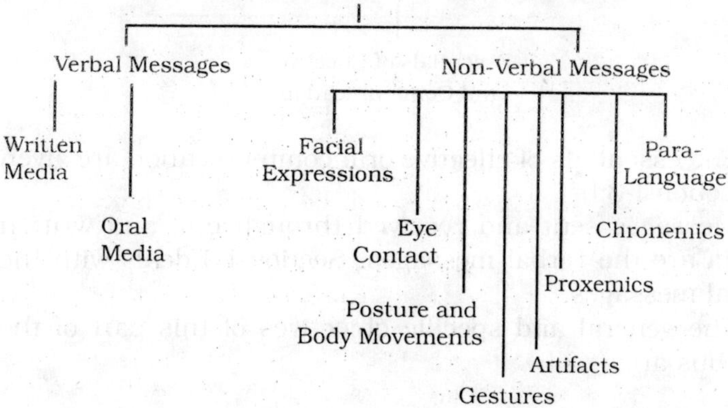

B. INTERPERSONAL AND INTRAPERSONAL COMMUNICATION

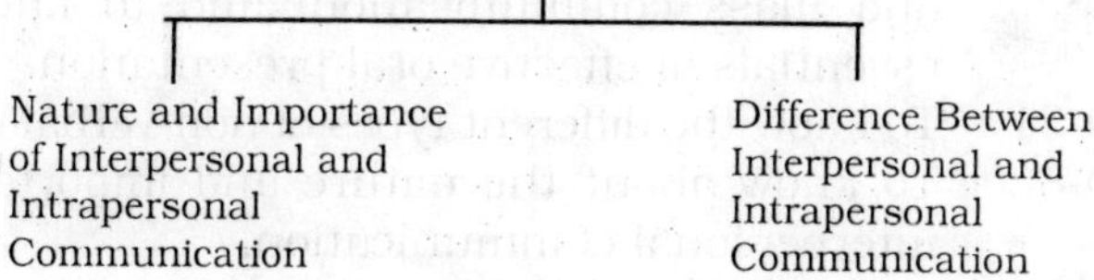

C. GROUP COMMUNICATION AND MASS COMMUNICATION

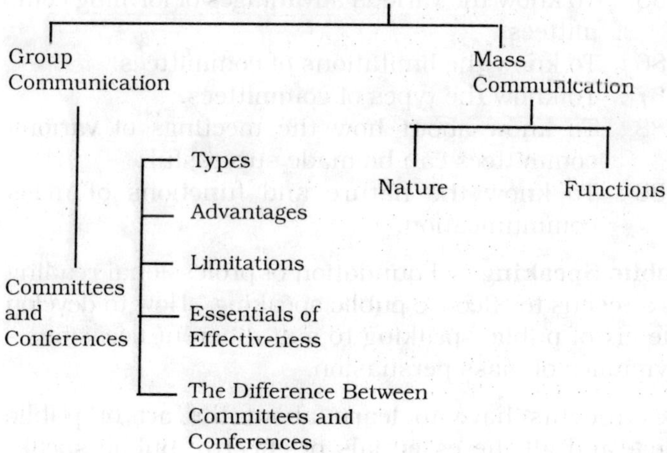

D. EFFECTIVE ORAL PRESENTATION

Essentials of Effective
Oral Communication

The essentials of effective oral communication are given in Section-I-3:b.

Messages sent and received through oral and written media are the verbal messages. Section-I:3 deals with the verbal messages.

The general and specific objectives of this part of the syllabus are —

GO-12 : To know the difference between the verbal and non-verbal messages, interpersonal and intrapersonal communication, the small group and mass communication; and to know the essentials of effective oral presentation.

SO-81 : To know the different types of non-verbal media.

SO-82 : To know about the nature and importance of interpersonal communication.

SO-83 : To know the difference between interpersonal and intra personal communication.

SO-84 : To know about the nature of the committees.

SO-85 : To know the various advantages of forming committees.

SO-86 : To know the limitations of committees.

SO-87 : To know the types of committees.

SO-88 : To know about how the meetings of various committees can be made successful.

SO-89 : To know the nature and functions of mass communication.

6. Public Speaking — Foundation of professional reading as a means to effective public speaking - How to develop the art of public speaking to suit different occasions - Dynamics of mass persuasion.

The students have to learn about the art of public speaking, and all the essentials of effective public speaking. The professional reading is one of the many essentials of effective public speaking. The students have to learn all these essentials which are helpful in mass persuasion. Thus the students are expected to know the essentials of effectiveness of the art of public speaking to suit different occasions.

PUBLIC SPEAKING

- Planning and Preparation
  - Understanding the Audience
  - Deciding the Purpose and Objectives
  - Acquiring Knowledge of the Subject
  - Selecting Suitable Pattern of Arrangement
    - Topical
    - Chronological
    - Spatial
    - Causal
    - Problem Solution
  - Determining Supporting Material
    - Analogies
    - Statistical Data
    - Examples
    - Quotations
  - Outline of Public Speech
    - Introduction
    - Body
    - Conclusion
- Essentials of Effective Oral Communication
- Presentation of Public Speech
  - Meaning of Speech Delivery
  - Modes of Delivery
    - Impromptu
    - Memorised
    - Extemporaneous
    - Manuscript
  - Using Visual Cues
    - Eye-Contact
    - Facial Expressions
    - Postures and Movements
    - Gestures
  - Using Vocal Cues
    - Volume
    - Rate
    - Pitch
    - Articulation

The essentials of effective oral communication are given in Section-I-3:b

Public Speech: The general and specific objectives of this part of the syllabus are —

GO-13 : To understand and develop the art of public speaking.

SO-90 : To know the nature and importance of public speech.

SO-91 : To know about how to prepare and present public speech.

The communicative functions in business communication situations through the selected media covered in the syllabus of WAC:

A) Identification and Interpretation of Communicative Functions.

B) Creating Discourse Units for Communicative Functions.

The Media covered in the syllabus of WAC are: (1) Business Letters, (2) Business reports, (3) Public Speech, (4) Group Communication, (5) Meeting minutes, (6) Journalistic writing.

The Communicative Functions in the selected media are - (1) Order (2) Persuasive appeal (3) Warning (4) Promise (5) Request (6) Acknowledgement (7) Appreciation (8) Opining (9) Inferring (10) Complaint (11) Inquiry (12) Suggestion (13) Advice (14) Invitation (15) Apology (16) Greeting (17) Motivation (18) Information (19) Instruction

A. Identification and Interpretation of Communicative Functions: The students are expected to identify and interpret the discourse units used for communication functions in business situations through selected media covered in the syllabus of WAC.

The general and specific objectives of this part of the syllabus are —

GO-14 : To identify and interpret communicative functions in discourse units which are used in business communicative situations through selected media.

SO-92 : To identify and interpret 19 communicative functions in 6 communication media given below.

Communication Media - (1) Business Letters (2) Business reports (3) Public Speech (4) Group Communication (5) Meeting minutes (6) Journalistic writing.

Communicative Functions - (1) Order (2) Persuasive appeal (3) Warning (4) Promise (5) Request (6) Acknowledgement (7) Appreciation (8) Opining (9) Inferring (10) Complaint (11) Inquiry (12) Suggestion (13) Advice (14) Invitation (15) Apology (16) Greeting (17) Motivation (18) Information (19) Instruction.

B. Creating Discourse Units for Communicative Functions: The students are expected to create discourse units for communicative functions in business situations through selected media covered in the syllabus of WAC.

The general and specific objectives of this part of the syllabus are —

GO-15 : To create discourse units for communicative functions in 6 communication media.

SO-93 : To create discourse units for 19 communicative functions in 6 communication media.

The 19 communicative functions and 6 communication media are already mentioned in SO-92 above.

References

Anastasi, A., 1988: *Psychological Testing*, (6th Edn.) New York: Macmillan.

Bloom, Benjamin, S. and D.R. Krathwohl. *Taxonomy of Educational Objective*, Handbook - I Cognitive Domain David Mckay Co. Inc. New York, 1956.

Boebe , Steven A., 1974: Eye Contact: A Nonverbal Determinant of Speaker Credibility, In *Speech Teacher*, (9174):23-21-25.

Gronlund, N.E. and Linn, R.L. (1990); *Measurement and Evalua-*

tion in Teaching; Macmillan Publishing Company, New York.

Harris, D.P. (1969); *Testing English as a Second Language*; McGraw-Hill Book Company, New York.

Lindeman, R. Chand, H., *Educational Measurement*, Scott, Foresman and Company, Glenview, Illinois-60025. 1967.

Mehrens, W.A. and Lehmann, I.J. *Using Standardized Tests in Education*, (4th Edn.); Macmillan, New York, 1987

Salvia, J. and Ysseldykc, *Assessment In Special and Remedial Education*, (4th Edn.) Houghton Mifflin, Boston. 1988.

Sekaran, U. Chicago, 1989 : *Organizational Behaviour*, New Delhi: Tata McGraw-Hill Publishing Co.Ltd.

Valette, R.M. (1967); *Modern Language Testing;* Harcourt Brace Jovanovich, Inc. New York.

14

EVALUATION AND DEVELOPMENT OF COMMUNICATIVE COMPETENCE TEST

"There is no substitute for talent. Indstry and all the virtues are of no avail."

— Aldous Huxley

This chapter is divided into two parts. The first part, 'Test evaluation and the development of CCCT' describes how the item analysis procedures were carried out after the assessment of the pilot tests. In all, four pilot tests of CCCT were administered and their results were assessed. Item analysis procedure was used after the assessment of pilot test responses. Item analysis results helped in the preparation and development of the final CCCT. The second part of 'Administration of CCCT' elaborates how the representative students of MBA-I students of eight MBA teaching centers of the selected University were selected. The final CCCT was administered to these representative students.

TEST EVALUATION AND DEVELOPMENT OF THE COMMUNICATIVE COMPETENCE TEST (CCCT)

The Steps Followed in Planning and Evaluating CCCT

Thus, before administering the final CCCT to the students at eight MBA teaching centers of the selected University, it was essential to confirm the fact that the most carefully and scientifically designed CCCT was the valid, reliable and comprehensive test of communicative competence of the students in WAC, the paper VIth. The likelihood of preparing a valid, reliable and useful CCCT was initially enhanced and finally confirmed by the series of steps followed in planning, administering and evaluating the test. The steps were as follows—

STEP-1: *Determining:* The Purpose of Designing the Comprehensive Communicative Competence Test of the MBA Subjects of the selected University in 'Written Analysis and Communication' (WAC): The purpose was to build comprehensive test design to test the achievements of the students in WAC, Paper-VIth.

STEP-2: *Developing The Test Specifications* : In order to build the table of test specifications the researcher had to— (i) Prepare a list of syllabus objectives, (ii) Outline the syllabus content, and (iii) relate the syllabus contents and instructional objectives to the test items.

STEP-3: *Selecting Appropriate Test Items*: It was decided to select the objective type test-items. 'The objective item includes a variety of different types, but they can be classified in to those that require the pupil to "supply" the answer and those that require the pupil to "select" the answer from a given number of alternatives.' (Gronlund & Linn, p.121). These two classes are commonly further divided into the following types of objective test items -

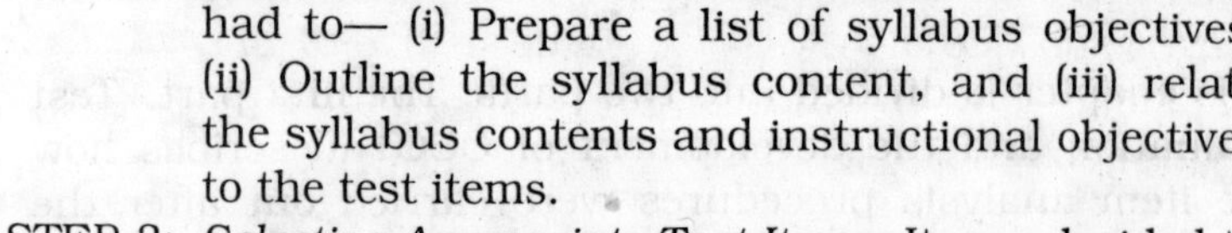

There are numerous modifications and combinations of these item types in addition to the basic types of objective test items. In CCCT both the 'supply' type of objective test items as well as 'selection type of objective test items with certain modifications and combinations of the basic types as described in the Pilot Test-2 and Pilot Test-3, has been used.

It is generally recognized that the multiple choice test-item is the most widely applicable and useful type of test-item. It can be effective in measuring many of the learning outcomes measured by the short answer items like the true-false items and the matching exercise. It can measure a variety of a more complex outcomes in the knowledge understanding and application areas. 'The multiple-choice item can measure at both the knowledge and understanding levels and is also free of many of the limitations of other forms of objective items. The flexibility plus the higher quality item usually found in the multiple choice from has led to its extensive use in achievement testing (Gronlund and Linn, 1990:166). Therefore, in comprehensive communicative competence test, multiple choice items were used to find the evidence of the students' achievements in the knowledge of the theory part of the paper -WAC (Section-I) and in the understanding of communicative functions of the discourse units in the business communicative situations (Section-II) in the first and second section, the third section. Beside multiple choice items the completion includes items that allows the students the required freedom to use any appropriate word to complete the discourse unit or utterance so as to make its communicative function evident and effective. The key word is dropped from an utterance which has same communication function in business situation whenever necessary, this communication function is given in the instruction below the utterance. When an instruction is not given the communication function is implied in the context of the given utterance. The students are expected to grasp this function and to use the most appropriate word in order to complete the utterance in such a way that the utterance is effective in its communicative function.

In section II & III the students are expected to identify, interpret and create the units of written and oral discourse in business communicative situations. They are the functional communicative units or the 'speech acts' carrying both locutionary and illocutionary meaning. A speech act is a sentence or an utterance which has both propositional meaning and illocutionary force. (Austin, 1962, Searle, 1981, Coulthard, 1977)

In philosophy, linguistics and semantics a proposition is the basic or literal meaning which a sentence expresses. Proposition consists of two factors — first, it consists of something which is named or talked about (an entity or argument), and secondly, it consists an assertion or predication which is made about an entity. A sentence may express or imply more than one proposition, for example—

'John's uncle, Michael, who is a poet, writes songs for films.'

This sentence can imply the following propositions:

John has an uncle.
His uncle's name is Michael
Michael is a poet
Michael writes songs
Michael writes songs for the films

A Propositional meaning of an utterance is also known as locutionary meaning. Locutionary meaning is the basic literal meaning of the utterance. It is conveyed by the particular words and structures which the utterance contains. The illocutionary meaning is also known as illocutionary force. This is the effect of the utterance on the communication receiver. This effect is associated with message transmission rather than with the message reception. It does not indicate the receiver's understanding of the encoded message, but on the other hand it indicates the effect the speaker or the communicator 'wants' the utterance to have on the listener or the receiver. For example, in the sentence 'I am tired', the propositional meaning is what the utterance says about the communicator's physical and/or mental state. What the speaker 'wants' to communicate may be a request to the listener to leave the room. There are many different kinds of speech acts or functional units of communication, such as orders, complaints, requests, commands, promises etc.

In 'Language Teaching' and 'Syllabus Design', speech

acts are often referred to as 'language functions' or 'functions' (Austin, 1962, Searle, 1981). Searle has classified speech acts in five groups:

a) Commissive — Promise, threat.
b) Declarative — declaration, pronouncement
c) Directive — suggestion, request, command
d) Expressive — apology, complaint, thanking.
e) Representative — assertion, claim, report.

(a) **Commissive** — The commissive speech acts commit the speakers to doing something in the future, such as a promise or a threat. For example — 'Though we are most anxious to avoid doing anything from which your credit and reputation might suffer, we are forced to inform you that unless we receive your cheque in full settlement by 30 September 1993, we shall be compelled, much against our will, to take legal steps to obtain payment' — Threat. 'Any information that you give us will be treated as strictly confidential.' — Promise.

(b) **Declarative** — Declarative speech acts change the state of affairs in the world. For example — 'We are pleased to inform you that we have been entrusted with the sole distributing agency of 'Mafatal Fabrics' and 'Bombay Textiles' in Ahmedabad, Baroda, Jaipur and Bikaner market.'

(c) **Directive** — Directive speech acts have the functions of getting the communication receivers to do something, such as a request, a command, a suggestion etc. For example — 'Please send the machines by S.T. parcel, carriage forward to Kolhapur Bus Stand.'

(d) **Expressive** — In expressive speech acts, the speakers express their feelings and attitudes about something, such as a complaint, an apology, thanking, congratulating etc. For example, 'We are very glad to receive your order of 5 October 1989 for the supply of twelve television sets.'

(e) **Representative** — The representative speech acts describe events or state of affairs in the world. They are informative, such as an assertion, a claim, a report etc. For example — 'They have been our regular suppliers for more than last three years'.

Thus speech acts serve various communicative functions of the languages (Searle, 1965, Wilkins, 1976). In language teaching, language functions are often described as categories of behaviour, e.g. requests, apologies, complaints, compliments. These functional uses of language cannot be determined simply by studying grammatical structures of the language (Wilkins, 1979). For example, imperative sentences may perform various other functions—

'Come for the party'. (Invitation)
'Try it for the second time'. (Suggestion)
'Read the passage carefully before answering the questions'. (Instruction)
'Sing a song for me'. (Request)
'Run fast'. (Order)

Therefore, the functional uses of language are studied in speech act theory, sociolinguistics and pragmatics. Lyons (1977, 1981) gives three main functions of Language—

(a) Descriptive
(b) Expressive
(c) Social.

(a) **Descriptive function** — The descriptive function of the language conveys factual information. This type of information can be stated or denied and in some cases even tested. For example, 'It must be well below fifteen degrees outside'.

(b) **Expressive function** — The expressive function of the language supplies information about the speaker — his feelings, attitudes, preferences etc. For example, the utterance 'I shall never contest for these elections,' may indicate that the speaker did not like the ugliness of politics.'

(c) **Social function** — The social function of the language serves to establish and maintain social relations. As language is a social phenomenon, every function of language can be justifiably called as social. Similarly, while expressing his thoughts and feelings, the speaker may convey factual information too. Thus, these functions are overlapping.

During early stages of language development a young child is able to master a number of elementary functions of language. According to Halliday (1978), each of these functions has a choice of meanings attached to it. He distinguishes seven initial functions.

(a) **Instrumental** : This function is used for satisfying material needs, ("I want")

(b) **Regulatory** : This function is used for controlling the behaviour of others, ("Do as I tell you")

(c) **Interactional** : This function is used for getting along with other people ("Me and You")

(d) **Personal** : This function is used for identifying and expressing the self, ("Here I come")

(e) **Heuristic** : This function is used for exploring the world around and inside one, ("Tell me why")

(f) **Imaginative** : This function is used for creating a world of one's own, ("Let's pretend")

(g) **Informative** : This function is used for communicating new information, ("I have got something to tell you")

Halliday (1978) gives three main functions of language:

(a) Ideational
(b) Interpersonal
(c) Textual

(a) **Ideational function** — The ideational function of the language organizes the communicator's experiences of the real or the imaginary world, i.e. language refers to real or imaginary things events, persons, actions and states.

(b) **Interpersonal function** — The interpersonal function indicates, establishes or maintains social relationships.

(c) **Textual function** — The textual function creates written or oral texts which cohere within themselves and which fit the particular situation in which they are used. (Halliday, 1978, de Joia and Stenton, 1980). These functions overlap each other. For example the textual function can be used for both interpersonal as well as ideational communicative purposes.

The investigator of this research study has identified nineteen communicative functions of oral and written discourse in business communicative situations. These functions are as follows —

Communicative function	Category
1. Enquiry	Heuristic Function
2. Information	Representative Function
3. Promise 4. Warning 5. Inference	Commissive Functions
6. Persuasive appeal 7. Suggestion 8. Order 9. Request 10. Motivation 11. Advice 12. Instruction 13. Invitation	Directive Functions
14. Appreciation 15. Apology 16. Complaint 17. Acknowledgement 18. Greeting 19. Opining	Expressive Functions

The Test-Items in Section-II are designed to test the students' ability to identify and interpret these communicative functions in the discourse units whereas in Section-III, the Test-Items are designed to test the students' ability to create discourse units for various communicative functions in business situations.

STEP-4: Considerations in Preparing Relevant Test items: It was believed that the CCCT was most likely to provide a valid measure of the achievement of the syllabus objectives of WAC if the test items were designed to measure the performance defined by the specific learning outcomes.

While constructing test-items of the CCCT, care was taken to eliminate the 'extraneous factors' or 'some possible barriers in test items' that might prevent the students from responding. If the students achieved a particular learning outcome, they can be enabled to answer correctly those test items that measure the attainment of that learning outcome. Therefore, it was essential to eliminate the possible barriers in the test items. While preparing Pilot tests-2, 3 and 4, the extraneous factors or barriers like 'ambiguous statements,' 'excessive wordiness', 'difficult vocabulary', 'complex sentence structure', 'unclear instructions' were eliminated. The superfluous instructions which were found to be the unintended clues to the answers were eliminated from the Section-III of the CCCT.

The effectiveness of evaluation depends on a careful description of 'what to evaluate', and secondly on the technical qualities of the evaluation instruments used. Therefore, it was necessary to analyze the syllabus, define the syllabus objectives in concrete terms and to carefully describe 'what to evaluate.' It was decided to test the students' acquisition and achievement of 'every' learning point in the syllabus. This clearly meant that the test of communicative competence of the students was not going to be the representative test but the comprehensive test. Finally, at the end of the item analysis of Pilot Test-4 it was confirmed that CCCT comprehensively tests the students achievement of each and every syllabus objective. Thus, when content validity of CCCT was confirmed the test was finalized and was administered to the selected students at all the MBA teaching centers of the selected University.

Item-analysis procedures of the Final CCCT, which were carried out after assessment of the results of the Final Test, indicated that all the items had an appropriate level of difficulty and discrimination.

Like the results of the item-analysis of Pilot Test-4, the results of the item analysis of the Final Test confirmed the fact that CCCT provided valid, reliable, comprehensive and useful information concerning the students' achievement of the instructional goals.

References

Austine, J.L., 1962: *How to do Things with Words*, Oxford, U.K.: Clarendon Press.

Coulthard, M., 1977: *An Introduction to Discourse Analysis*, London: Longman.

De Joia, A. and A. Stenton, 1980: *Terms in Systemic Linguistics, A Guide to Haliday*, London: Batesford.

Ebel, R. and D.A. Frisbie, 1991: *Essentials of Educational Measurements*, New Delhi: Prentice-Hall of India Pvt. Ltd.

Gronlund, N.E., and R.L. Linn, 1990: *Measurement and Evaluation in Teaching*, New York: Macmillan Publishing Co.

Halliday, M.A.K., 1978: *Language As Social Semiotic*, London: Edward Arnold.

Lyons, J., 1977: *Semantics I & II*, London: Cambridge University Press.

Lyons, J., 1981: *Language, Meaning and Context*, London: Fontana.

Searle, J.R., 1981: *Speech Acts*, 2nd Edition, London: Cambridge University Press.

Searle, J.R., 1965: What Is A Speech Act? In M. Black (ed.) *Philosophy in America*, London: Allen & Unwin.

Wilkins, D.A., 1976: *National Syllabuses*, Oxford: Oxford University Press.

15

ANALYSIS OF THE COMMUNICATIVE COMPETENCE TEST RESULTS

"For everyone who asks receives, and he who seeks finds, and to him who knocks it will be opened."

— Mathew 7.8

The present chapter is divided into four parts. The first part presents the details of the eleven variables of the 40 representative students. Each representative subject is treated as a case. The second part deals with the statistical analysis and interpretation of the frequency and standard deviation of the scores obtained by the students in WAC-70 and CCCT. The third part deals with the statistical analysis and interpretation of the correlation coefficient of the students' scores in eight tests. This study has helped to obtain the criterion related validation evidence of CCCT and WAC-70. In the fourth part of this chapter, the representative students are classified in twelve groups according to their mothertongues, graduation degrees and sex; and their comparative performances in eight tests are statistically analyzed and interpreted.

THE REPRESENTATIVE SUBJECTS AND VARIABLES

The 40 representative students were selected from the eight MBA teaching centers of the selected University. Each representative subject is treated as a case. The details of their mothertongues, sex, names of the graduation degrees, and the marks obtained in the eight tests are in total the eleven variables of each case.

The variables of each case are specified below :

1. Mothertongue (MTNG).
2. Sex (Male/Female).
3. Name of the Graduation Degrees obtained (GDE).
4. Percentage of the Graduation Degree Marks (DMK).
5. Total marks obtained out of 850 in all the papers of MBA-I Examination, April, 1993 (MBA-I).
6. Written Analysis and Communication, Paper VIth, MBA-I Examination, April, 1993 + Internal Credit; marks obtained out of 100 (WAC%).
7. Written Analysis and Communication, Paper VIth, MBA-I Examination, April, 1993; marks obtained out of 70 (WAC-70).
8. Comprehensive Communicative Competence Test (CCCT% or CCCT).
9. Comprehensive Communicative Competence Test, Section - I (CCCT-I).
10. Comprehensive Communicative Competence Test, Section-II (CCCT-II).
11. Comprehensive Communicative Competence Test, Section-III (CCCT-III).

The above variables of each case are given below :

	Variables	Case No.1	Case No.2	Case No.3	Case No.4
1	Mothertongue	Marathi & Other	Kannada	Mala-yalam	Kannada
2	Sex	Male	Male	Male	Male
3	Graduation Degree	B.E.	B.A.	B.Sc.	B.Sc.
4	Graduation Degree Scores	71.5	55	61.5	79
5	MBA-1 Scores	497	492	530	563
6	WAC % Scores	50	61	57	55
7	WAC 70 Scores	32	40	38	37
8	CCCT % Scores	53	47	61	60.5
9	CCCT-I Scores	54	55	61	60
10	CCCT-II Scores	10	09	13	15
11	CCCT-III Scores -	42	30	48	46

Variables		Case No.5	Case No.6	Case No.7	Case No.8
1	Mothertongue	Mala yalam	Mala-yalam	Mala-yalam	Marathi & Other
2	Sex	Male	Male	Male	Male
3	Graduation Degree	B.Sc.	B.Sc.	B.Com. & Other	B.Com. & Other
4	Graduation Degree Scores	64	59	68	58
5	MBA-1 Scores	536	578	459	472
6	WAC % Scores	58	65	62	55
7	WAC 70 Scores	38	40	36	35
8	CCCT % Scores	58.5	77	66.5	39.5
9	CCCT-I Scores	57	71	69	37
10	CCCT-II Scores	16	17	13	09
11	CCCT-III Scores	44	66	51	33

Variables		Case No.9	Case No.10	Case No.11	Case No.12
1	Mothertongue	Mala-yalam	Hindi	Marathi & Other	Marathi & Other
2	Sex	Male	Female	Female	Male
3	Graduation Degree	B.Sc.	B.Com. & Other	B.Sc.	B.Sc.
4	Graduation Degree Scores	59	50	65	62
5	MBA-1 Scores	552	503	527	550
6	WAC % Scores	58	62	53	61
7	WAC 70 Scores	38	40	29	37
8	CCCT % Scores	64	69.5	51	38
9	CCCT-I Scores	64	65	57	43
10	CCCT-II Scores	12	15	10	03
11	CCCT-III Scores	52	59	35	30

Variables		Case No.13	Case No.14	Case No.15	Case No.16
1	Mothertongue	Telugu	Telugu	Marathi & Other	Kannada
2	Sex	Male	Male	Female	Male
3	Graduation Degree	B.Com.	B.Sc.	B.Sc.	B.Sc.
4	Graduation Degree Scores	59.9	68	70	45

5	MBA-1 Scores	553	605	560	521
6	WAC % Scores	59	62	60	61
7	WAC 70 Scores	37	39	37	34
8	CCCT % Scores	37	48.5	53.5	33
9	CCCT-I Scores	38	49	41	42
10	CCCT-II Scores	07	15	16	10
11	CCCT-III Scores	29	33	50	14

Variables		Case No.17	Case No.18	Case No.19	Case No.20
1	Mothertongue	Marathi & Other	Telugu	Marathi & Other	Hindi
2	Sex	Male	Male	Male	Male
3	Graduation Degree	B.E.	B.Com. & Other	B.Sc.	B.Sc.
4	Graduation Degree Scores	64.5	49	59	47
5	MBA-1 Scores	576	525	555	589
6	WAC % Scores	59	60	62	66
7	WAC 70 Scores	37	33	36	38
8	CCCT % Scores	62	54	32.5	66
9	CCCT-I Scores	64	45	37	62
10	CCCT-II Scores	17	14	08	18
11	CCCT-III Scores	43	49	20	52

Variables		Case No.21	Case No.22	Case No.23	Case No.24
1	Mothertongue	Telugu	Telugu	Telugu	Malayalam
2	Sex	Female	Male	Male	Male
3	Graduation Degree	B.Sc.	B.Com. & Other	B.A.	B.Com. & Other
4	Graduation Degree Scores	69	57	60	63
5	MBA-1 Scores	579	535	556	585
6	WAC % Scores	59	61	59	63
7	WAC 70 Scores	36	38	37	40
8	CCCT % Scores	44.5	39	45	47.5
9	CCCT-I Scores	43	37	36	39
10	CCCT-II Scores	08	07	11	06
11	CCCT-III Scores	38	34	43	50

	Variables	Case No.25	Case No.26	Case No.27	Case No.28
1	Mothertongue	Marathi & Other	Punjabi	Marathi & Other	Telugu
2	Sex	Male	Male	Male	Male
3	Graduation Degree	B.Com. & Other	B.Com. & Other	B.Sc.	B.Com. & Other
4	Graduation Degree Scores	52	60.1	69	59.9
5	MBA-1 Scores	491	598	595	491
6	WAC % Scores	60	61	62	57
7	WAC 70 Scores	37	38	37	35
8	CCCT % Scores	25.5	70	72	62
9	CCCT-I Scores	33	65	68	50
10	CCCT-II Scores	03	15	15	15
11	CCCT-III Scores	15	60	61	59

	Variables	Case No.29	Case No.30	Case No.31	Case No.32
1	Mothertongue	Marathi & Other	Kannada	Telugu	Telugu
2	Sex	Male	Male	Male	Male
3	Graduation Degree	B.Com. & Other	B.Com. & Other	B.Com. & Other	B.Com. & Other
4	Graduation Degree Scores	72	62	50	71.5
5	MBA1 Scores	574	569	535	591
6	WAC % Scores	62	52	66	65
7	WAC 70 Scores	36	29	39	37
8	CCCT % Scores	66.5	47	29	55
9	CCCT-I Scores	58	51	36	54
10	CCCT-II Scores	15	15	08	13
11	CCCT-III Scores	60	28	14	43

	Variables	Case No.33	Case No.34	Case No.35	Case No.36
1	Mothertongue	Telugu	Malayalam	Telugu	Marathi & Other
2	Sex	Male	Male	Male	Male
3	Graduation Degree	B.Sc.	B.Com. & Other	B.Com. & Other	B.Sc.
4	Graduation Degree Scores	59	45	72	67
5	MBA-1 Scores	524	496	512	554

6	WAC % Scores	62	61	60	60
7	WAC 70 Scores	36	36	35	34
8	CCCT % Scores	46.5	69	28	32.5
9	CCCT-I Scores	55	71	38	25
10	CCCT-II Scores	15	16	09	09
11	CCCT-III Scores	23	51	09	31

Variables		Case No.37	Case No.38	Case No.39	Case No.40
1	Mothertongue	Punjabi	Telugu	Marathi & Other	Marathi & Other
2	Sex	Male	Male	Male	Male
3	Graduation Degree	B.Com. & Other	B.Com. & Other	B.Com. & Other	B.Sc.
4	Graduation Degree Scores	41	57	54	55
5	MBA-1 Scores	484	484	503	531
6	WAC % Scores	67	64	62	64
7	WAC 70 Scores	41	37	37	40
8	CCCT % Scores	19	34.5	21	23
9	CCCT-I Scores	27	29	23	19
10	CCCT-II Scores	04	09	05	03
11	CCCT-III Scores	07	31	14	24

STATISTICAL ANALYSIS OF THE FREQUENCY AND STANDARD DEVIATION OF THE SCORES OBTAINED IN WAC-70 AND CCCT

The Frequency of The Scores of The Population in WAC, Paper-VIth, MBA-I Examination, April, 1993

TABLE 15.1 : Frequency of the Scores of the Population in WAC, Paper-VIth, MBA-I Examination, April, 1993

Range of the Scores Upper Bound		Lower Bound	Frequency
00	to	21	0
22	to	28	10
29	to	35	142
36	to	42	390
43	to	49	5
50	to	70	0

The Table 15.1 and the Fig. 15.1 indicate the scatteredness of scores of the population in WAC, MBA-I Examination, April 1993. The maximum marks for this paper were out of 70. The total number of students who registered for the MBA-I Exam 564. Six students remained absent. The total number of students who appeared for the exam was 558. The results of 11 students were kept reserved for the copying cases. Thus, there were a total of 547 students who appeared for this examination and whose results were declared. Three students failed in the paper. The total number of successful students was 545. Thus the result was 99.45 per cent. Out of 547 students 5 students scored in the range of 43 to 49 marks; 390 students scored in the range of 36 to 42 marks; 142 students scored in the range of 29 to 35 marks; and 10 students scored in the range 22 to 28 marks. There is very high concentration of scores in the range of 36 to 42 marks. Out of total population, 71.167 per cent population scored between 36 to 42 marks. This concentration of scores in the limited range in itself clearly indicates uneven distribution of scores. 25.912 per cent students scored in the ranges of 29 to 35 marks. Only 1.8 per cent students scored in the range of 22 to 28 marks, whereas only 0.91 per cent students scored in the range of 43 to 49 marks. No one of the population has scored in the range of 0 to 21 and 50 to 70 marks.

Conclusions

These figures indicate as shown in the Fig. 15.1, that the degree of the scatteredness of scores is very low, the distribution of scores is uneven, and the level of concentration of scores in the ranges of 29 to 35 and 36 to 42 marks is very high.

The study of the scores of the population in WAC-70 reveals that the highest level of the concentration of scores is in the range of 36 to 42 marks followed by the second highest level of concentration of scores in the range of 29 to 35 per cent marks. The study of the representative students' scores in WAC-70 reveal exactly the same trend.

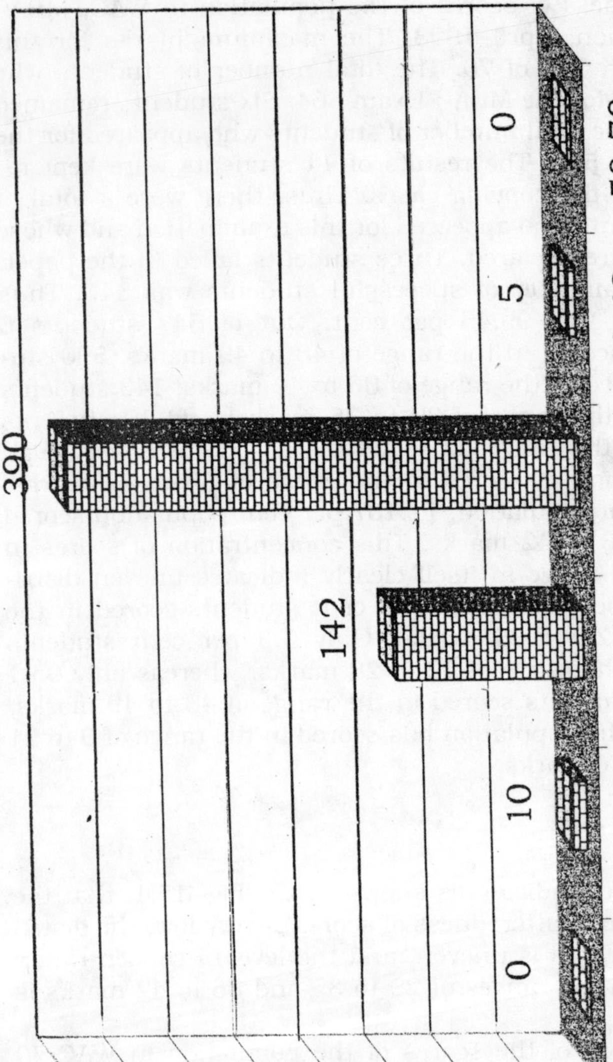

Fig. 15.1: The frequency of the scores of the population in WAC, MBA-I Exam. April 1993

The highest level of the concentration of scores obtained by the representative students is in the range of 36 to 42 marks followed by the second highest level of the concentration of scores in the range of 29 to 35 marks. This indicates that the sample truly represent the population.

Secondly, the objective of achievement test is to discriminate the achievement levels of the students. If the degree of the scatteredness of scores obtained by the students is very low, and the distribution of scores is uneven, the test is ineffective in differentiating the achievement levels of the students. WAC-70 does not discriminate or differentiate the achievement levels of the students effectively and thus it does not serve the objective of achievement test.

Thirdly, it has been found that WAC-70 does not correlate with DMK, MBA-I test, CCCT%, CCCT-I, CCCT-II and CCCT-III. This is mainly because the scores obtained by the students in WAC-70 are concentrated in a limited range. The 85 per cent of the representative students scored in the range of 36 to 42 marks out of the maximum 70 marks. It seems impossible that such a large number of students would score in such a limited range.

Therefore, it can be concluded that the assessment of WAC-70 is not reliable. The examiner's tendency to boost the University results is evident. The intention seems to help the students to get through. The evidence of this tendency is also indicated by the 99.45 per cent University result of WAC-70. Even if we take WAC per cent we find the same tendency of boosting the University results.

Comparison of the Frequency of Marks of the Sample in WAC-70 And CCCT:

The Table 15.2 and the Fig. 15.2 indicate the scatteredness of scores of the representative students in WAC-70 and CCCT (percentagewise).

The maximum marks for the Paper VIth, Written Analysis and Communication, were out of 70. The performance of the representative students in Written Analysis & Communication is compared with their performance in Comprehensive Communicative Competence Test. As the maximum marks for Written Analysis and Communication, Pa-

TABLE 15.2 : Frequency of The Scores of the Representative Subjects in WAC-70 and CCCT.

Range of the Scores			Frequency in WAC	Frequency in CCCT
Upper Bound		Lower Bound		
00	to	10	0	0
11	to	20	0	1
21	to	30	0	5
31	to	40	0	8
41	to	50	6	7
51	to	60	34	6
61	to	70	0	10
71	to	80	0	3
81	to	90	0	0
91	to	100	0	0

per VIth MBA-I Exam. April, 1993 (WAC-70) were out of 70 and the maximum marks for Comprehensive Communicative Competence Test (CCCT) were out of 200, it was essential to convert both of these into percentage. In WAC, paper VIth, MBA-I Exam. April, 1993, out of 40 selected students 34 students scored in the range of 50 to 60 per cent marks and the remaining 6 students scored in the range of 40 to 50 per cent marks. No one of the students scored in the ranges of 00 to 40 per cent, and 60 to 100 per cent marks. Percentagewise, there is very high concentration of scores in the range of 50 to 60 per cent marks. Out of 40 students 85 per cent scored between 36 to 43 (50 to 60 per cent) marks and the remaining 15 per cent students scored in the range of 29 to 35 (40 to 50 per cent) marks. No one of the population has scored in the range of 00 to 40 and 60 to 100 per cent marks. These figures indicate, as shown in the Fig. 15.2 that the degree of scatteredness of scores is very low, the distribution of scores is uneven, and, the level of concentration of scores in the limited ranges of marks, is very high.

The objective of the achievement test is to discriminate the achievement levels of the students. WAC-70 does not discriminate or differentiate the achievement levels of the

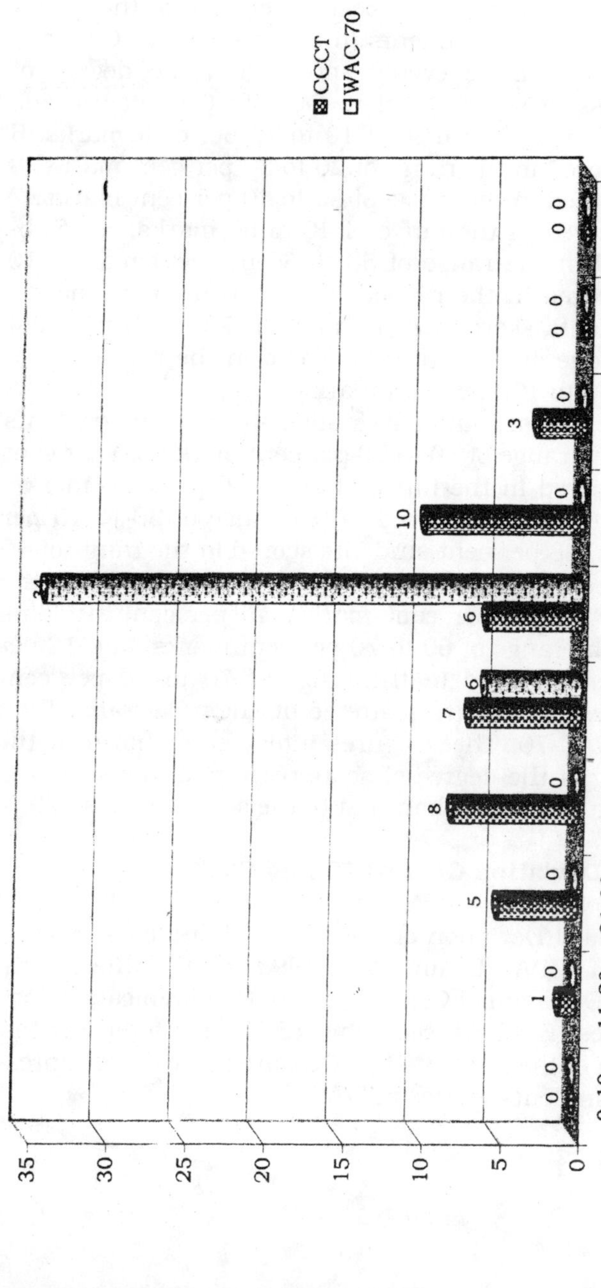

Fig. 15.2: The frequency of the scores of the Representative Subjects in WAC, MBA-I Exam. 1993 and in CCCT

students effectively. Therefore, WAC-70 is not a valid and reliable measure of the students' achievements.

On the other hand, it has been observed that the scores of the representative students in Comprehensive Communicative Test is more evenly spread and the degree of scatteredness of scores is high. Out of 40 students, one subject scored in the range of 10 to 20 per cent marks, 5 students scored in the range of 20 to 30 per cent marks, 8 students scored in the range of 30 to 40 per cent marks, 7 students scored in the range of 40 to 50 marks. Six Subjects scored in the range of 50 to 60 per cent marks, 10 students scored in the range of 60 to 70 per cent marks, and 3 students scored in the range of 70 to 80 per cent marks. No one of the students scored in the ranges of 00 to 10 and 80 to 100 per cent marks.

Percentagewise, out of 40 students 4 per cent students scored in the range of 10 to 20 per cent marks, 20 per cent students scored in the range of 20 to 30 per cent marks, 32 per cent students scored in the range of 30 to 40 per cent marks, 28 per cent students scored in the range of 40 to 50 per cent marks, 24 per cent students scored in the range of 50 to 60 per cent marks, 40 per cent students scored in the range of 60 to 70 per cent marks, and 12 per cent students scored in the range of 70 to 80 per cent marks. These scores are scattered on the wider range than those of WAC-70. These figures indicate as shown in the Fig. 15.2 that the degree of scatteredness of the scores in CCCT is much higher than that of the scores in WAC-70.

Standard Deviation Of WAC-70 And CCCT

The Standard Deviation of the scores of students in WAC, Paper-VIth, MBA-I Exam. April, 1993 is 2.65, whereas the Standard Deviation of Comprehensive Communicative Competence Test is 15.83 (see Table 15.3). This indicates that the scores of the students in CCCT are move evenly spread than the students' scores in WAC-70.

TABLE 15.3 : Table of Descriptive Statistics of the Scores Obtained in Eight Tests (Standard Deviation, Mean, Range, etc.)

The Tests	Mean	Standard Deviation	Range	Minimum	Maximum	Standard Error
1. Graduation Degree Marks (DMK)	60.24	08.63	38	41	79	1.36
2. MBA-I (All Papers)	538.25	38.87	146	459	605	6.14
3. WAC%	60.32	03.71	17	50	67	0.58
4. WAC-70	36.65	02.65	12	29	41	0.41
5. CCCT%	48.71	15.83	58	19	77	2.50
6. CCCT-I	48.20	14.35	52	19	71	2.27
7. CCCT-II	11.20	04.69	15	03	18	0.69
8. CCCT-III	38.02	15.91	59	07	66	2.51

'*Standard Deviation*' (SD) is a measure of the spread of scores in a group. It is used to indicate a pupils' relative position in a group by showing how far the raw scores are above or below the mean. The 'Mean' is the arithmetic of the scores average. The standard deviation of WAC-70 is much lower than that of the CCCT. This proves that the scores of the students in CCCT are more scattered than those of the WAC-70, and secondly, they are more evenly spread than those of the WAC-70. If the degree of the scatteredness of scores obtained by the students is high and the distribution of scores is even, the test is effective in discriminating the achievement levels of the students.

Conclusion

The objective of the achievement test is to discriminate the achievement levels of the students. It has been found that WAC-70 does not discriminate the achievement levels of the students. The scores of the students in WAC-70 are neither well-scattered nor evenly spread. The low standard deviation of these scores proves that WAC-70 does not discriminate the achievement levels of the students. The scores obtained by the students in WAC-70 are concentrated in narrow range. It seems impossible that such a large number of students would score in such a short range.

Therefore, it can be concluded that the assessment of WAC-70 is not reliable. The examiner's tendency to boost the University results is evident. The intention seems to be to help the students to get through. The evidence of this tendency is also indicated by the 99.45 per cent. University result of the population and 100 per cent University result of the representative students in WAC-70.

On the other hand, the scores obtained by the students in CCCT per cent are well-spread and evenly scattered, and thereby the test effectively serves the objective of the achievement test. The CCCT per cent effectively differentiates the achievement levels of the students' Communicative Competence. The standard deviation of CCCT per cent scores shown in the standard normal curve (see Fig. 15.3) also proves that the scores of CCCT% are evenly spread and normally distributed. Therefore, the scores obtained by the students in CCCT% are valid, realistic and reliable.

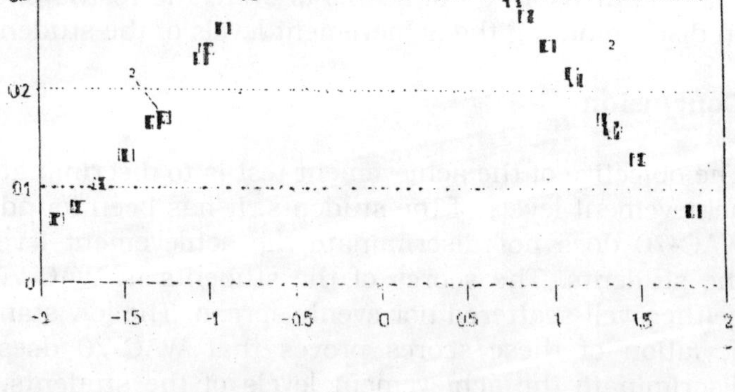

Fig 15.3 : The Normal Curve of the Scores of the Subjects in CCCT Indicating Standard Deviation

Comparison of the Passing Percentage of the Results Of CCCT and WAC-70

The minimum marks required for passing in CCCT are 40 per cent. Out of 40 representative students to whom the CCCT was administered 26 students passed. Thus the result of CCCT was 65 per cent. Fourteen students secured marks below 40 per cent in CCCT. Thus, 35 per cent of the representative students failed to attain the standards they are expected to attain. Yet in WAC-70, all the representative students passed. As the validity and reliability of CCCT was established, it can be safely concluded that there was 35 per cent boosting in the results of the WAC-70.

THE CRITERION-RELATED VALIDATION EVIDENCE OF CCCT% AND WAC-70: A STUDY OF THE CORRELATION COEFFICIENTS OF THE EIGHT TESTS

What is Correlation Coefficient?

In this part of the study, the objective is to find out and interpret the correlation coefficients of the scores of the students in eight tests. Correlation coefficient is a statistical method which is employed to determine if there exists any relationship between two variables and to express this relationship numerically. 'When in a given group of individuals, measures of two characteristics for each individual are obtained, it may frequently be observed that the two measures of each individual have a tendency to occupy almost the same relative position in their respective distributions' (Gupta: 1992, 443). For example, if the measures of heights and weights of the pupils of a class are secured, it will be found that, if the height of a pupil is considerably above the average height, his weight will, more often than not, also be considerably above the average weight. On the other hand, if the height of a pupil is below the average, his weight will also tend to be correspondingly below the average. When this kind of a phenomenon is observed, it is said that the two characteristics are mutually related or correlated. Thus, we can conclude that the two variables will be said to be correlated if an increase in one variable is on an average accompanied by an increase (or decrease) of the other.

Positive Correlation : When the higher values of the one variable are associated with higher values of the other values, or when lower values of the one are accompanied by the lower values of the other, they are said to have positive correlation. In other words, when the movements of the two variables are in the same direction, there is a positive correlation between them. For examples, If a company declares higher dividend, the market prices of its shares will also be relatively higher.

Negative Correlation : When the higher values of the one variable are associated with the lower values of the other, they have negative correlation. In other words, when the movements of the two variables are in opposite directions, there is negative correlation between them. For example, if the prices increase, the demand decreases.

The purpose of finding out correlation coefficients of the scores obtained by the students in eight tests is to know if the scores of one test can be used to predict future performance and to estimate current performance on some valued measure other than the test itself. 'The correlation between test and criterion scores has been regarded by many as the best kind of evidence to support valid achievement test use' (Ebel & Frisbie, 1991: 106). The evidence regarding the degree of relationship between the scores of different tests can be obtained from correlation coefficients. 'The degree of relationship can be described more precisely by statistically correlating the two sets of scores' (Gronlund & Linn, 1990: 58).

The following correlation coefficients indicate the extreme degree of relationship possible between the variables:

1.00 = perfect positive relationship
0.00 = no relationship
-1.00 = perfect negative relationship

The correlation coefficient is used to obtain evidence of criterion related predictive validity and criterion lated concurrent validity.

Criterion-Related Predictive and Concurrent Validation

It was decided to find out and interpret the correlation coefficients of the scores of the students in eight tests. Given below is the list of the tests:

(i) Graduation Degree Exam. (GDE)
(ii) MBA-I Exam. All Papers (Paper 1 to 11), April, 1993 (MBA-I).
(iii) Written Analysis & Communication, Paper-VIth, MBA-I Exam. April, 1993 + Internal credit, i.e. 70+30=100 marks (WAC%).
(iv) Written Analysis & Communication Paper VIth, MBA-I Exam. April, 1993, max. 70 marks (WAC-70).
(v) Comprehensive Communicative Competence Test (CCCT%).
(vi) Comprehensive Communicative Competence Test, Section-I (CCCT-I).
(vii) Comprehensive Communicative Competence Test, Section-II, (CCCT-II).
(vii) Comprehensive Communicative Competence Test, Section-III (CCCT-III).

In this study, the correlation between the two sets of scores: GDE Vs WAC-70 and GDE Vs CCCT% calls for Predictive Validation Study, whereas the correlation between the following sets of scores calls for a Concurrent Validation Study:

CCCT% Vs. CCCT-I; CCCT% Vs. CCCT-II;
CCCT% Vs. CCCT-III; CCCT-I Vs. CCCT-II;
CCCT-I Vs. CCCT-III; CCCT-II Vs. CCCT-III;
MBA-I (All papers) Vs. CCCT%; MBA-I (All papers) Vs. WAC-70;
MBA-I (All papers) Vs. CCCT-I; MBA-I (All papers) Vs. CCCT-II;
MBA-I (All papers) Vs. CCCT-III; CCCT% Vs. WAC-70.

In finding out the correlation coefficients between the above given sets, we are concerned about the Criterion

Related Validity. 'Criterion-related validation may be defined as the process of determining the extent to which test performance is related to some other valued measure of performance' (Gronlund & Linn, 1990: 56).

There are two types of criterion-related validities:

1. The Criterion - Related Predictive Validity.
2. The Criterion - Related Concurrent Validity.

Criterion - Related Predictive Validity

The predictive validation of any test depends on the correlation between the students' performance in the present test and their performance in some other test in the past. To know the criterion-related predictive validity means to know if the students' performance in one test (criterion) can be used to predict their future performance in some other test. For example, the students' scores in the S.S.C. examination can be used to predict their scores in the H.S.C. examination. Similarly, in the present study, the performance of the students in their Graduation Degree Examination (GDE) is accepted as a criterion or standard to predict their performance in WAC-70 and CCCT%. If the students' performance in WAC-70 and CCCT% are predictable on the criterion of their performance in GDE both WAC-70 and CCCT can have the criterion-related predictive validity. However, it has been found that WAC-70 does not have the criterion-related predictive validity, but on the other hand, CCCT% has proved its criterion related predictive validity.

Criterion - Related Concurrent Validity

Concurrent validation depends on the correlation between the students' performance in two or more concurrent tests. To know the criterion — related concurrent validity means to know if the students' performance in one test depends on their performance in some other concurrent test. For example, the students' scores in the Dictation Test of spelling Achievement can be accepted as a criterion on which their scores in an another test like True-false Spelling Test may depend. If the students' performance in True-false Spelling Test depends on their performance in Dictation Test of Spelling Achievement, the True-false Spelling Test has the Criterion — related concurrent validity. Similarly, in the present study, it has been found that WAC-70 does not have the criterion - related concurrent validity because students' performance in WAC-70 does not correlate with other concurrent tests like MBA-I (All Papers). On the other hand, CCCT% has criterion related concurrent validity because students' performance in CCCT% correlates with their performance in MBA-I (All papers).

Thus, WAC-70 hardly seems to have both the predictive validity and the concurrent validity. This proves that the scores of WAC-70 are unrealistic. In WAC-70, 85 per cent students scored in the range of 36 to 42 marks and the remaining 15 per cent students scored in the range of 29 to 35 marks. It seems impossible that the students' scores would concentrate in such a limited range. Practically, it is impossible that such a large number of students may scores in the same range of marks. It is because of this reason the scores of WAC-70 do not correlate with GDE, MBA-I (All papers), CCCT%, CCCT-I, CCCT-II and CCCT-III. The assessment of WAC-70 is not reliable. The examiners' tendency to boost the University results is evident. The intention seems to be to help the students to get through.

The high correlation between WAC-70 and WAC% proves that in WAC% too, there is the same of boosting of the University results.

On the other hand, CCCT% has both the predictive as well as concurrent validities. This proves that the scores obtained by the students in CCCT% are realistic and reliable. The students' scores in CCCT% are well-spread and widely scattered. This allows CCCT% to discriminate the achievement levels of the students. CCCT% positively correlates with GDE, MBA-I (All papers), CCCT-I, CCCT-II and CCCT-III because its scores are valid, realistic and its assessment is reliable.

TABLE 15.4 : Correlation Coefficients of The Eight Tests
(Each cell shows the correlation, sample size,and one- tailed significance.)

	GDE	MBA-1	WAC%	WAC-70	CT%	CT-I	CT-II	CT-III
GDE	1.0000	0.3857	-0.4132	-0.2451	0.2656	0.2048	0.2229	0.2824
	40	40	40	40	40	40	40	40
	0.0000	0.0070	0.0040	0.0637	0.0488	0.1025	0.0834	0.0387
MBA-1	0.3857	1.0000	0.1302	0.1102	0.3223	0.2268	0.3378	0.3438
	40	40	40	40	40	40	40	40
	0.0070	0.0000	0.2116	0.2493	0.0213	0.0796	0.0165	0.0149
WAC%	-0.4132	0.1302	1.0000	0.7001	-0.1400	-0.1646	-0.1210	-0.0968
	40	40	40	40	40	40	40	40
	0.0040	0.2116	0.0000	0.0000	0.1945	0.1551	0.2286	0.2762
WAC-70	-0.2451	0.1102	0.7001	1.0000	0.0107	-0.0351	-0.1198	0.0857
	40	40	40	40	40	40	40	40
	0.0637	0.2493	0.0000	0.0000	0.4740	0.4149	0.2308	0.2994
CT%	0.2656	0.3223	-0.1400	0.0107	1.0000	0.9240	0.8385	0.9257
	40	40	40	40	40	40	40	40
	0.0488	0.213	0.1945	0.4740	0.0000	0.0000	0.0000	0.0000
CT-I	0.2048	0.2268	-0.1646	-0.0351	0.9240	1.0000	0.7780	0.7226
	40	40	40	40	40	40	40	40
	0.1025	0.0796	0.1551	0.4149	0.0000	0.0000	0.0000	0.0000
CT-II	0.2229	0.3378	-0.1210	-0.1198	0.8385	0.7780	1.0000	0.6917
	40	40	40	40	40	40	40	40
	0.0834	0.0165	0.2286	0.2308	0.0000	0.0000	0.0000	0.0000
CT-III	0.2824	0.3438	-0.0968	0.0857	0.9257	0.7226	0.6917	1.0000
	40	40	40	40	40	40	40	40
	0.0387	0.0149	0.2762	0.2994	0.0000	0.0000	0.0000	0.0000

The findings and interpretations of the correlation coefficients of the eight tests are given below:

Correlation Coefficients of the Eight Tests

1. Correlation: Graduation Degree Test Vs. The Other Tests

The correlation between the marks obtained by the students in the graduation degree and the marks obtained in other tests

Positive Correlation: There is positive correlation between the graduation degree marks and the marks obtained in —

1. MBA-I (All papers); Correlation: 0.3857.
2. Comprehensive Communicative Competence Test; Correlation: 0.2656.
3. Section-I of the Comprehensive Communicative Competence Test; Correlation: 0.2048.
4. Section-II of the Comprehensive Communicative Competence Test; Correlation : 0.2824
5. Section-III of the Comprehensive Communicative Competence Test; Correlation: 0.2824.

Negative Correlation: There is negative correlation between the graduation degree marks and the marks obtained in —

1. WAC%, Correlation: -0.4132
2. WAC-70, Correlation: -0.2451

Conclusions

WAC-70 does not correlate with GDE, therefore WAC-70 does not have the predictive validity. This proves that the scores obtained by the students in WAC-70 are unrealistic. This is mainly because the scores obtained by the students in WAC-70 are concentrated in a limited range. 85 per cent of the representative students scored in the range of 36 to 42 marks out of the maximum 70 marks. It seems impossible that such a large number of students would score in such a short range.

Therefore, it can concluded that the assessment of WAC-

70 is not reliable. The examiner's motivation to boost the University results is evident. The intention seems to be to help the students to get through. The evidence of this tendency is also indicated by the 100 per cent University result of WAC-70.

On the other hand, the CCCT per cent correlates with the GDE. This proves that CCCT per cent has predictive validity and its scores are realistic and reliable.

2. Correlation: MBA-I (All papers) Test Vs. The Other Tests

Correlation between the marks obtained in all students of MBA-I Exam. April, 1993 (Paper 1 to 11) and the marks obtained in the other tests.

Positive Correlation: There is positive correlation between the marks obtained in all students of MBA-I Exam. April, 1993 (Paper 1 to 11) and the marks obtained in —

1. GDE; Correlation: 0.3857.
2. CCCT%; Correlation: 0.3223.
3. CCCT-I; Correlation: 0.2268.
4. CCCT-II; Correlation: 0.3378.
5. CCCT-III; Correlation: 0.3438.

Low Correlation: In comparison with the positive correlations between and among the five variables i.e. GDE marks, MBA-I (All papers) marks, CCCT% marks, CCCT-I marks, CCCT-II marks, CCCT-III marks, there is lower degree correlation between the marks obtained in MBA-I (All papers) and the marks obtained in -

1. WAC%; Correlation: 0.1302. This is very low and negligible correlation.
2. WAC-70; Correlation: 0.1102. This is very low and negligible correlation.

Conclusion

WAC-70 does not correlate with MBA-I (All papers) test. Therefore, WAC-70 does not have the concurrent validity. This proves that the scores obtained by the students in WAC-70 are unrealistic. (This is mainly because the scores obtained by the students in WAC-70 are concentrated in a limited range. 85 per cent of the representative students scored in the range of 36 to 42 marks out of the maximum 70 marks. It seems impossible that such a large number of students would score in such a short range.

Therefore, it can be concluded that the assessment of WAC is not reliable and realistic. The examiner's motivation to boost the University results is evident. The intention seems to be to help the students to get through. The evidence of this tendency is also indicated by the 100 per cent University result of WAC-70.

On the other hand, the CCCT% correlates with MBA-I (All papers) test. This proves that CCCT% has concurrent validity and its scores are reliable and realistic

3. Correlation: WAC% Vs. The Other Tests

Correlation between the marks obtained by the students in WAC% and the marks obtained in other tests.

Positive Correlation: There is positive correlation between the marks obtained in WAC% and the marks obtained in -

1. WAC-70; Correlation:- 0.7001

Low Correlation: In comparison with the positive correlations between and among the six variables i.e. GDE marks, MBA-I (All papers) marks, CCCT% marks, CCCT-I marks, CCCT-II marks, CCCT-III marks, there is low degree positive correlation between the marks obtained in WAC% and the marks obtained in —

1. MBA-I (All papers); Correlation: 0.1302. This is very low and negligible correlation.

Negative Correlation: There is negative correlation between the marks obtained in WAC% and the marks obtained in —

1. GDE; Correlation: -0.4132
2. CCCT%; Correlation: -0.1400.
3. CCCT-I; Correlation: -0.1646.
4. CCCT-II; Correlation : -0.1210.
5. CCCT-III; Correlation : -0.0968.

Conclusion

The high positive correlation between WAC% and WAC-70 prove that both of these tests have the same tendencies. WAC% does not correlate with MBA-I (All papers) test effectively. Therefore, WAC% does not have the concurrent validity. This proves that the scores obtained by the students in WAC% are unrealistic.

Therefore, it can be concluded that the assessment of WAC% is not reliable and realistic. The examiner's motivation to boost the University results is evident. The intention seems to be to help the students to get through. The evidence of this tendency is also indicated by the 100 per cent University result of WAC%.

On the other hand, the CCCT% correlates with MBA-I (All papers) test. This proves that CCCT% has concurrent validity and its scores are realistic and reliable.

4. Correlation: WAC-70 Vs. The Other Tests

Correlation between the marks obtained by the students in Written Analysis & Communication, Paper IVth MBA-I Exam. April, 1993, and the marks obtained in the other tests.

Positive Correlation: There is positive correlation between the marks obtained in WAC-70 and the marks obtained in -

1. WAC%; Correlation:- 0.7001

Low Correlation: In comparison with the positive correlations between and among the variables - GDE marks, CCCT-I marks, CCCT-II marks, CCCT-III marks, there is lower degree positive correlation between the marks obtained in WAC-70 and the marks obtained in —

1. MBA-I (All Papers); Correlation: 0.1102. This is very low and negligible correlation.
2. CCCT%; Correlation- 0.0107. This is very low and negligible correlation.
3. CCCT-III; Correlation:- 0.0857. This is very low and negligible correlation.

Negative Correlation: There is negative correlation between the marks obtained in Written Analysis and Communication, Paper VIth MBA-I Exam. April, 1993 and the marks obtained in —

1. GDE; Correlation: -0.2451.
2. CCCT-I; Correlation: -0.0351.
3. CCCT-II; Correlation: -0.1198.

Conclusion

WAC-70 does not correlate with GDE, MBA-I (All Papers) test, CCCT%, CCCT-I, CCCT-II and CCCT-III. Therefore, WAC-70 has neither predictive validity nor concurrent validity. This proves that the scores obtained by the students in WAC-70 are unrealistic. (This is mainly because the scores obtained by the students in WAC-70 are concentrated in a limited range. 85 per cent of the representative students scored in the range of 36 to 42 marks out of the maximum 70 marks. It seems impossible that such a large number of students would score in such a short range).

Therefore, as mentioned earlier, it can be concluded that the assessment of WAC-70 is not reliable and realistic. The examiners intention to boost the University results is evident. The intention seems to be to help the students to get through. The evidence of this tendency is also obtained by 100% University result of WAC-70.

5. Correlation: CCCT% Vs. The Other Tests

Correlation between the marks obtained by the students in CCCT% and the marks obtained in other tests.

Positive Correlation: There is positive correlation between the marks obtained in CCCT% and the marks obtained in —

1. GDE; Correlation: 0.2656.
2. MBA-I (All Papers); Correlation:- 0.3223.
3. CCCT-I; Correlation: 9240.
4. CCCT-II; Correlation: 0.8385.
5. CCCT-III; Correlation: 0.9257.

Low Correlation: In comparison with the positive correlations between and among the six variables i.e. GDE marks, MBA-I (All Papers) marks, CCCT% marks, CCCT-I marks, CCCT-II marks, CCCT-III marks, there is lower degree correlation between the marks obtained in CCCT% and the marks obtained in -

1. WAC-70; Correlation:- 0.0107. This is extremely low and negligible correlation.

Negative Correlation: There is negative correlation between the marks obtained in CCCT% and the marks obtained in —

1. WAC%; Correlation: -0.1400.

Conclusion

The CCCT% correlates with GDE, MBA-I (All Papers) test, CCCT-I, CCCT-II and CCCT-III. Therefore, CCCT% has both the predictive as well as the concurrent validity. This proves that the scores obtained by the students in CCCT% are realistic and reliable. This is mainly because the scores obtained by the students are well-spread and evenly distributed. The well-spread and evenly distributed scores of CCCT% effectively show the difference in the achievement levels of the students. The objective of every achievement test is to show difference or to discriminate the achievement levels of the pupils. As the scores of CCCT% discriminate the achievement levels of the students in an effective manner, the objective of the achievements test is rightly served. Thus, the scores obtained by the students in CCCT% are valid, realistic and reliable

6. Correlation: CCCT-I Vs. The Other Tests

Correlation between the marks obtained by the students in CCCT-I and the marks obtained in other tests.

Positive Correlation: There is positive correlation between the marks obtained in CCCT-I and the marks obtained in —

1. GDE; Correlation: 0.2048.
2. MBA-I (All Papers); Correlation: 0.2268.
3. CCCT%; Correlation: 0.9240.

4. CCCT-II; Correlation: 0.7780.
5. CCCT-III; Correlation: 0.7226.

Negative Correlation: There is negative correlation between the marks obtained in CCCT-I and the marks obtained in —

1. WAC%; Correlation: -0.1646.
2. WAC-70; Correlation: -0.0351.

Conclusion

The CCCT-I correlates with GDE, MBA-I (All Papers) test, CCCT%, CCCT-II and CCCT-III. Therefore, CCCT-I has both predictive validity as well as the concurrent validity. This is mainly because the scores obtained by the students in CCCT-I discriminate the achievements levels of the students and thereby serve the objective of the achievement test in an effective manner. Thus the scores obtained by the students in CCCT-I are valid, realistic and reliable.

7. Correlation: CCCT-II Vs. The Other Tests

Correlation between the marks obtained by the students in CCCT-II and the marks obtained in the other tests.

Positive Correlation: There is positive correlation between the marks obtained in Comprehensive Communicative Competence Test, Section-II and the marks obtained in —

1. GDE; correlation: 0.2229.
2. MBA-I (All Papers); Correlation:- 0.3378.
3. CCCT%; Correlation: 0.8385.
4. CCCT-I; Correlation: 0.7780.
5. CCCT-III; Correlation: 0.6917.

Negative Correlation: There is negative correlation between the marks obtained in CCCT-II and the marks obtained in -

1. WAC%; Correlation:- -0.1210.
2. WAC-70; Correlation:- -0.1198.

Conclusion

The CCCT-II correlates with GDE, MBA-I (All Papers) test,

CCCT%, CCCT-I and CCCT-III. Therefore, CCCT-II has both the predictive validity as well as the concurrent validity. This is mainly because the scores obtained by the students in CCCT-II discriminate the achievement levels of the students and thereby serve the objective of the achievement test. Thus, the scores obtained by the students in CCCT-II are valid, realistic and reliable.

8. Correlation: CCCT-III Vs. The Other Tests

Correlation between the marks obtained by the students in CCCT-III and the marks obtained in other tests —

Positive Correlation: There is positive correlation between the marks obtained in CCCT-III and the marks obtained in —

1. GDE; Correlation: 0.2824.
2. MBA-I (All Papers); Correlation: 0.3438.
3. CCCT%; Correlation: 0.9257.
4. CCCT-I; Correlation: 0.7226.
5. CCCT-II; Correlation: 0.6917.

Low Correlation: In comparison with the positive correlation between and among the six variables, i.e. GDE marks, MBA-I (All Papers) marks, CCCT% marks, CCCT-I marks, CCCT-II marks, CCCT-III marks, there is lower degree correlation between the marks obtained in CCCT-III and the marks obtained in —

1. WAC-70; Correlation: 0.0857. This is extremely low and negligible correlation.

Negative Correlation: There is negative correlation between the marks obtained in CCCT-III and the marks obtained in —

1. WAC%; Correlation: -0.0968.

Conclusion

The CCCT-III correlates with GDE, MBA-I (All Papers) test, CCCT%, CCCT-I and CCCT-II. Therefore CCCT-III has both the predictive as well as the concurrent validity. This is mainly because the scores obtained by the students in CCCT-III discriminate the achievement levels of the students and thereby serve the objective of the achievement test in an effective manner. Thus, the scores obtained by the students in CCCT-III are valid realistic and reliable.

COMPARATIVE PERFORMANCE OF CLASSIFIED SUBJECTS IN EIGHT TESTS

Classification of The Subjects in Twelve Groups

It was noticed that the representative students could be classified in various groups according to their mothertongues, graduation degrees and sex. Therefore, on the criteria of their mothertongues, graduation degrees and sex, the 40 students were distributed in the twelve groups.

However, the computation of the students' sexwise, degreewise and mothertonguewise performance in eight tests was only incidental. This computation of the comparisons of the average scores of different groups does not fall under our present study. As the population of some of these groups is inadequate, it was obvious that the performance of these groups in the eight tests with that of the students in rest of the groups cannot be compared.

The 40 students were distributed in the following twelve groups on the criteria of their mothertongues, graduation degrees and sex.

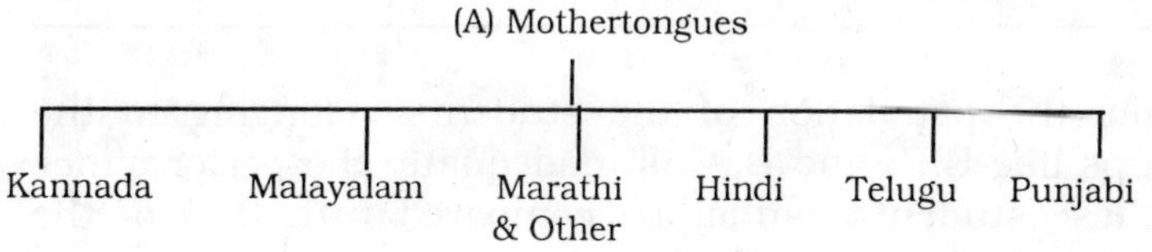

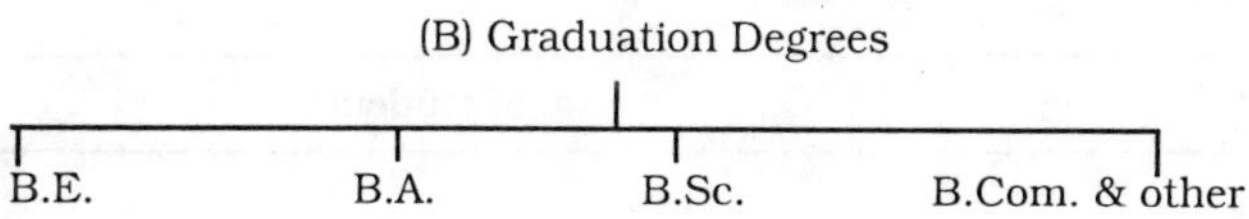

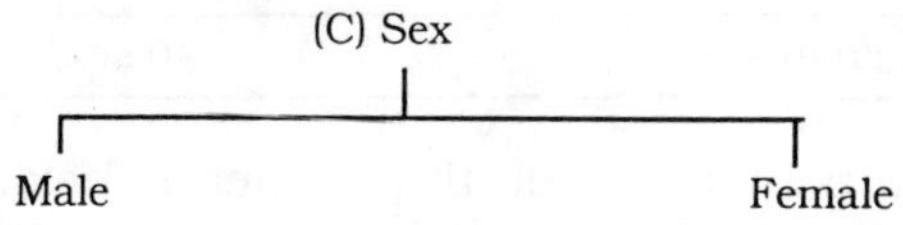

The number of students in each one of these groups is given in the table below.

TABLE 15.5 : Classification of the Subjects According to Their (A) Mothertongues (B) Graduation Degrees (C) Sex.

(A) Mothertongues	No. of students
Kannada	3
Malayalam	8
Marathi & Other	13
Hindi	2
Telugu	12
Punjabi	2
Total: 6 groups	40 students

As the population of the students in the groups like Kannada, Hindi and Punjabi is inadequate, the performance of these students cannot be compared with that of the students in the rest of the groups.

(B) Graduation Degree	No. of students
B.E.	2
B.A.	2
B.Sc.	17
B.Com & Other	19
Total: 4 groups	40 students

As the population of the students belonging to the groups like B.E. and B.A. is inadequate, the performance of these students cannot be compared with that of the students in the rest of the groups.

(C) Sex	No. of students
Male	36
Female	4
Total: 2 groups	40 students

As the population of the students belonging to the group like Female group is inadequate, the performance of this group cannot be compared with that of the Male group.

As the representative students belonged to the six mothertongues, four graduation degrees and both the sexes, it was decided to form different groups of them. The twelve groups based on the criteria of sex, mothertongues and graduation degrees were formed. Then, we decided to compare the performance of the students of one group with the performance of the students of the other groups in each one of the eight tests given below —

1. DMK; 2. MBA-I (All Papers); 3. WAC%; 4. WAC-70; 5. CCCT; 6. CCCT-I; 7. CCCT-II; 8. CCCT-III.

However, as mentioned earlier, some of the comparisons were dropped due to inadequate population of the students in groups specified earlier.

The comparative figures of the mean of the scores of twelve variables (representative students in 12 groups) in eight tests is given in the table.

The average scores of twelve variables in eight tests given in the table 15.6 above is shown in the Fig. 15.4.

The average scores of the students belonging to the twelve groups, in the eight tests were calculated. However, the average scores of the five groups in each test were compared with the average scores of the rest of the students. Thus, the following comparisons were made —

1. The average scores of the Malayalam students with the average scores of the non-Malayalam students in each one of the eight tests.
2. The average scores of the Marathi & other students with the average scores of the non-Marathi & other students in each one of the eight tests.
3. The average scores of the Telugu students with the average scores of the non-Telugu students in each one of the eight tests.
4. The average scores of the B.Sc. students with the average scores of the non-B.Sc. students in each one of the eight tests.
5. The average scores of the B.Com & other students with the average scores of the non-B.Com. & other students in each one of the eight tests.

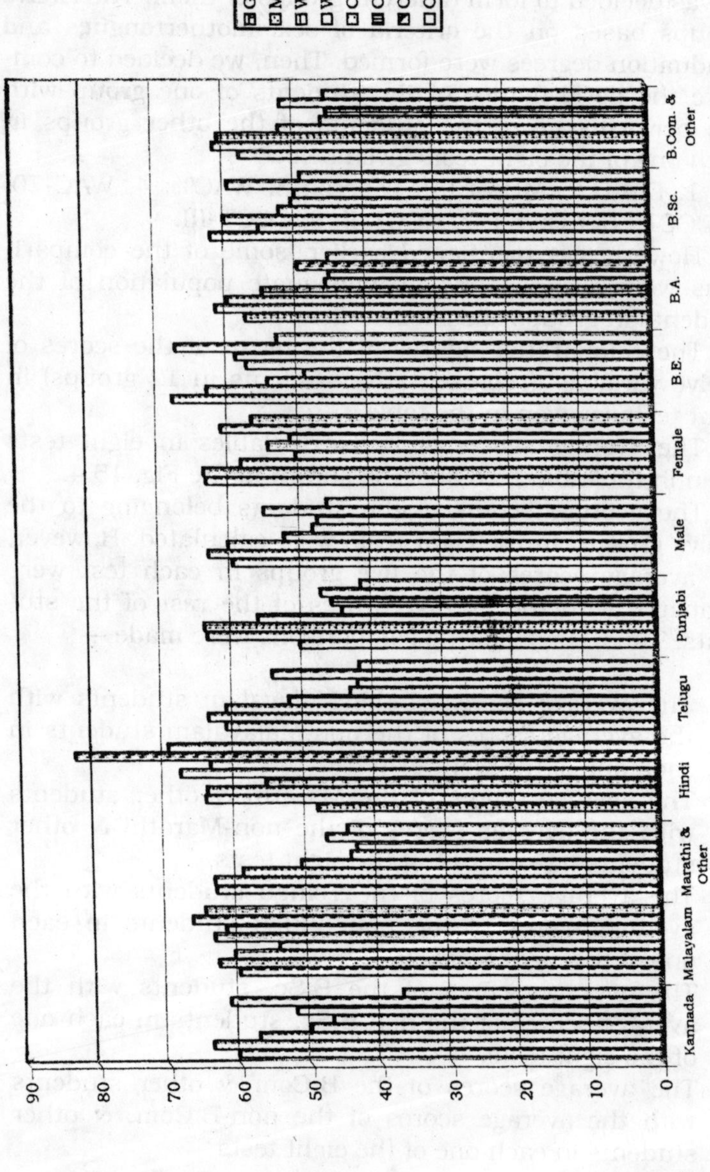

Fig. 15.4 : Comparative Performance of Twelve variables in Eight Tests

TABLE 15.6 : Comparative Performance of Twelve Variables (representative students in 12 groups) in Eight Tests (average scores of each group).

Name of the Group	GDE	MBA-1	WAC%	WAC-70	CT%	CT-I	CT-II	CT-III
1. Kannada	60.25	63.08	57.25	50	46.87	52	61.25	36.87
2. Malayalam	59.92	62.78	60.57	54.28	63.35	61.71	66.40	64.64
3. Marathi & Other	63	63.21	59.23	50.98	43.84	43	47.30	44.03
4. Hindi	48.50	64.23	64	55.71	67.75	63.50	82.50	69.37
5. Telugu	61.02	63.62	61.16	52.26	43.58	42.50	54.55	42.19
6. Punjabi	50.55	63.64	64	56.43	44.50	46	47.50	41.87
7. Male	59.88	63.27	60.52	52.53	48.05	47.83	55.40	46.48
8. Female	63.50	63.79	58.50	50.71	54.62	51.50	61.25	56.88
9. B.E.	68	63.12	54.50	49.28	57.50	59	67.50	53.12
10. B.A.	57.50	61.65	60	55	46	45.50	50	45.62
11. B.Sc.	62.20	65.39	60.29	52.43	50.70	50.23	59.70	49.04
12. B.Com. & Other	57.96	61.67	61	52.32	46.28	45.52	52.10	45.79

The results of the comparison of the average scores of five variables in eight tests were statistically calculated and the conclusions drawn therefrom are summed up in the following section.

QUALITATIVE ANALYSIS OF COMMUNICATIVE COMPETENCE TEST RESULTS

The results of the CCCT and other tests are computed and statistically analyzed in the section-A of the present chapter. Yet it was desirable to make qualitative analysis of the results of CCCT beside the quantitative analysis which was already accomplished. Therefore, it was decided to deal with the errors made by the students in the three sections of CCCT separately. The errors were identified and later classified under different headings. The analysis of the errors and the post-test discussion with the students about the errors made by them revealed the facts which are given in this part of the study.

Analysis of The Errors In Section-I

The First Section of the CCCT deals with various concepts in business communication. These concepts cover the nature of communication process, various functions of business communication, media of business communication, channels of business communication, barriers to business communication, essentials of effective business communication, business letters, business reports, minutes-writing, journalistic writing, public speeches, group and mass communication, intrapersonal and interpersonal communication etc. (See 'The Coverage of CCCT' in Chapter-7 for further details). The analysis of the errors and the post-test discussion with the students about the errors made by them in the first section of CCCT reveal the following facts.

(1) *The Lack of Understanding of the Concepts* : There are some students who have not understood some concepts in business communication. For example: In Item-1, 17 students have selected the distracter 'a'. They have failed to conceptualize the process of communication. In

Item-3, 23 students have selected the distracter 'd'. They do not seem to have understood the concept of communication situation. In Item-8, 17 students have selected the distracter 'c'. They do not seem to have understood the criteria of reliable information. In Item -9, 11 students have selected the distracter 'c'. They have failed to understand the significance and function of 'advice' in business communication. In Item-12, 12 students have selected the distracter 'a'. During post-test discussion, most of these students expressed their disliking of the very concept of 'order' even in the downward channel of communication. They thought it to be dictatorial. They have failed to understand the significance of 'order' in business communication. In Item-14, 27 students have selected the distracter 'a'. They seem to have contrasted 'order' against 'friendliness'. They have misconceptualized that the order and friendliness cannot coexist in a business situation. In Item-18, 14 students have selected the distracter 'd'. It has been revealed that they have not understood the essentials of the art of persuasion in business communication. They have not understood the fact that the argumentation has a limit in persuasion. Beyond that limit it ceases to be objective and becomes subjective. In Item-19, 21 students have selected the distracter 'c'. In business situation, 'outside public' is connected with business house. The students seem to have stretched the meaning of 'outside'. They have not understood the relevance of educating of the 'outside public' in a business situation. In Item-22, situation students have selected the distracter 'a'. They do not seem to have understood that warning has demoralizing effect if it is given publicly and frequently. They may have taken the surface meaning of the 'effectiveness of warning'. If warning is given as punishment it becomes effective when it is given publicly and frequently. This is what they might have thought about the 'effectiveness of warning'. In Item-25, 21 students have selected the distracter 'd'. They were under the impression that the motivator has to give commands and orders to motivate the receiver. It seems tha they have not understood the concept of motivation. In Item-32, 10 students have selected the distracter 'a'.

Distracter 'a' is a commonly used method of upward communication. These students do not know that are the commonly used methods of upward communication. In Item-33, 12 students have selected the distracter 'a'. They are under the impression that on one who communicates with his/her superior, can have any 'awe of authority'. They do not seem to have understood the limitations of upward communication. In Item-40, 21 students have selected the distracter 'b'. They do not seem to know the ways of controlling grapevine. In Item-41, 15 students have selected the distracter 'd'. They think that they can have consensus without avoiding dissent. They do not seem to have understood the concept of 'consensus'. In Item-50, 15 students have selected the distracter 'd'. They do not seem to know the different types of business letters. In Item-56, 19 students have selected the distracter 'c'. They are not aware of the fact that the meeting minutes do not offer verbatim report of the proceedings. Secondly, they do not know that the minutes are more analogous to a telegram than to a letter. They do not seem to have understood the concept of minutes-writing. In Item-59, 12 students have selected the distracter 'c'. This indicates that they have not understood the nature of the 'lead' of a press report. Secondly, their failure to select the alternative 'a' suggests that they do not know that the 'caption' of the press report should be catchy and suggestive. In short, they do not appear to have an adequate knowledge of the nature of journalistic writing. In Item-67, 13 students have selected the distracter 'd'. They do not seem to have understood the concepts 'intrapersonal communication' and 'interpersonal communication'. They are unable to distinguish between them. In item-68, 14 students have selected the distracter 'a' and some students have selected the alternative 'd'. They are unable to understand that the statements in both of these alternatives are correct. They do not seem to know the limitations of the working of the committees. In Item-73, 12 students have selected the distracter 'a'. They lack the knowledge that the advisory committees do not have the executive powers. In Item-84, 22 students have selected the distracter 'a'. They show poor understanding of the major activities of mass communication. In Item-89, 11 students have selected the distracter 'd'. They are unaware of the fact that 'status consciousness' is a barrier to effective business communication. The post-test discussion with them has revealed that they were under the impression that status consciousness helps the participants to communicate effectively. Secondly, by selecting the distracter 'd', they show their lack of knowledge about 'inference' as a barrier to communication. In Item-90, 9 students have selected the distracter 'a'. They do not seem to have understood the concept 'abstracting'. Secondly, their failure to select the alternative 'c' indicates that they do not know that translations, interpretations and explanations allow distortion of the message. In Item-96, some students have selected the distracter 'a'. They do not seem to have understood that the business communicator has to vary the tone and style of his message, keeping in view the relation and psychology of the receiver and the need of the occasion. They have failed to understand the importance of the occasion and its context in a communication event. Finally, in Item-98, 23 students have selected the distracter 'd'. They do not seem to have understood the concept of 'You attitude' and its importance in business communication.

(2) *Failure to Distinguish Between Various Concepts*: There were some students who were found unable to distinguish between various concepts in business communication. For example: In Item-11, 16 students have selected the distracter 'b'. They seem to be unable to distinguish between counselling and advice. In Item-67, 13 students have selected the distracter 'd'. This indicates that they were enable to differentiate between the interpersonal communication and intrapersonal communication. In Item-76. 17 students have selected the distracter 'b'. They were unable to distinguish between the conferences and the committees. In Item-77, 9 students have selected the distracter 'a'. They were unable to distinguish gestures from various facial expressions. In Item-79, 13 students have selected the distracter 'a'. They were unable to distinguish between the gestures and postures. Finally, in Item-80, 13 students have selected the distracter 'd'. They were

unable to distinguish body movements from the postures.

(3) *The Lack of Linguistic Competence*: These were some students who made some linguistic errors, especially of semantic nature. For example: In Item-3, 24 students have selected the distracter 'd'. They do not seem to have understood the meaning of this distracter. This distracter has double negative which they may have failed to understand. This is a linguistic error. In Item-8, 16 students have selected the distracter 'c'. In a post-test discussion many of those students showed inability to understanding the meaning of the word 'bearing'. This indicates that they did not have language proficiency. In Item-56, 19 students have selected the distracter 'd'. It was revealed that many of those students did not understand the meaning of the word 'analogous'. In Item-73, 12 students have selected the distracter 'a'. It was revealed that they did not understand the meaning of the word 'confer'. In Item-84, 22 students have selected the distracter 'a'. The post-test discussion with the students has revealed that many students did not know the meaning of the word 'surveillance'.

The post-test discussions also revealed that the students' lack of attention of some key concepts and to the distinctions of the concepts was due to the poor weightage given to these items in the annual University examinations. Further, there is no inclusion of the aspect of linguistic competence in the syllabus. Some students who have taken their degrees from those colleges that impart instruction in their regional languages, thought that the aspect of linguistic competence i.e. the study of grammar and composition should be included in the syllabus.

Analysis of the Errors in Section-II

The test items in Section-II are designed to test the students' ability to identify and interpret the communication functions in the discourse units. These discourse units have various communicative functions in business situations. The coverage of the test-items on this section is given in Chapter-7. (See 'The Coverage of CCCT' in Chapter-7 for further details). The post-test discussions with the students about the errors made by them in this section, revealed the following facts —

In Item-101, 10 students have selected the distracter 'd'. They seemed to be unable to identify and interpret the communication function in the discourse unit in the stem. They were neither able to differentiate between 'information in circular letter' and 'instruction in circular letter', nor they have understood how discourse units are used for these communicative functions. In Item-102, 9 students have selected the distracter 'c'. They were unable to identify and interpret the communicative function in the discourse unit in the stem.

They were neither able to differentiate between the 'appreciation' and 'suggestion' in quotation letter, nor they have under stood how discourse units were used for these communicative functions. In Item-105, 17 students have selected the distracter 'a'. They were unable to identity and interpret the communication function of the discourse unit in the stem. They seemed to be unable to differentiate between 'inquiry in trade and bank reference correspondence' and 'inference in status and credit enquiry letter'. They did not understand how discourse units were used for these communicative functions. In Item-108, 16 students have selected the distracter 'a'. They were unable to identify and interpret the communication function in the discourse unit in the stem. They seemed to be unable to differentiate between 'persuasive appeal in business speech' and 'Inquiry in business speech'. They did not understand how discourse unit were used for these communicative functions. In Item-112, 15 students have selected the distracter 'd'. They could not identify and interpret the communication function in the discourse unit in the stem. They were unable to distinguish between 'appreciation in journalistic writing' and 'persuasive appeal in journalistic writing'. They did not understand how discourse units were used for these communicative functions. In Item-113, 16 students have selected the distracter 'b'. They were unable to identify and interpret the communication function in the discourse units in the stem. They could not distinguish between 'inference in journalistic writing' and 'warning in journalistic writing'.

In Item-117, 15 students have selected the distracter 'b'. They could not identify and interpret the communicative function in the discourse unit in the stem. They were unable to distinguish between 'inference in group communication' and 'motivation in group communication'. They did not understand how discourse units were used for these communicative functions. In Item-19, 15 students have selected the distracter 'a'. They were unable to identify and interpret the communication function in the discourse unit in the stem. They were unable to distinguish between 'suggestion in business report' and 'persuasive appeal in business report'.

In post-test discussion, several students attributed their inability to identify communicative functions and to distinguish between the functions to the fact that they did not have much practical orientation in business communication.

Some students lack linguistic competence. In other words, they were weak in identifying the linguistic expressions for various functions. So they expressed their need for the orientation in linguistic component of business communication. They expressed their inability to follow linguistic cues in identifying the various functions.

Analysis of The Errors In Section-III

The Section-III in CCCT deals with the creative ability of the students. There are eighty test items consisting of eighty discourse units which are taken from various oral and written media of business communication like - business letters, business reports, journalistic writing, public speeches, minutes writing, group communication (meetings of the committees and conferences) etc. In these units, there are blanks to be completed by the students as per the instructions given. The instructions are given at the end of each test item regarding how to fill in the blanks by choosing vocabulary items. The responses are expected to express various functions of the discourse units in business communicative situations. The coverage of these test-items is given in the earlier Chapter.

The errors made by the students in this section were mainly analyzed on three axes —

(1) Syntactic errors
(2) Semantic errors
(3) Pragmatic errors

The syntactic and semantic errors are the linguistic errors, but the pragmatic error is an error in recognition and use of an appropriate language function in the discourse unit. In this section the students are instructed to use a linguistic expression for filling in the blanks so that the discourse unit acquires one of the language functions like warning, suggestion, request, greeting etc.

The syntactic error is an error which is grammatical. If the subject fails to observe the grammar rules and like pluralization, word-order, agreement of the subject with the verb etc., it is a syntactic error. The semantic error is one in which the subject fails to create the proposition. The pragmatic error is essentially the error in identifying and assigning the appropriate elocutionary force to the proposition. That is, the discourse unit must have the intended function like — promise, warning, conveying information etc. The syntactic and semantic errors are both linguistic errors. If the subject fails to absence conventional rules of syntax and meaning, he commits the linguistic error. The pragmatic errors are nonconventional in the sense that there are no conventional rules for a discourse unit to have a communicative function. However, discourse unit takes on a communicative function in communicative situation. If the subject fails to identify and assign an appropriate communicative function to the discourse unit, he commits the pragmatic error

The analysis of the errors and the post-test discussions with the students revealed that they need orientation in communicative grammar. They also need the practical orientation in using language functions in various discourse units. This section highlights the practical aspect of the competence of the students in business communication. The following table gives the analysis of the errors —

Item No.	Wrong Response	Types of Errors: Syntactically acceptable (A)/ unacceptable (U)	Semantically acceptable (A)/ unacceptable (U)	Pragmatically acceptable (A)/ unacceptable (U)	Instruction followed (F)/ not followed (NF)
1	2	3	4	5	6
121	notice	A	U	U	F
	announce	U	A	U	F
	know	U	A	A	F
122	get	A	U	U	F
	give	A	A	U	F
123	make	A	U	U	F
124	made	U	U	U	F
125	Start	A	U	U	F
	come	U	A	U	F
126	inviting	U	A	A	F
127	thank	A	U		F
	know	U	A	A	F
	welcome	A	U	U	F
	offer	A	A	U	F
127	also	U	A	U	F
	must	A	A	U	F
	usually	U	A	U	F
	list	U	A	U	F
	quoted	U	A	U	F
	are	U	U	U	F
	given	U	A	U	F
	have	U	U	U	F
	will	A	A	U	F
128	came	U	A	A	F
	pay	U	U	U	F
	now hurry	U	A	A	N F
	rush	A	A	U	F
	send	U	U	U	F
	get	A	A	U	F

Contd.

1	2	3	4	5	6
129	Fill in	A	A	U	N F
	Take	A	A	U	F
	Present	A	A	U	F
	Draw	A	A	U	F
	Exchange	A	U	U	F
	Get	A	A	U	F
130	try to	A	A	U	N F
	urgently	A	A	U	F
	able of	U	A	U	N F
	will	A	A	U	F
131	found	U	A	U	F
	admit	A	U	U	F
	regret	A	U	U	F
	inform	A	A	U	F
	infer	A	A	U	F
	state	A	A	U	F
	told	U	A	U	F
	knew	U	A	U	F
	considered	U	A	A	F
132	Not satisfied	A	A	U	N F
	sorry	A	A	U	F
	annoyed	A	A	U	F
	inconvenient	A	A	U	F
	dejected	A	A	U	F
	dismood	U	A	U	F
	of the	U	U	U	N F
	dissatisfied	A	U	U	F
133	sorry	A	A	U	N F
	felt very sorry	A	A	U	F
	hope	A	A	U	F
	know	A	A	U	F
	found	A	A	U	F
	condolence	U	U	U	F
	are sorry	A	A	A	N F
134	can	A	A	U	F
	will	A	A	U	F
	facilitate	U	U	U	F
	promise	U	A	A	F
	replace	U	U	U	F
	should	A	A	U	F
	assure	U	A	A	F

Contd.

1	2	3	4	5	6
135	considered	U	U	U	F
	discuss	A	U	U	F
	cover	U	U	U	F
136	inform	U	U	U	F
137	very	U	U	U	F
	moved to	U	U	U	N F
	might	A	A	U	F
	shall	A	A	U	F
138	hear	A	A	U	F
	understand	A	U	U	F
139	appreciate	A	A	U	F
	received	U	A	A	F
	reference to	U	U	U	N F
	have received	A	A	U	N F
	thanks	U	U	U	F
	welcome	A	A	U	F
	know	A	A	U	F
140	inviting	A	A	U	F
	addressing	A	A	U	F
	giving	A	U	U	F
141	grateful	U	U	U	F
	thanking	U	A	A	F
	glad	U	U	U	F
142	extend	A	U	U	F
	profit	A	U	U	F
	cover	A	A	U	F
143	So	U	A	A	F
	If	U	U	U	F
	Please	U	A	U	F
	Hope	U	A	U	F
144	quality	A	A	U	F
	character	A	U	U	F
	brand	A	U	U	F
	use	A	U	U	F
	purpose	A	U	U	F
	features	U	A	U	F
	strangeness	A	U	U	F

Contd...

1	2	3	4	5	6
145	early	U	A	A	F
	before time	A	A	A	N F
	with	U	U	U	F
146	prices	A	U	U	F
	value	A	U	U	F
	rate	U	A	A	F
	time	A	U	U	F
147	greatly	A	A	U	F
	now	A	A	U	F
148	plan	A	A	U	F
	take	U	U	U	F
	decided	A	A	U	F
	suggest	A	A	U	F
	advice	A	A	U	F
	happy	U	A	U	F
149	shall	A	A	U	F
	better	U	A	U	F
	must	A	A	U	F
	could	A	A	U	F
150	years	U	U	U	F
	strive	A	A	U	F
	start	U	A	U	F
	progress	A	A	U	F
	look	A	A	U	F
	this inform	U	U	U	N F
151	should	A	A	U	F
	leave to	U	U	U	N F
	have to	A	A	A	N F
152	Can	A	A	U	F
	Believe	U	U	U	F
	If	U	U	U	F
	I request	U	A	A	N F
153	very good	A	A	A	N F
	friendship	U	A	A	F
154	detectives	U	A	A	F
	rules	U	U	U	F

Contd.

1	2	3	4	5	6
155	should	A	U	U	F
	wouldn't	A	A	U	F
156	strive to	A	A	U	N F
	promise to	A	U	A	N F
	give	U	U	U	F
	first	A	A	U	F
	together	A	A	U	F
	must	A	A	U	F
157	must	A	A	U	F
158	note	A	A	U	F
	report	A	A	U	F
	speech	A	A	U	F
	inquiring	A	A	U	F
	account of	A	A	A	N F
	sorry	A	A	U	F
	remark	U	U	U	F
159	a great				
	pleasure	U	U	U	N F
	surprise	U	U	U	F
	only recently	U	U	U	N F
	suggested	A	A	U	F
	informed	U	U	U	F
160	taking change	A	A	A	N F
161	switch	A	U	U	F
	take	A	A	U	F
162	I must	U	U	U	N F
	will	U	U	U	F
	ready	U	U	U	F
	shall	U	U	U	F
163	vital	U	A	A	F
	major	U	A	A	F
	remarkable	U	A	A	F
	prominent	U	A	A	F
	key	U	A	A	F
	significant	U	A	A	F
164	may	A	A	U	F
	must	A	A	U	F
	might	A	A	U	F
	have to	A	A	U	N F

Contd.

1	2	3	4	5	6
165	could	A	A	U	F
	had	U	U	U	F
	have to	A	A	U	N F
	decided	U	U	U	F
	can	A	A	U	F
	plans to	U	A	U	N F
	must	A	A	U	F
	will	A	A	U	F
166	should	A	A	U	F
	will	A	A	U	F
	definitely	A	A	U	F
	may	A	A	U	F
167	can't	A	A	U	F
	therefore	U	U	U	F
	can	A	A	U	F
168	have	A	A	U	F
	gave	A	A	U	F
	important	U	U	U	F
169	certainly	U	U	U	F
	promised	A	A	U	F
	been	U	U	U	F
	compelled	A	U	U	F
	ready	U	A	A	F
	right	A	A	U	F
	going	U	A	A	F
170	suppose	U	A	U	F
	showing	A	A	U	F
	essentially	U	U	U	F
	try	U	U	U	F
171	announce	A	A	U	F
	declare	A	A	U	F
	know	U	A	U	F
172	has	U	U	U	F
	must	U	U	U	F
	will	U	U	U	F
	can	U	U	U	F
	already	U	U	U	F
	start	U	U	U	F

Contd.

1	2	3	4	5	6
173	we	A	U	U	F
	you	U	U	U	F
174	accessible	A	U	U	F
	paramount	U	U	U	F
	different	U	A	U	F
175	presence	A	U	U	F
	to come	U	U	U	N F
	function	U	U	U	F
176	promise	U	U	U	F
	know	A	A	U	F
177	must	U	U	U	F
	likely	U	U	U	F
	try	A	A	U	F
178	immediate	U	U	U	F
	helping hand	A	A	A	N F
	them	A	U	U	F
	royally	A	A	U	F
179	should	A	A	U	F
	do	A	A	U	F
180	inform	U	U	U	F
	get	U	U	U	F
	call	A	A	U	F
	look	A	A	U	F
	suggest	A	A	U	F
181	is quite	A	A	A	N F
	may	U	U	U	F
	all night	U	U	U	N F
	perfectly	U	U	U	F
182	results	U	U	U	F
	progress	U	U	U	F
	attitude	A	U	U	F
183	for	U	U	U	F
	when	A	A	U	F
184	sure to	U	U	U	N F
	surely	A	A	U	F
	promise to	A	A	A	N F
	can	A	A	U	F
	must	A	A	U	F

Contd.

1	2	3	4	5	6
185	go	A	U	U	F
	have to	A	A	A	N F
	put	A	A	U	F
186	you all	A	A	A	N F
	every day	A	A	U	F
	every one	A	A	U	F
187	continuous	U	U	U	F
	going on	U	U	U	N F
	goes on	U	U	U	N F
	would	A	A	U	F
	could	A	A	U	F
188	require	U	U	U	F
	required	U	U	U	F
189	happy	A	U	U	F
	kind	A	A	U	F
190	ensures	U	U	U	F
	sure	U	U	U	F
	shocking	A	A	U	F
191	be happy	U	U	U	N F
	that	U	U	U	F
	see	U	U	U	F
192	very noticeable	A	A	U	N F
	very good	A	A	U	N F
193	raise	U	U	U	F
	will	A	A	U	F
	should	A	A	U	F
	may	A	A	U	F
194	released	U	U	U	F
	effectively	U	A	U	F
	has	U	A	U	F
	must	A	A	U	F
195	motivated	U	A	A	F
	have	A	A	U	F
	willing	U	A	A	F
	must be persuaded	A	A	U	N F

Contd.

1	2	3	4	5	6
	account of	U	A	A	F
	sorry	A	A	U	F
	remark	U	A	A	F
196	to	U	U	U	F
	surely	U	U	U	F
	will	U	U	U	F
	should	U	U	U	F
	since	A	A	U	F
	when	A	A	U	F
	with	U	U	U	F
197	If	A	A	U	F
	Remember	U	U	U	F
	Without	U	U	U	F
198	harsh	A	U	U	F
199	move	U	A	U	F
	sleepy	U	A	U	F
	definitely	U	A	U	F
200	reply	U	A	A	F
	reference	U	A	A	F
	report	U	U	U	F
	response	U	A	A	F

Thus, the analysis of the errors found in the students' responses to the test-items in CCCT, and the post-test discussions with the students about those errors has revealed that many students lack knowledge of some key concepts in business communication. It was also found that their lack of attention of those concepts and to the distinctions of the concepts was due to the poor weightage given to these items in the annual University examination. Thirdly, the linguistic errors made by some students who have taken their degrees from those colleges that impart instruction in their regional languages, suggest that they require to enhance their linguistic competence. In the post-test discussion many of them expressed their need of studying grammar and composition. Thus it is necessary to include the aspect of linguistic competence in the syllabus. Fourthly, their errors in Section-II reveal that many students are unable to identify the communicative functions and also to distinguish between them. In post-test discussion, several students have attributed their inability to identify and distinguish the communicative functions to the fact that they did not have much practical orientation in business communication. Finally, the syntactic, semantic and pragmatic errors in the Section-III, and the post-test discussions with the students revealed that they need orientation in communication grammar.

References

Ebel, R. and D.A. Frisbie, 1991: *Essentials of Educational Measurements*, New Delhi: Prentice-Hall of India Pvt. Ltd.

Gronlund, N.E. and Linn, R.L. (1990); *Measurement and Evaluation in Teaching*; Macmillan Publishing Company, New York.

Gupta, C.B., 1992: *An Introduction to Statistical Methods* (18th Edn.), New Delhi: Vikas Publishing House Pvt. Ltd.

16

SUMMARY OF THE CONCLUSIONS AND PEDAGOGICAL IMPLICATIONS

"Let them to good, that they be rich in good works, ready to give, willing to share."

— Timothy 6:18

Introduction

In the previous chapter the various results of the investigation of comprehensive communication competence achievement testing of the MBAs in Written Analysis and Communication (WAC) has been noted. It may be useful now to summarize the findings and view them in the larger pedagogical perspectives. Therefore, the present chapter consists the summary of the conclusions and the pedagogical implications.

Summary of Conclusions

1. The syllabus of WAC does not prove that the syllabus designer has identified the communicative needs of the MBAs especially in the view of their future on the job performance requirements.
2. The syllabus of WAC does not contain the clear statements of specified objectives as learning outcomes. The syllabus designer did not decide what constitutes an acceptable set of criteria in evaluating outcomes of the curricular programme.

The communicative competence evaluation of the students in WAC through University examination system presents a host of difficulties mainly because the syllabus of WAC does not give specifications of the instructional objectives. The achievements of the students in the specified areas of the instructional objectives are discovered through the achievement test conducted at the end of the academic year.

3. The annual University examination system of WAC is inadequate because it fails to evaluate the subject's achievement of the instructional objectives in a comprehensive manner.

   Secondly, the question paper does not allow the inclusion of sufficient number of test-items to give even the representational coverage to all the content areas of the syllabus of WAC. The questions included in the University question paper do not represent all the content areas of the syllabus of WAC.

   Thus the University examination system of WAC is neither comprehensive nor adequately representative.

4. The annual University examination system of WAC is incompatible with the teaching goals and procedures. The students' ability of understanding and creating various discourse units in business communicative situations is not evaluated.

5. The annual University examination system of WAC involves essay type of written answers which do not measure the students' communicative competence in oral expressions.

6. Though the annual University examination of WAC tests only the written performance of the students, it does not test all the aspects of the students' written communicative competence in business communicative situations.

7. Though the annual University examination of WAC is administered according to the standardized procedure, the assessment of the students' essay-type of responses is subjective and its reliability is limited. In subjective assessment, the scores are influenced by the opinion or judgement of the person assessing the answers.

The answer to essay type questions are scored differently by different teachers and even the same teachers score the answers differently at different times. Such results hardly foster confidence in the essay-type of test. Thus, unreliability of the scoring is a serious limitation of the University examination system of WAC.

8. The scores of the population of MBA-I in WAC-70 doesn't differentiate the achievement levels of the students in an effective manner.
9. The scores of the representative students in WAC-70 are concentrated between the minimum 29 marks and maximum 41 marks. The standard deviation of the scores is 2.65. The scores are not evenly distributed and scattered even within a narrow range of 12 marks. The scores of WAC-70 do not differentiate the students' achievement levels in an effective manner.

   The test which does not differentiate or discriminate the achievement levels of the students effectively, is not a valid and reliable measure of the students' achievement of the instructional objectives. Thus, WAC-70 is not a valid and reliable achievement test.

   On the other hand, the scores of the representative students in CCCT are spread between the minimum 19 marks and the maximum 77 marks. The Standard Deviation of the scores is 15.83. The scores are evenly distributed and scattered within a broad range of 58 marks. The scores of CCCT differentiate the students' achievement levels in an effective manner.

   The test which differentiates or discriminates the achievement levels of the students, is a valid and reliable measure of the students' achievement of the instructional objectives. Thus, CCCT is a valid and reliable test.
10. The purpose of finding out the correlation coefficient of the scores obtained by the students in the eight test — (i) GDE, (ii) MBA-I, (iii) WAC%, (iv) WAC 70, (v) CCCT %, (vi) CCCT-I, (vii) CCCT-II, (viii) CCCT-III was to find out the criterion related evidence which proves or disproves the predictive validation as well as the

concurrent validation of the two tests — (i) WAC -70 and (ii) CCCT %.

WAC-70 has positive correlation with WAC%, but it has negative and negligible correlation with the remaining six tests. Especially the negative correlation of WAC 70 with GDE indicates that WAC-70 does not have criterion related predictive validity and secondly its negligible correlation with MBA-I indicates that it does not have the criterion related concurrent validity. On the other hand, CCCT% has negative and negligible correlation with WAC% and WAC 70 respectively. But, it correlates positively with all the remaining six tests. Especially its positive correlative with the universal GDE ensures that CCCT% has criterion related predictive validity. The positive correlation of CCCT% with MBA-I, CCCT-I, CCCT-II, and CCCT-III gives evidence that the students' performance in CCCT% is correlated with other four current measures of performance. Thus the criterion related concurrent validity of CCCT % is proved.

In short, it is concluded that WAC 70 has neither the criterion related predictive validity nor it has the criterion related concurrent validity. On the other hand, the CCCT has both the criterion related predictive validity as well as the criterion related concurrent validity.

11. The CCCT comprehensively tests the students' acquisition of every learning point. It tests the students' achievement of all the operationally stated syllabus objectives. Thus CCCT was proved to be the valid, reliable and comprehensive test of communicative competence of the students in Written Analysis & Communication, paper VIth MBA-I.
12. Incidentally, the students' performance in the eight tests mentioned earlier was compared mother-tonguewise. The following conclusions were drawn from the comparisons. (i) On an average the Malayalam students performance in the eight tests is better than the performance of the non-Malayalam students. (ii) On an average the non Marathi & other students' performance in the eight tests is better than the

performance of the Marathi and other students. (iii) On an average the non Telugu students' performance in the eight test is better than the performance of the Telugu students.

13. When the students' performance in the eight tests mentioned earlier was compared on the basis of their Graduation Degrees the following conclusions were drawn from the comparisons: (i) On an average, the B.Sc. students' performance in the eight tests is better than the performance of the non-B.Sc. students. The scores of the B.Sc. students are almost equal to the scores of the non-B.Sc. students in (1) WAC-70 and (2) WAC%. The results of these two tests are not compatible with the results of the remaining six tests in which the scores of B.Sc. students are clearly higher than the scores of the non-B.Sc. students. This indicates that the WAC-70 does not have the reliability and validity. (ii) On an average, the non-B.Com & Other students' performance in the eight tests is better than the performance of the B.Com & Other students. The scores of the B.Com & Other students are almost equal to the scores of the non-B.Com & Other students in WAC-70. And, the scores of the B.Com & Other students are higher than the non-B. Com & Other students in WAC%. The results of these two tests are not compatible with the results of the remaining six tests in which the scores of the non-B.Com & Other students are clearly higher than the scores of B.Com & Other students. This indicates that the WAC-70 does not have the reliability and validity.

However, the computation of the students' graduation degreewise performance in the eight tests was only incidental and the results of these comparisons can be ignored as the population of some of these groups is inadequate.

PEDAGOGICAL IMPLICATIONS AND RECOMMENDATIONS

1. Achievement test plays a central role in the evaluation of pupil learning. It provides relevant measures of many

important learning outcomes. However, the validity of the information provided by it depends upon the care that goes into the planning and preparation of the test. WAC-70 has not been prepared with adequate carefulness and planning. The likelihood of preparing a valid, reliable and useful achievement test of 'Written Analysis and Communication' will be greatly enhanced if the test writer determines the objectives of testing, develops the test specifications, selects apprcpriate item types, and finally, prepares the relevant test items of appropriate difficulty level.

2. In order to the test students' achievement in 'Written Analysis and Communication' comprehensively the test must be designed to provide an evidence of the students' achievement of each and every instructional objective.
3. The content related validity, criterion related validity and the reliability of the achievement test of WAC must be proved before its final administration. This can be done through item analysis procedures and through statistical analysis of the pilot test results, the study of test correlations, the study of the standard deviation of the scores, frequency of the scores, and, scatteredness of the scores.
4. The annual University examination system of WAC needs to be made compatible with the teaching goals and procedures.
5. The syllabus designer of 'Written Analysis and Communication' has to prepare the operationally stated syllabus objectives. It ought to be decided what constitutes an acceptable set of criteria in evaluating outcomes of the curricular programme.
6. The syllabus designer of 'Written Analysis and Communication' has to identify the communicative needs of the MBAs, especially in the view of their future on the job performance requirements.
7. Bearing in mind the communicative needs of the students in oral media, it is essential to select the suitable items types in adequate number to test their oral communicative competence achievement. The

annual University exam. of WAC involves only paragraph or essay type of questions which do not measure the students' communicative competence in oral expressions.

8. Items measuring the subject's competence in every written media, especially those which are used in business communicative situations, must be included in the final achievement test. Though the annual University examination of WAC tests only the written performance of the students, it does not test all the aspects of the students' written communicative competence.
9. Although the subjective scoring of essay type of questions in the present annual University examination system of WAC will always include some uncontrolled variations (Answers to essay questions are scored differently by different teachers, and even the same teachers score the answers differently at different times), the scoring reliability can be increased by clearly defining the outcomes to be measured, properly framing the questions, and carefully following the scoring rules.
10. The theory part of the syllabus consists of some concepts in business communication. The students must know how these concepts are realized in business communication. It is practically impossible for them to experience the business situation where the business communication takes place. Such situations cannot be created in the classroom, though such situation can be artificially created by presenting certain cases and by making the students to play certain roles. But this has a limitation. All situations cannot be presented in a classroom. However, some genuine channel of business communication can be made available in the form of the written materials, audio-visual cassettes etc. The students should be exposed to these channel of genuine business communication.

    The students should be guided in analyzing these genuine channels of discourse and in identifying the various concepts in business communication. This practical aspect of teaching should supplement the reading material on theory.

11. The teaching of grammar at this level will only be remedial though some students coming from the rural colleges where the instruction is imparted in their regional languages, certainly need some help in achieving linguistic competence.
    However, they should be given some orientation in the functional aspect of language study. They should be guided in understanding the language functions which are carried out through various linguistic expressions. For example, certain linguistic expressions like 'will you...', 'Please...', carry out the function of requesting. They should be made conversant with basic communicative functions in business communication and in their corresponding linguistic expressions.
12. The productive aspect of business communication is not given proper weightage in the syllabus and also in the annual examination. The students should be able to produce the materials for business communication—business letters, business reports, meeting minutes, business articles, business speeches, conversations in committee and conference meetings etc. To achieve this, they should be well-motivated. The proper weightage for this aspect should be given in the syllabus and also in the examination. This aspect should cover at least 50 per cent of the syllabus and the examination (whereas, it is only 15 per cent at present).

The students should be made to produce various oral as well as written discourse units in business situations. Communication is essentially problem solving activity. At one end, it is the problem of sending the message through a code, and at the other end, it is the problem of interpreting the message. The productive aspect should cover both. The students should be taught to produce as well as to interpret the discourse units. This productive aspect consists of not only producing the discourse unit but also responding meaningfully to them. For this the technique of role playing would be very useful.

APPENDIX-I

FINAL TEST

COMPREHENSIVE COMMUNICATIVE COMPETENCE TEST (CCCT)

Comprehensive Test of Communicative Competence in 'Written Analysis and Communication' — MBA Part-I

INSTRUCTIONS

i) All the questions are compulsory
ii) All the questions carry equal marks.

SECTION - I

i) Select the correct answer from the alternatives given below each item, and
ii) Complete the incomplete statements by selecting correct answer from the alternatives given below each item.

1. Communication can be defined as ______ and exact replication of thoughts, feelings, facts, beliefs and ideas between and among the individuals through a common system of symbols to cause some actions or change in behaviour.

   a) a transmission
   b) an exchange
   c) a reception
   d) an understanding

2. Effective communication is extremely important in the field of business. One of the following reasons does not contribute to this importance. Find it out.
   a) Business activity has become extremely complex.
   b) Business has grown in size.
   c) There is no need to show concern for employees and customers.
   d) There is a need of participation, co-operation and team-work of the management and employees.
3. The communication situation exists when all of the following components except one are present. Find out an irrelevant component.
   a) There is a sender and a receiver of the message.
   b) There is an interpreter of the message.
   c) The receiver understands the message.
   d) The receiver does not restrain feedback to the message.
4. The process of decoding of signals is ___________
   a) encoding signals.
   b) retranslation or interpretation of signals.
   c) symbolizing signals
   d) semantic noise
5. One of the following is not an internal information required in the business houses. Point it out.
   a) Information about the exact designation and decision-making powers of the employees.
   b) Information about the strong and weak points of the rival companies.
   c) Information about the purchase, production and sales, job assignments and efficiency of the workers.
   d) Information about the capital, investments and accounts.
6. One of the following is not an external information required by the business houses. Point it out.
   a) Information about political, climatic and socio-eonomic conditions.
   b) Information about the availability of credit, raw material, electricity etc. and about the demands of the market.

c) Information about the latest rules and regulations made by the government and local authorities.
d) Information about the procedures governing job assignments.

7. The only reliable source of collecting information about the nature of an employee is ______________.
   a) library research and office files.
   b) interviews, seminars, committees and conferences.
   c) letters, questionnaires, trade exhibitions and mass media.
   d) personal observation.
8. One of the following criteria of reliable information is not correct. Point it out.
   a) Reliable source.
   b) Completeness and correctness.
   c) Current bearing.
   d) Brevity and conciseness.
9. One of the following statements about advice is wrong. Point it out.
   a) In business, each individual activity needs specialized handling which can be fulfilled only through expert advice.
   b) Advice flows horizontally and downward.
   c) Advice is given to a person either to influence his opinion or his behaviour; therefore, advice cannot be neutral.
   d) Advice flows vertically upward.
10. One of the following statements about advice is wrong. Point it out.
   a) The only justified motive of giving advice in business is the betterment of the receiver.
   b) Advice should be work-oriented, but the advisor should consider the over-all competence of the receiver.
   c) Advice should not create a feeling of inferiority in the receiver.
   d) Adviser should not seek feedback from the receiver.
11. Counselling is very similar to giving advice. But, counselling is ______________.

a) subjective and factual
b) objective and personal
c) impersonal
d) personal

12. One of the following statements about order is wrong. Point it out.
    a) The downward flow of communication is dominated by order.
    b) Order is a directive to the superior.
    c) It is a directive to modify, start or stop an activity.
    d) It should be issued to achieve organizational goals.
13. ________________ given in the following cases: (i) It is repetitive, (ii) It is highly responsible, (iii) It is essential to keep the record of it.
    a) Only oral order is
    b) Usually written order is
    c) Often oral order is
    d) Oral and written orders are
14. One of the following statements about order is wrong. Point it out.
    a) An order should be given in a friendly manner.
    b) Before an order is issued, the order given should ensure if its execution is possible.
    c) The order given should take into consideration the anticipated reaction of the receiver before giving the order.
    d) The order must be given in such a tone and language that it sounds authentic and brings resentment.
15. One of the following statements about suggestions is wrong. Point it out.
    a) The acceptance of suggestion is almost a foregone conclusion.
    b) Suggestion can be turned down by the receiver.
    c) Suggestion puts forward an idea for the other person's approval.
    d) Suggestion clearly indicates the authority of the receiver to evaluate, appreciate or criticize the proposed idea.
16. One of the following statements is wrong. Identify the

wrong statement.

a) Workers are to be encouraged to drop suggestions in suggestion boxes.
b) Suggestion boxes are placed in the chambers of business executives.
c) Suggestions must be scrutinized.
d) Employees offering best suggestions are awarded prizes.

17. In persuasion, effort is not made to influence one of the following factors. Find it out.
    a) Attitudes and beliefs of others.
    b) Suggestions of others.
    c) Feelings and emotions of others.
    d) Actions of others.
18. One of the following statements about the art of effective persuasion is correct. Find it out.
    a) Persuasion does not need conviction on the part of the communicator.
    b) Communicator must try to persuade others from a selfish motive.
    c) Communicator must give indirect hints and subtle suggestions.
    d) Communicator must overwhelm the receiver with arguments.
19. In business houses, education is carried on at three levels. One of the following does not indicate any one of these levels. Point it out.
    a) Education at management level.
    b) Education for different age-groups.
    c) Education for outside public.
    d) Education for the employees.
20. If an accounts officer asks one of his clerks to prepare a voucher, he has issued an order. If he shows the clerk how to prepare a voucher and asks him to prepare more, he has issued _______.
    a) suggestion.
    b) opinion.
    c) instruction.
    d) second order.

21. Warning which communicates a person of unfavourable and unpleasant consequences of the workers undesirable behaviour is not given for one of the following reasons. Point it out.
    a) Tardiness and negligence
    b) Defiance and pilfering
    c) Spreading rumours and mishandling equipment
    d) Regularity and punctuality
22. In order to retain effectiveness of warning, it should be administered ____________.
    a) publicly and frequently.
    b) for morale raising.
    c) for demoralizing effects.
    d) for evoking resentment.
23. Morale is a powerful, intangible factor representing the sum of several qualities. One of the qualities given below does not indicate high morale. Point it out.
    a) Defiance.
    b) Fortitude
    c) Resolution.
    d) Confidence.
24. One of the following factors is not conducive to the creation of high morale. Point it out.
    a) The employee's work is suited to his caliber and he is given sufficient freedom in his work.
    b) The executives do not neglect the physical comfort and general facilities to the workers.
    c) The employees have a sense of belonging to the organization and their good work is rewarded.
    d) The employees carry a feeling that their work carries little significance.
25. One of the following statements about motivation is wrong. Point it out.
    a) A motivated worker does not need much supervision.
    b) Motivation is an inner state that energizes, activates and directs behaviour towards goals.
    c) In motivation, communicator keeps himself in foreground and centre.

d) In motivation, communicator keeps himself in back ground.

26. One of the following factors is not conducive to motivation. Point it out.
    a) Clarity of purpose, objectives and procedures.
    b) Lack of needs and aspirations.
    c) Worker's active participation in decision-making process.
    d) An urge to fulfil the primary and secondary needs.
27. One of the following is not an example of downward communication. Point it out.
    a) Managing Director Communicating with the General Manager.
    b) Departmental Head Communicating with the Foreman.
    c) Production Manager giving directives to the purchase officer.
    d) Foreman giving instructions to the operator.
28. One of the purposes of downward communication given below is incorrect. Point it out.
    a) To give the suggestions.
    b) To appraise the subordinates.
    c) To inform the superiors.
    d) To give orders and warnings.
29. Downward communication may be both oral and written, but the downward flow of communication is dominated by ___________ means.
    a) oral
    b) written
    c) gestural
    d) written and non-verbal
30. One of the following items does not state the limitation of downward channel. Point it out.
    a) Under-communication or over-communication.
    b) Delay in transmitting information.
    c) Fear of authority.
    d) Loss and distortion of information.
31. Upward communication provides the ___________ with necessary feedback.
    a) management

b) employees
c) customers
d) subordinates

32. One of the items given below does not constitute commonly used method of upward communication. Point it out.
    a) Open door policy and counselling
    b) Complaints and suggestion boxes
    c) Meeting of the Board of Directors
    d) Letters, reports and minutes
33. One of the items given below does not indicate limitations of upward communication. Point it out.
    a) Employees do experience awe of authority.
    b) Employees feel that if they communicate their problems upward, it may adversely reflect on their own efficiency.
    c) Employees do not like to receive orders and warnings.
    d) Upward communication is deliberately distorted.
34. Workers communicating with the other workers, clerks exchanging information with one another, supervisors holding a coffee-break session to discuss some organizational problems are all engaged in ____________ communication that promotes co-ordination.
    a) upward
    b) downward
    c) lateral
    d) vertical
35. Horizontal communication is extremely important for ____________________.
    a) giving directives.
    b) promoting co-ordination
    c) giving suggestions.
    d) persuasion.
36. Horizontal communication is most effectively carried on through ____________________ means.
    a) only oral
    b) written
    c) oral and non-verbal
    d) visual

37. Periodical meetings among the departmental heads are used for ________________.
    a) oral upward communication.
    b) horizontal verbal and non-verbal communication.
    c) oral horizontal communication only.
    d) oral and non-verbal upward communication.
38. Some managers discourage horizontal communication feeling that ______________.
    a) workers may quarrel and create problems.
    b) workers may get friendly with one another and pose problems for the management.
    c) workers may keep on talking and neglect their duties.
    d) workers may spread rumours.
39. One of the following statements about grapevine is wrong. Point it out.
    a) Grapevine is a formal channel of communication which follows definite directions.
    b) Grapevine acts as a safety valve for the pent-up emotions of the subordinates.
    c) Grapevine has damaging swiftness in spreading secret messages.
    d) Grapevine indicates organizational solidarity.
40. Management can control grapevine by using ______________ channels.
    a) official or formal
    b) informal
    c) only upward
    d) horizontal
41. One of the following statements about consensus is wrong. Point it out.
    a) Consensus is a common agreement of people among a group.
    b) In consensus, members express divergent views.
    c) In consensus, members subordinate their private views.
    d) In consensus, members avoid dissent.
42. One of the following statements about consensus is wrong. Point it out.
    a) Consensus indicates unity and harmony.

b) Consensus allows divergent views and splits.

c) Consensus is used to bring about agreement between management and trade unions.

d) A member is forced to subscribe to a view he does not hold.

43. One of the following statements about written communication is wrong. Point it out.

a) Promptness in replying the letter is absolutely necessary.

b) Correspondent must have and adequate knowledge of the receiver and the subject.

c) Appropriateness of style and tone in writing leads to friendliness and good feeling.

d) Accuracy and completeness do not go together in avoiding mistakes.

44. One of the following statements about written communication is wrong. Point it out.

a) A persuasive style is mainly aimed at arousing a reader's interest in what the correspondent says.

b) Brevity should be effected at the cost of clarity, completeness, courtesy ad correctness.

c) A letter which has an unpleasant appearance fails to catch the reader's eye even if it contains an attrac tive proposition.

d) A positive and pleasant approach builds and retains the customer's goodwill.

45. ______________ and complimentary close should correspond to each other.

a) Sender

b) Salutation

c) Receiver

d) Signature

46. One of the following items of commonly used salutations is rather formal. Point it out.

a) Sir or Madam

b) Dear Mr. Smith

c) Dear Sirs/Mesdames

d) Gentlemen

47. 'Messrs' is an abbreviation of __________ and it is

used as a plural for 'Mr.'

a) Mrs.
b) Messieurs
c) Mesdames
d) Mmes

48. One of the following items is a part of the body of business letter. Point it out.
    a) Subject or reference line
    b) Enclosures
    c) Heading of the letter
    d) Complimentary close
49. One of the following items does not indicate the types and functions of business letters. Point it out.
    a) Adjustment for customer's grievances
    b) A letter to promote sales
    c) Correspondence with government's departments and insurance companies
    d) An editor's apology to reader's complaints
50. One of the following items does not indicate the type and/or function of business letters. Point it out.
    a) Making and/or soliciting inquiries for the supply of goods and services.
    b) Placing of order for goods.
    c) Requesting newspaper editor to publish an article.
    d) Acknowledging and executing orders.
51. One of the following items does not indicate the types and functions of business letters. Point it out.
    a) Granting or applying for credit
    b) Requesting for settlement of accounts
    c) Complaining about the delay or mistake in the supply of goods
    d) Complaining about delay in receiving photographs from a friend
52. One of the following statements about business report is wrong. Point it out.
    a) A report is a basic management tool used in decision-making.
    b) If a report analyses the facts, draws conclusions and makes recommendations, it is an interpretative report.

c) If a report merely presents facts pertinent to an issue or a situation, it is an objective report.
d) The interpretative or analytical reports and objective or factual reports are not used in decision-making.

53. We can have five types of business reports: (i) Periodic reports, (ii) Progress reports, (iii) Examination reports, (iv) Recommendation reports, (v) Statistical reports. These are classified on the basis of the ______________.
 a) written formalities.
 b) nature of reports.
 c) legal formalities.
 d) number of persons drafting reports.
54. Once the report-writer is clear about the purpose of writing a report, the persons for whom it is meant, the facts to be examined and the time at his disposal, the step in writing a report is ____________.
 a) making outline and taking notes.
 b) collaborating and analysing data.
 c) finding out the sources of information.
 d) drafting the report.
55. Every business report must invariably contain __________.
 a) the title page, Summary and Bibliography.
 b) the definition of problem, findings and conclusions.
 c) the contents page and Index.
 d) solutions of the problem.
56. One of the following statements about minutes writing is wrong. Point it out.
 a) Minutes must communicate what was done and ultimately decided upon.
 b) Minutes offer a verbatim report of the proceedings.
 c) Minutes are more analogous to a telegram than to a letter.
 d) Once approved and signed, minutes are acceptable in a court of law as evidence of proceedings.
57. One of the items given below is not included in the minutes of each meeting. Point it out.
 a) The place, date and time of the meeting.

b) The signature of the chairman on each page of the minute.
c) The names of all those who are present and the capacity in which they are present. A brief account of their discussion and voting pattern is given.
d) The names of the movers and seconders of the resolutions are mentioned.

58. One of the following statements about journalistic writing is wrong. Point it out.
a) A press report on commercial and economic matters should cover an event that has news value.
b) The larger the number of the people affected by an event, the smaller is its news value.
c) Faithful representation in press reports includes two things — accuracy and comprehensiveness.
d) A press report is expected to mobilize public opinion on certain current issues.

59. One of the following statements about journalistic writing is wrong. Point it out.
a) The headline or caption of a press report should not be catchy and suggestive.
b) The first one or two paragraphs that give the gist of the reports constitute its lead.
c) The lead is like the synopsis of a long report.
d) A good press report is written in a simple and lucid style.

60. One of the following statement about oral communication is wrong. Point it out.
a) Oral means of communication are more adequate for factual and statistical messages.
b) Oral means of communication are more adequate for immediate action of the receiver.
c) Oral means of communication are more adequate for persuasive messages.
d) Oral means of communication are more adequate for group interactions.

61. One of the following statements about oral communication is correct. Point it out.
a) Oral communication is extremely useful when the

communicator and receiver are far removed from each other.

b) Lengthy messages are suitable for oral communication.

c) Oral messages can be retained for a long time.

d) Oral messages do not have legal validity unless they are taped.

62. One of the following statements about oral communication is wrong. Point it out.

a) Clear and correct pronunciation is the first prerequisite of effective oral communication.

b) Speakers, often when they are groping for words, make use of hackneyed phrases.

c) Clarity of thought and expression, completeness, correctness, conciseness, adaptability are the essentials of effective written communication only. They are not applicable to oral communication.

d) Some essentials of effective communication are common to both the written and oral communications.

63. One of the following statements about public speech is wrong. Point it out.

a) Extemporaneous speeches are more spontaneous than the manuscript and memorized speeches.

b) The greater his speech making ability, the better salesman he will be.

c) Speeches are powerful means of persuasive and imperative message but are unsuitable for lengthy informative messages.

d) The topical, chronological, spatial and causal patterns of arrangement are confined to written presentation only.

64. One of the items given below does not contribute to the failure of the speaker. Point it out.

a) He shows no feeling for or against his subject.

b) He does not slant his material to suit his audience. He doesn't keep the strong points at the beginning.

c) He assumes that his audience already know much about the subject. He indulges in abstractions.

d) He has a sense of responsibility to his audience

and his subject.

65. One of the following items contribute to the failure of the speaker. Point it out.
    a) He stands up tall, he talks eye to eye; he speaks
    b) Responsibly and with authority, as a leader should.
    c) He speaks in order to show off, to impress his audience.
    d) He is not carried off by his over-enthusiasm or over-confidence.
66. As interpersonal communication is ________, the response and reaction of the listener can be easily and instantly evaluated.
    a) audio-visual
    b) face-to-face
    c) non-verbal
    d) oral
67. ________ 'communication is a dialogue or a conversation without the intervention of a machine like telephone.
    a) Impersonal
    b) Interpersonal
    c) Intrapersonal
    d) Personal
68. One of the following statements about committees is wrong. Point it out.
    a) Committee is a small group with its common purposes and objectives.
    b) The term 'committee' covers the activities of any group of people who deliberate about certain matters with a view to action.
    c) The committee with even number of members cannot function more effectively than the committee of odd numbers.
    d) The committee meeting can be effective if its members do not follow the agenda of the meeting.
69. One of the following statements about the committees is wrong. Point it out.
    a) Committees offer expert opinion.
    b) Committees help to generate new ideas.

c) Committees enable managements to find out the response of the employees to proposed policies.
d) Employees need not be associated with the decision making committees of the management.

70. One of the following statements about the committees is wrong. Point it out.
a) The employee's interest is safeguarded through proper representation.
b) Committees promote co-ordination.
c) Committees do not draw out latent talent.
d) Committees do not allow authoritarian trends.

71. One of the following statements about the working of the committees is wrong. Point it out.
a) If committees are appointed to take decisions, it definitely causes delay.
b) In decision-making process, committees prove inexpensive.
c) Committee members often tend to drift into trivialities and irrelevancies.
d) Committees transmit information uniformly.

72. One of the following statements about the working of committees is wrong. Point it out.
a) The authority of the committee is divided among its members.
b) Committees following formalities in there procedures are failure.
c) Committees suffer from the minority tyranny.
d) Committees consisting inadequate, large or incompetent membership are failure.

73. One of the following committees has the executive powers. Point it out.
a) Advisory committees
b) Standing committees
c) Informal committees
d) Ad-hoc committees

74. One of the following items does not add to the effective working of the committees. Point it out.
a) Capable chairman of the committee.
b) Large size of the committee.
c) Competent membership.

d) Preparation and distribution of agenda.

75. One of the following items is not synonymous to 'confer'. Point it out.
    a) To give
    b) To consult
    c) To converse
    d) To discuss

76. One of the following statements about conference is wrong. Point it out.
    a) A conference may suggest solutions to the problem, but those solutions are not binding upon the executives.
    b) A conference is a kind of informal committee meeting.
    c) The conference members have to follow the formal meeting procedures more rigidly than the committee members.
    d) Conferences are similar to committees. Conferences pool knowledge and experience, define problems and help to solve them.

77. Point an odd item out.
    a) Eye-contact and eye-movement
    b) Frowning
    c) Twisting of the lips
    d) Movements of the head

78. Nervousness, anger, fear, scorn, determination, lack of understanding, sympathy, horror, pity, disinterestedness, resentment can be better expressed through __________ than through verbal means.
    a) verbal language
    b) non-verbal language
    c) oral language
    d) written language

79. Point an odd item out.
    a) Raising the fist and thumping the table.
    b) Fumbling the pockets.
    c) Moving about restlessly in the seat.
    d) Biting the nails.

80. Point an odd item out.

a) Sitting with relaxed alertness.
b) Sitting stiffly.
c) Pacing up and down.
d) Awkward drooping posture.

81. Point an odd item out.
a) Articulation and pronunciation.
b) Volume and audibility.
c) Staring at the floor.
d) Stressing and diving.

82. One of the following statements about mass communication is wrong. Point it out.
a) The term 'mass communication' refers to the communication with the masses through mass media.
b) Mass communication is well-planned and rapid public communicational arrangement.
c) Mass communication does not require elaborated organizational arrangements.
d) The audience of mass communication is large, heterogeneous and anonymous.

83. One of the following items is not a mass medium. Point it out.
a) Television
b) Telephone and telegram
c) Radio and motion pictures
d) Newspapers and newsmagazines

84. One of the following items does not mention major activities of mass communication. Point it out.
a) Surveillance of the environment.
b) Educating the masses.
c) Political canvassing.
d) Public entertainment.

85. One of the following statements about communication barriers is wrong. Point it out.
a) There is no such thing as perfect communication.
b) The natural result of obstacles in the process of communication is the misunderstanding of message.
c) The barriers to communication are dangerous to any business organization if they are not removed

in time.

d) The process of 'perfect' communication exists due to the barriers to communication.

86. One of the following statements about organizational barriers is wrong. Point it out.
    a) Hierarchical barriers are organizational barriers.
    b) Increasing specialization of the workforce poses a serious barrier to internal communication.
    c) Sales manager's wrong choice of medium in communicating with the prospective buyer is an organizational barrier to communication.
    d) Communication overload or underload is not an organizational barrier to communication.
87. One of the following statements about physical barriers is wrong. Point is out.
    a) Noise refer to the 'unwanted' signals of messages which interfere and disturb the reception of the 'wanted' signals.
    b) 'Faulty sitting arrangement in the office' and 'A phone call at midnight' refer to the barriers of 'distance' and 'time' respectively.
    c) 'Age' or 'generation gap' does not come in the way of human communication.
    d) Men and women communicate with one another according to their sex.
88. One of the following is not a language barrier. Point it out.
    a) Lack of common language.
    b) Semantic barrier.
    c) Adequate knowledge of vocabulary, punctuation and grammar.
    d) Roundabout verbiage.
89. One of the following statements about socio-psychological barriers is wrong. Point it out.
    a) When the employees are status conscious, it helps them to communicate effectively.
    b) Messages are interpreted by the people in terms of their attitudes and values.
    c) The individual experiences and their interpretations are never identical. They are

different perceptions of reality.

d) As inferences go beyond the facts in making certain statements, they can give wrong signals also.

90. One of the following statements about socio-psychological barriers is wrong. Point it out.

a) Abstracting is a process of focussing attention on some details and omitting others.

b) The reason behind closed mindedness of a person is his deeply rooted prejudice.

c) Translations, interpretations, and explanations do not allow distortion.

d) Our manners of thinking, feeling and acting are influenced by our experience in the past.

91. One of the following statements about communication barriers is wrong. Point it out.

a) Most people do not listen very well due to distractions, emotions, indifference and aggressiveness.

b) Negative emotions and inattentiveness do not interfere with effective communication.

c) The halo effect is the listener's trust or distrust in the speaker.

d) The average human mind which resists change does not accept the new ideas from the communicator.

92. One of the following statements about 'clarity of thought and expression' is wrong. Point it out.

a) For clarity of thought and expression the communicator must be clear about the objective of communication, content of message and suitable medium.

b) For clarity of expression, the communication should use jargon.

c) Ambiguities destroy clarity and create confusion.

d) Colloquialisms are expressions common in speech but supposed to be unsuitable for written communication.

93. Conciseness does not sacrifice ______________ for the sake of brevity.

a) utopian language.

b) completeness and correctness.
c) lengthy constructions.
d) abstractions and round-about verbiage.

94. Whether you are transmitting message or receiving it, you must be very __________.
a) sensitive and impulsive.
b) argumentative.
c) attentive and positive.
d) closed-minded.

95. All messages must be transmitted and responded __________.
a) in urgency.
b) at the most appropriate time.
c) when somebody asks for it.
d) when communicator desires it.

96. Business communicator should vary the tone and style of his message, keeping in view the relation and psychology of the receiver and the need of the __________.
a) delivery.
b) organization.
c) occasion.
d) communicator.

97. One of the following statements about 'objectivity' is wrong. Point it out.
a) While preparing and transmitting messages, the communicator must exclude his emotions, attitudes and opinions.
b) While receiving messages, the receiver's mental set, attitudes and opinions cannot affect his understanding of the messages.
c) The hostile, suspicious and prejudiced receiver is likely to draw a negative and distorted meaning of the message.
d) A high level of trust and mutual respect between the sender and the receiver facilitates objective communication.

98. To make our communication more effective, we must avoid I's and We's and have as many __________ as possible.

a) He's and She's
b) They's and It's
c) You's
d) Our's

99. To say "Thank you" for a service performed or work done or order booked or complaint adjusted is the essence of________.
a) showy mannerism.
b) style of speech.
c) courtesy.
d) pompish behaviour.

100. ____________ is very essential for one who undertakes to transmit message orally or through written media.
a) Basic knowledge of psychology
b) General knowledge of linguistics
c) Knowledge of the subject and the receiver
d) Knowledge of literature

SECTION - II

The alternative answers provide identification and interpre tation of the discourse units in the items. Select the correct answer from the given alternatives.

101. We are proud and delighted to announce the opening of our New England Service Centre in Boston.
a) Instruction in circular letter.
b) Information in circular letter.
c) Opining in adjustment letter.
d) Persuasive appeal in sales letter.

102. If you visit to our showroom, we could then demonstrate the various machines and show you our very wide range of modern office appliances and equipments.
a) Order in an adjustment letter
b) Suggestion in quotation letter
c) Appreciation in quotation letter
d) Warning in collection letter

103. Walk into your grocer's shop with the enclosed coupon to get your pocket of Yummy Breakfast Food at 25 per cent discount. Hurry: The offer expires on the 6th.
   a) Request in sales letter
   b) Motivation in sales letter
   c) Advice in agency letter
   d) Greeting in business inquiry
104. After carefully examining the dress materials supplied to our order of 15th April. 19..., we must express surprise and disappointment at their quality. They certainly do not match the sample you sent us.
   a) Apology in business adjustment
   b) Acknowledgement to business inquiry
   c) Promise in bargaining letter
   d) Complaint in business letter
105. Whatever information you can provide us will be of immense help to us and we assure that such information will be treated strictly confidential.
   a) Inquiry in trade and bank reference correspondence
   b) Inference in status and credit inquiry letter
   c) Invitation in agency correspondence
   d) Information in meeting minutes
106. On my own behalf and on behalf of the Board of Directors of the Company, I have much pleasure in welcoming you at the 29th Annual General meeting of the company.
   a) Information in business speech
   b) Greeting in business speech
   c) Suggestion in business speech
   d) Inference in business speech
107. Let me express my gratitude to the organizing committee of the Nehru Research Centre for giving me the privilege of inaugurating this prestigious institution.
   a) Acknowledgement in business speech
   b) Motivation in business speech
   c) Apology in business speech
   d) Opining in business speech

108. Can you name some more techniques which the advertising companies employ? Is it possible to save customers from buying products which they do not need?
    a) Persuasive appeal in business speech
    b) Request in business speech
    c) Order in business speech
    d) Inquiry in business speech
109. Set and accomplish ambitious goals. Optimize resource utilization and lead the organization to achieve superior results.
    a) Inference in business report
    b) Instruction in business speech
    c) Warning in business speech
    d) Order in business speech
110. You have successfully tackled both the food and unemployment problems by controlling the population explosion.
    a) Promise in business speech
    b) Advice in business speech
    c) Complaint in business speech
    d) Appreciation in business speech
111. Philip A. Clement, President of the Video Group of Bell and Howell Company, has been elected a corporate Vice-President, the company announced today.
    a) Instruction in journalistic writing
    b) Suggestion in journalistic writing
    c) Motivation in journalistic writing
    d) Information in journalistic writing
112. It's every issue is resplendent with articles on current national and world affairs, industry, management and health and also humour and fiction.
    a) Appreciation in journalistic writing
    b) Complaint in journalistic writing
    c) Advice in journalistic writing
    d) Persuasive appeal in journalistic writing
113. The usual insistence of multinationals on 51 per cent equity to keep control can often poison the relationship.

a) Acknowledgement in business report
b) Inferring in journalistic writing
c) Request in journalistic writing
d) Warning in journalistic writing

114. Mr. Verma, draft a short speech of the chairman for the Annual General Meeting. This speech should deal with three major points in addition to other matters. Have you noted those points?
a) Instruction in group communication
b) Appreciation in group communication
c) Opining in group communication
d) Promise in group communication

115. Your Deccan Fiance is of the top ten leasing companies in the country. Your efforts can take it even higher during the next financial year.
a) Order in group communication
b) Warning in group communication
c) Request in group communication
d) Persuasive appeal in group communication

116. I think we should have two rounds and each should get minimum two chances to speak.
a) Advice in group communication
b) Suggestion in group communication
c) Complaint in group communication
d) Acknowledgement in group communication

117. Nothing can replace him, but the least we can and should do is to contribute generously to this fund so that we can at least share the misery of his family.
a) Information in group communication
b) Inference in group communication
c) Invitation in group communication
d) Motivation in group communication

118. Would you like to say something about the time limit; I mean, how much time each one can take?
a) Warning in business report
b) Inquiry in group communication
c) Greeting in group communication
d) Apology in group communication

119. A temporary loan upto Rs. 2,00,000 ought to be sanctioned as this loan is not only very safe but also

profitable.

a) Suggestion in business report
b) Persuasive appeal in business report
c) Appreciation in business report
d) Promise in business report

120. The company should make special arrangements with the Vivid Bharati and Doordarshan to advertise their products.

a) Information in business report
b) Opining in business report
c) Advice in business report
d) Complaint in business report

SECTION - III

Complete the following discourse units by filling in the gaps with one word only.

121. We are proud and delighted to _________ you that we are opening a branch of Bajaj Service Centre at Kolhapur.
122. As these saris are urgently required, make an arrangement to _________ the consignment on or before 14th January 1993. (Give the instruction)
123. We shall give you a special discount of 7 per cent on the readymade garments if you ___________ an order for readymade garments.
124. Our readymade garments are of ________ designs and excellent qualities. (Appreciate readymade garments).
125. If you ______ our showroom, we shall show you a very wide variety of readymade garments. (Give a suggestion)
126. We cordially _______ you to grace the occasion of the tenth anniversary of our company. (Ask formally and politely to grace the occasion)
127. The quotation of prices _______ include packing and delivery charges. (Advice the supplier).
128. Just _______ into our shop with the enclosed coupon and you will get as much as 20 per cent discount on

dress material upto 24th February (Motivate your customer).

129. ________ the cheque for the full amount. (Give an order to your customer).
130. We shall be glad if you _________ send an illustrated catalogue of sewing machines. (Make request to the supplier).
131. We therefore, _________ that your complaint is wrong. (Express your opinion)
132. We were both ________ and disappointed to find that you have supplied low quality goods. (Make complaint, but don't display anger at the inconvenience).
133. We _________ that the goods we sent have reached in a damaged condition. (Express your apology).
134. We ________ immediately replace the wrong goods supplied to you. (Give promise to your customer).
135. We shall ________ over the matter to our lawyer if you don't clear the account on or before 21st March, 1993. (Give warning)
136. Hearty _________ on your appointment on the Board of Electronics Industries. (Convey your greetings).
137. The information which you would provide us about this customer, __________ be of immense help to us. (Express inference).
138. We shall be glad to ______ whether you will be able to supply Asbestos sheets in the size of 55cm X 30cms X 1cm. (Make an inquiry).
139. We ________ with thanks your letter of 5th Dec. 1992. (Admit knowledge)
140. On behalf of the Board of Directors of this company, I have the pleasure in ________ you at the annual general meeting of the company. (Express salutation).
141. I am _________ to the organizing committee of this programme for giving me an opportunity to inaugurate this prestigious institution. (Acknowledge this opportunity with gratitude).
142. The annual turnover of this company is 40 crores and might ____________ over 50 crores in next two years. (Express inference).

143. I have employed all these techniques in advertising and I would like to know some more from you. ______ you tell me some more techniques of advertising? (Make inquiry)
144. The special ________ of our toilet soap is that it is specifically made for soft and glowing skin. (Impart information about the product).
145. The employees must arrive fifteen minutes ________ in the premises of the company to maintain discipline. (Give an instruction regarding how to maintain discipline).
146. Family Medical Services Centre of this company is started in the premises of our company to make these services available to you at reasonable ________. (Make persuasive appeal).
147. All the workers of this company had been facing this serious problem. Mr. Kambale, our friend and colleague, had ______ tacked this problem. (Appreciate Mr. Kambale's performance.)
148. We ____________ to start a canteen in the company. (Give a constructive suggestion).
149. You __________ greet your supervisor and obey his commands. (Give your employees an advice).
150. Let us ________ forward to increase the production and obey his commands. (Give your employees an advice).
151. You ________ finish the given work before you leave. (Give an order).
152. ________ you, therefore, raise the percentage of subsidies upto 7 per cent during 1993-94. (Make a request).
153. The management's attitude towards us is _________. (As an employee express your opinion about the management's attitude towards the employees in your company).
154. The serious recession in Indian industry is due to government's ______________ economic policies. (Express your complaint).
155. I am every sorry to tell you that I ________ keep an appointment with you because I shall be in a very important meeting at that time.

156. We shall ________ strengthen the public distribution system of essential commodities. (Give promise).
157. ____ anyone of you is found pilfering office stationery, a serious action will be taken against him.
158. The chairman made a brief __________ of company's progress and answered questions relating to company's plans for expansion.
159. It was __________ that Mr. Alexander be appointed as 'Joint-Director of the Association.
160. Roger Smith, the president of M/s. Smith and Company is _______ to-day as a vice-president of Stanford Corporation.
161. ________ the machine on the table, plug the wire and press the button. (Give instructions regarding how to operate the machine).
162. To make rapid progress in agriculture and industry we ______ to open our doors for the multinationals.
163. The workers' trade union has played an __________ role in solving the labour problems in Iron and Steel Industries of Kolhapur. (Appreciate the role of Trade Union).
164. The small-scale industries ________ expand, diversify or modernize their business with financial assistance from certain agencies. (Give suggestions).
165. The managements of textile industries in Maharashtra _______ modernize their industries. (Give an advice).
166. You ________ choose a way to become rich in shortest possible time by reading Business Today's Special Issue on Investments. (Motivate the readers).
167. Considering the shortcomings of the policy of privatisation, __________ the government make some changes in the policy?
168. The Government has played a _______ of pass on looker, when a violent mob has set seventy cloth shops on fire. (Express your complaint).
169. The company has ________ to take legal action against those who imitate brand names of the products of our company. (Give warning).
170. In the near future the interlinked economy is ______ to grow faster. (Express your inference).

171. Friends, I am very glad to ______ you that your company's exports totaled Rs.90 crores this year.
172. Mr. Smith ________ write this progress report, you have to collect data from the office files. (Give instruction).
173. Friends, our company is one of the five top exporting companies in the country, ______ can take it even higher with your efforts. (Make a persuasive appeal).
174. Mr.Jacob's performance as an assistant marketing manager of our company was of an _________ quality. (Appreciate Mr. Jacob's performance).
175. Friends, I request the ________ of your company for a dinner at Hotel Ashoka on 5th March.
176. I _______ we should give three chances to each participants. (Give suggestion).
177. You _______ to work hard with consistency. (Give an advice).
178. What we can do for the riot-affected people i Bombay is to give ________ to the relief fund.
179. You _______ open your shop from tomorrow. (Give order).
180. Friends, may I __________ for your kind attention?
181. The pattern developed by our research division ________ allright and it can be introduced in the market.
182. The prolonged strike of the workers of this company has a negative __________ on the company's export performance. (Express your complaint)
183. I am very sorry; you made mistake only _______ didn't give you clear instructions.
184. We ________ give you the amount of bonus before Divali. (Give promise).
185. If your strike continues, we shall ______ down the unit. (Give warning).
186. Good morning to _________. (Greet all the committee members on your arrival in the meeting hall).
187. We shall have to increase the prices of our products if the communal riots in the country _________ result in raising prices of the raw material. (Express your inference).

188. How much time ________ you grant us to prepare and present this report? (Make an inquiry)
189. Friends, I am very ________ to you for your whole-hearted support to my plan.
190. It has been ________ that NTPC has already two major private sector participation power projects pending execution. (State this information in your report).
191. You ought to sanction a temporary loan of five lakhs to this industry ________ this loan is not only safe, but also profitable. (Make a persuasive appeal).
192. The performance of Mr. R.V. Anthony in increasing production during the year 1992-93 is ________. (Appreciate the performance).
193. The limits of loans to these grains merchants ________ be safely raised to 5 lakhs. (Give suggestion).
194. The company ________ make special arrangement to advertise their products on TV. (Give an advice).
195. A large number of the prospective buyers of refrigerators ________ to buy them on the recommendations of the present owners.
196. ________ these suggestions are put into affect promptly, the adverse conditions in trading will disappear. (Give promise).
197. ________ these suggestions are put into effect promptly, the adverse conditions in trading will not disappear. (Give warning).
198. A large number of consumers are not satisfied with the quality of our product. This recent brand of beauty soap of our company leaves the skin ________ and rough. (Express complaint)
199. A careful study of the present market indicates that the prices of the products of petrochemical industries will rise ________ the year ahead. (Express inference).
200. In ________ with your letter dated 21st January 1993, I am submitted a report on market demands of inorganic chemicals in Pune division.

APPENDIX-II

SYLLABUS OF WRITTEN ANALYSIS AND COMMUNICATION (WAC)

Introduction

The Master of Business Administration course in the selected University is of two years duration and is divided into two parts. Part one is taught during the first year and part two during the second year course. MBA programme provides participants with techniques and understanding required for successful managerial careers for the public and private profit or non-profit sectors of the economy. The basic objectives of the MBA programme are:

1. To introduce basic tools and concepts for analysis and decision making and to train the students in their use and application in managerial context.
2. To instill problem-solving attitude in the practice of management.
3. To develop the social-skills needed for the implementation of decisions.
4. To provide a broader socio-economic scope against which a particular managerial problem can be assessed. The emphasis is on decision-making process with reference to Indian situation.

Proficiency in English is an essential eligibility factor for the graduates of the following faculties to get admission to this course. Arts, commerce, Science, Engineering, Social Sciences and Agriculture. In selection procedure, the applicant's proficiency in English and his potential to shoulder the responsibility of managerial positions is tested in the Written Test, Group Discussion Test and Personal Interview.

The Syllabus of WAC

The syllabus of 'Written Analysis and Communication' for the course of MBA is only for the first year. The paper of WAC is for 100 marks and it is divided in two Units. Three sessions of 70 minutes each are allotted per week for the teaching programme of this paper. The syllabus of WAC is reproduced below.

UNIT COURSE - 6

Written Analysis and Communication

Section - I

i) Communication in Organization - Nature, Function, Scope and Limitations - Management communication.

ii) Downward communication - Upward communication - Horizontal communication - purpose, kinds, and methods - constraints and limitations - psychological variables, personal variables, structural variables - Effectiveness of communication.

iii) Communication skills - Written Media - Advantages and Usefulness - Oral media - Advantages and usefulness - Aids to communication.

Section - II

iv) Foundations of effective writing:

AIDS

a) Letters - How to write - Types of Letters

b) Reports - Format of a report - steps in writing the report - different types of reports.

c) Meetings and conferences

d) Journalistic style - Writing procedures - General knowledge - Organizing the writing - specialization in style.

v) Verbal Messages - Non-verbal messages - Interpersonal

communication - Intrapersonal communication - Small group communication - Mass communication - Foundation of effective oral presentation Analysis and presentation.

vi) Public speaking - Foundation of professional reading as a means to effective public speaking - How to develop the art of public speaking to suit different occasions - Dynamics of mass persuasion.

Notes

1. The general approach is to give broad idea of business communication.
2. Practical work consists of writing reports on the organiza tional information — case studies or information of real life situations supplied to the students from different functional areas; and are evaluated on the basis of knowledge and skills in communication. The minimum of six reports are to be written in classroom sessions.
   Every student has to deliver in English language a minimum of three extempore and three prepared speeches during academic year.
3. Out of the total 100 marks, internal credit is of 30 marks for the performance in written and oral communication work detailed in (2) above. The written final examination is of 70 marks divided as follows:

Section I : 30 marks
Section II : 40 marks

The Question Paper of WAC

The question paper of WAC, MBA (Part-1) final examination is divided in two sections Section - I consists of two case passages. The student is expected to comprehend and analyze any one of the case on the basis of his knowledge and skills of business communication 'Question-1' is the only question in the first section. It is compulsory and it carries twenty-five marks. One-fourth of the case, and remaining marks arc distributed over questions on the case to be answered.

Section — II consists of six questions out of which any three questions are to be answered. 'Each question carries 15 marks. The weightage given at the examination to different topics in the syllabus is not specified. but, the weightage given to different skills and sub-skills of written and oral communication is specified in the 'internal credit' of 30 marks.

Recommended Books for WAC

1. Harold Koontz & Cyril O'Donnell: 'Management' International student's Edn. McGraw-Hill KogaKusha Ltd., 6th Edn. (1976).
2. Harold Koontz and Cyril O'Donnell. '*Essentials of Management*' - Tata McGraw-Hill Pub. Co. Ltd.' New Delhi. (1971).
3. Joseph, L. Massie: *Essentials of Management* - Prentice-Hall of India Pvt. Ltd. New Delhi. (1987)
4. S.G.Bapat & S.G.Datar: '*A Text Book of Business Correspondence*', Anmol Prakashan. (1977).
5. L.M. Goud & K.R. Dixit: '*Advanced Commercial Correspondence*' - Universal Publications, Kolhapur. (1976).
6. V.N. Mugali: '*Business English*,' Book Centre, Hubli (1975).
7. Robert Zatter and W. George Gronch: *Successful Communication in Science and Industry* - McGraw-Hill Co. Inc. (1961).
8. Edited by Elizabeth Marting & Others: '*Effective Communication on the Job* - Taraporwala Publishing Industries Pvt. Ltd. (1977).
9. Edited by Jean M. Gurky: *A Reader in Human Communication* 'Random House, New York.
10. Charles R. Wright: *Mass Communication, a Sociological Perspective*, Random House New York. (1974).
11. Adelstein, M.E. : '*Contemporary Business Writing*,' Random House, New York. (1971).

Analysis of Question Paper of Written Analysis & Communication

The Question Paper of Written Analysis and Communication

M.B.A. Part-I Examination & M.B.A. with Specialization in Agriculture & Rural Development Part I

WRITTEN ANALYSIS AND COMMUNICATION-Paper VI

Day & Date: Wednesday, 02/05/90 Total Marks:70

Time : 11.00 a.m. to 2.00 p.m.

INSTRUCTIONS:

1) All questions are COMPULSORY.
2) Figures to the RIGHT indicate FULL marks.
3) Answers to the questions from both the Sections should be written in the SAME answer book.

SECTION I

1. A well known financial house started an industrial unit using new technology under the name General Electronics Co., Their system of management in general was of the old type where everything was centralized on a personal level. However, in the case of the new industry, due to various factors like distance, time etc., the industry was allowed to develop on autonomous lines and was put in charge of a well trained Engineer.

Considering the various aspects, the industry was developing well. But due to lack of adequate attention to labour and lack of downward communication, a strike developed. It generated tension and fear among the executives, both on the production side as well as in other departments. Several Engineers and Executives left jobs including the Labour Officer because of lack of communication.

QUESTIONS

1) Give a brief analysis of the case. 7
2) Why did the Executives leave the job? 6

3) Explain the reasons for fear and tension. 6
4) Suggest solution for the problem. 6

OR

A Company manufacturing Engineering items had Mr. Joshi as Production Manager, who was worried about cost of production. He decided to consult the experts. But before doing this he thought of meeting the foremen of the company. Accordingly he met the foremen and started the discussion by stating that the new production control system will surely eliminate our current problem of excessive cost of production due to less of rejection because of the quality. He insisted that every one should ensure the success of new system of production. A senior foreman replied that after consulting the other foremen he had come to the conclusion that they had a list of 12 changes to be made in the new system otherwise it would not work effectively. The Production Manager got annoyed and told the foremen that either he did as he was asked to do or he will have to leave the job. He was not ready to listen to any argument. He further shouted that the system had worked in other plants, it must work here too. He felt that the foremen were against the system. Turning to them he asked if there were any other questions. Seeing that no one among the foremen was ready to talk, he once again shouted and announced that the meeting was adjourned.

QUESTIONS

1) Give a brief analysis of the case. 6
2) Do you feel that the Production Manager did not use the skill of communication effectively? If yes, comment on it. 6
3) Explain the problem. 7
4) Suggest a proper solution. 6

2. Write short note on any ONE: 5
1) Objective of communication.
2) Signs and signals.

3) Persuasion and propaganda.
4) Open door policies.

SECTION II

3. Describe the role of Audio-Visuals in communication, its advantages and disadvantages. 15

OR

How can Sales Letters help in building up goodwill?

4. Prepare a speech on the prospects of the Electronic Industry in India. 15

OR

Draft the minutes of the Annual General Meeting of Bharat Chemicals Ltd.

5. Write short notes on any TWO: 10
   1) Use of microphone in public speaking.
   2) Language of communication.
   3) Salutation in Letter writing.
   4) Physical barrier.

BIBLIOGRAPHY

Adelstein, Michael E., 1971 : *Contemporary Business Writing*, New York : Random House.

Alderson, J. 1979 : The Cloze Procedure and Proficiency in English as a Foreign Language. *TESOL Quarterly*, 13, 219-227.

Allen, Louis, 1958 : *Managemet and Organization*, Tokoy : McGraw-Hill Kogakusha Ltd.

Allen, E.D., 1975 : *Communicative Competence*, Eric Clearing house on Language and Linguishtics; Arlington, Virginia; Centre for Applied Linguistics.

Anastasi, A., 1988: *Psychological Testing*, 6th ed., New York : Macmillan.

Anastasi, T.E., (Jr.), 1974: *Desk Guide to Communication*, New York : Random House.

Applbaum, R.L., Bodaken E.M., Sereno K.K. and K.W.E., Anatol, 1974: *The Process of Group Communication*, Science Research Associates, Chicago.

Austine, J.L. 1962; *How to do things with Words*, Oxford, UK: Clarendon Press.

Bachman, L.F., 1982: 'The trait structure of close test scores'. *TESOL Quarterly*, 16, 61-70.

Bachman, L. 1985: 'Performance On Cloze Tests with Fixed Ration and Rational Deletions'. *TESOL Quarterly*, 19, 535-556.

Bachman, L.F., 1989: 'Language Testing — SLA Research Interface', In *Annual Review of Applied Linguistics*, 9, 193-209, 1989.

Bapat, S.G. & Datar, S.G. 1973: *A textbook of Business Correspondence*, Poona : Anmol Prakashan.

Barnlund, D.C., 1970: 'A Transactional Model of Communication,' In J. Akin, A. Goldberg, G.E. Myers and J. Stewart (Eds.) *Language Behaviour : A Book of Readings*, Mouton, The Hague.

Barnlund, D.C. and F.S. Haiman, 1960: *The Dynamics of*

Discussion, Boston : Houghton Miffin Company.

Bartz, W.H., 1974: 'A study of the relationship of certain learner factors with the ability to communicate in a second language for the development of measures of communicative competence', Ph.D. Diss., Chio state University.

Benson, M.J., 1987 : 'The Construction of Curriculums in ECL and EFL, Artful Tasks' *FORUM*, Vol. XXV/1 Jan.

Berlo, David, 1960: *The Process of Communication*, New York : Holt, Rinehart and Winston, Inc.,

Bettinghaus, E.P., 1968 : *Persuasive Communication*, New York : Holt, Rinehart and Winston, Inc.

Birdwhistell, R.L., 1970: *Kinesics and Context*, Philadelphia: University of Pennsylvania Press.

Birrvenu, 1987 : 'Definition of Communication' In Doctor, R. and A. Doctor, *Principles and Practice of Business Communication*, Bombay : Sheth Publishers.

Biswas, A. and J.C. Agarwal, 1971 : *Encyclopedic Dictionary and Directory of Education*, Vol 1. New Delhi : The Academic Publishers (Indian).

Bloom, B.B., J.T. Hastings, G.F. Madans, (Eds.), 1971 : *Handbook on Formative and Summative Evaluation of Learner Learning*'. New York : McGraw Hill.

Bloom, Benjamin, S. and D.R. Krathwohl, *Taxonomy of Educational Objective*, Handbook-I, Cognitive Domain David Mckay Co., Inc. New York, 1956.

Boebe, Steven A., 1974: *Eye Contact : A Non-verbal Determinant of Speaker Credibility*, Speech Teacher, (1974): 23-21-25.

Bormann, E.G. and N.C. Borman, 1972 : *Speech Communication*, New York : Harper & Row, Publishers, Inc.

— —, 1986 : *Speech Communication. A Basic Approach*. New York : Harper & Row, Publishers.

Bowman, J.P. and B.P. Branchaw, 1984 : *Business Report Writing*, Tokyo : The Dryden Press, Holt-Sounders, Japan.

Brown, J., 1983 : A Closer Look at Cloze: Validity and Reliability. In J. Oller, Jr. Ed., *Issues in Language Testing Research* (pp. 237-250). Rowley, Mass; Newburg House Publishers.

Breen, M.P.,(1984), 'Process syllabuses of the language classroom. In C.J. Brumfit (Ed.). *General English Syllabus Design* (ELT Documents No. 118, pp. 47-60), Pergamon Press and British Council, London.

— —, (1987), 'Learners contributions to task design.' In C.N. Candlin and D. Murphy (Eds.) *Lancaster Practical Papers in English Languages Education* : Vol. 7 Language learning tasks, (pp. 23-46) Prentice Hall, Englewood Chiff, N.J.

Breen, M.P. and Candlin, C. (1980). 'The Essentials of a Communicative Curriculum in Language Teaching'. *Applied Linguistics*, 1(2), 89-112.

Brooks, C. and R.P. Warren, 1961: *Modern Rhetoric*, New York : Harcourt Brace.

Brown, C.A., 1975: in *Write Better, Speak Better*, Readers Digest Publication, p. 278.

Brown, C.T. and C.V. Riper, 1966: *Speech and Man*, Englewood Cliffs, N.J. : Prentice-Hall, Inc.

Brown, J. 1988 : 'Tailored Cloze : Improved with Classical Item Analysis Techniques.' *Language Testing* 5, 19-31.

— —, 1989 : 'Cloze Item Difficulty' *JALT Journal*, 11, 46-67.

Burgoon, M., Heston J.K., and J. McCroskey, 1974 : 'Small Group Communication' : A Functional Approach, New York : Holt, Rinehart and Winston, Inc, 1, Biswas, A. and Agarwal, J.C. *Encyclopedic Dictionary and Directory of Education*, Vol 1, New Delhi : The Academice Publishers (Indian); (1971).

Campbell, J.H. and H.W. Helper, 1971 : *Dimensions in Communication*, Belmont, Calif : Wadsworth Publishing Company.

Camphell, R. and R. Wales, 1970: 'The Study of Language Acquisition'. In Lyons, John, ed. *New Horizons in Linguistics*, Penguin.

Canale, M., 1983 : 'Communicative competence of communicative language Pedagogy' London : Longman, In J. Richards and R. Schmidt (Eds.) *Language and Communications*, pp. 2-27.

Canalc, M. and Swain M., 1980 : 'Theoretical Bases of Communicative Approaches to second Language

Teaching and Testing' in *Applied Linguistics*, 1 pp 1-47.

Candlin, C.N., 1984 : *Syllabus Design as a Critical Process* (ELT Documents No. 118, pp 29-36). London : Pergamon Press and the British Council.

— —, 1987 : 'Towards Task-Based Language Learning'. In C.N. Candlin & D. Murphy (Eds.), *Lancaster Practical Paper in English Language Education*. Col. 7, Englewood Cliffs, N.J. : Language learning tasks (pp. 5-22). Prentice Hall.

Candlin, C.N., and D. Murphy, 1987 : *Language Practical Papers in English Language Education*, Vol. 7, Language Learning tasks. Engleood Cliff, N.J. : Prentice Hall.

Carr, Jacqueline, 1984 : *Communication and Relating*, Dubuque, Iowa : Brown.

Cartier, F.A. and K.A. Harwood, 1953 : 'Definition of Communication', *The Journal of Communication*, November, 1953 in Doctor, R and A. Doctor, 1977 : *Principles and Practice of Business Communication*, Bombay : Sheth Publishers.

Carroll, B.S., 1982 : 'Language Testing — Is There Another Way'? in J.B. Heaton (Ed.) 1982. *Language Testing* Hays: Modern English Publications.

— —, 1984 : 'Psychometric Theory and Language Testing' in J.W. Oller (Ed.) 1983, *Issues in Language Testing Research*. Massachusetts : Newsburg House.

Carroll, J.B., 1961 : 'Fundamental Considerations in Testing for English Language Proficiency for Foreign Learners'. In J.E. Alatis (Ed.), *Testing the English Proficiency of Foreign Learners*. Washington D.C.:Centre for Applied Linguistic, 31-40.

Cartier, F.A., 1968 : 'Criterion-Referenced Testing of Language Skills'. *TESOL Quarterly*, 2, 27-32.

Chavez, Oller, M., Chihara, T. Weaver, K. & J. Oller, 1985 : 'When Are Cloze Items Sensitive to Constraints Across Sentences?' *Language Learning* 35, 181-203.

Chappell, R.T., and Read, W.L., 1979 : 'A Textbook of Business Communication' In Pal, R. and J.S. Korlahalli, *Essentials of Business Communication*, New Delhi : Sultan Chand & Sons.

Chase, Stuart, 1954 : *The Power of Words*, New York :

Harcourt, Brace and World.

Chen-Si-Quing, 1990 : 'A study of Communicative Strategies in Interlanguage Production by Chineses EFL Learners' In Language, Learning, *Journal of Applied Linguistics*, Vol. 40, No. 2, June 1990.

Chomsky, N, 1965 : *Aspects of the Theory of Synax*, MIT Press.

— —, 1970 : 'Remarks on Nominalisation'. In Jacobs, R. and P. Rosenabaum, (Eds.) *Readings in English Transformational Grammer*, Ginn.

Clark, L.R., Zimmer, K., Tinervia, J., 1988 : *Business English and Communication*, New York : English Language series. McGraw Hill International Editions.

Clevenger, Theodore, Jr., 1966 : *Audience Analysis*, Indianapolis : The Bobbs-Merril Company, Inc.

Cooper, R.L., 1968 : *An Elaborated Language Testing Model: Language Learning* — Special Issue No. 3 on Problems in Foreign Language Testing.

Corder, P., 1983 : 'Strategies of Communication', London: Longman, In Faerch, C and G. Kasper (Eds) *Strategies in Interlanguage Communication*, pp 15-19.

Coulthard, M., 1977 : *An Introduction to Discourse Analysis*, London: Longman.

Cziko, G.A., 1982: 'Improving the Psychometric, Criterion Refers Need and Practical Qualities of Integrative Language Tests'. *TESOL Quarterly* Vol. 16/3, Sept. 1982.

Cziko, G.A. & N.J. Lin, 1984 : 'The Construction and Analysis of the Short Scales of Language Proficiency'. Classical Psychometric, Latent Trait and Nonparasitic Approaches. *TESOL Quarterly* 18 : 4, 627-647.

Davar, R.S., 1980 : *Principles of Managements*, Bombay; Progressive Corporation Pvt. Ltd.

Davies, A. (1989) 'Communicative Competence as language use : *Applied Linguistics*, 10(2), 157-170.

Davis, Keith, 1981 : *Human Relations at work*, New Delhi : Tata McGraw-Hill Book Company.

Davis, Keith and J..W. Newstrom, 1989 : *Human Behaviour at Work*, New York : McGraw Hill Book Company.

De Fleur, Melvin L., 1970 : *Theories of Mass Communication*, New York : David Mckay Company, Inc.

De Joia, A. and A. Stenton, 1980 : *Terms in Systemic Linguistics, A Guide to Halliday*, London : Batesford.

Doctor, R. & Doctor, A. 1977 : *Principles and Practice of Business Communicational*, Bombay : Sheth Publishers.

Dwivedi, R.S., 1989 : *Human Relations and Organisational Behaviour*, New Delhi : Oxford & IBH Publishing Co. Pvt. Ltd.

Ebel, R. and D.A. Frisbie, 1991 : *Essentials of Educational Measurements*, New Delhi :Prentice-Hall of India Pvt. Ltd.

Eisher, E.W., 1967 : 'Educational Objectives : Help of Hindrance?' *School Review*, 75.

Ellis, R., 1985 : 'Understanding Second Language Acquisition, Oxford : Oxford University Press 13. Ellis, R. (1985), *Understanding Second Language Acquisition*. Oxford University Press, Oxford.

Fabun, Don, 1968 : *Communication : The Transfer of Meaning*, New York : Glencoe Press, The Macmillan Company.

Faerch, C. Kasper, G., 1983, *Strategies in Interlanguage Communication*, London : Longman.

Ferguson, C.A., 1959 : 'Diglossia', In Giglioli (Ed.) *Language and Social Context*, Pengion, 1972 (Reprinted from Word, Vol. 15).

Farhady, H. 1979, 'The Disjunctive Fallacy Between Discreet Point and Integrative Tests' *TESOL Quarterly* 13, 347-357.

Fisher, B.A., 1974 : *Small Group Decision-Making : Communication and the Group Process*, New York; McGraw-Hill Book Company.

Fishman, J.A., 1965: 'Who Speaks What Language to Whom ,d When?' *La Lingistique*, 67, 88.

Fod and Garrett, 1966; 'Some Reflections on Competence ad Performance,' In Psycholinguistic Papers, Edinburgh University Press.

Fotos, S.S. 1991 : 'The Cloze Test As an Integrative Measure of EFL Proficiency A Substitute for Essays on College Entrance Examination?' *Language Learning* 41:3, 313-336.

Fouly, K.A., L.A., Bachman & G.A., Czikø, 1990: 'The Divisibility of Language Competence : Confirmatory

Approach,' In *Language Learning* 40:1 March, pp 1-21.

Galbraith, J.K., 1956 : 'Problems of Communication,' Bangalore : In the Symposium on 'Organisation and Management of Public Enterprises' — Organised by Indian Statistical Institute, Bangalore, on 17th and 18th April, 1956.

Gardiner, J.C. 1971 : 'A Synthesis of Experimental studies of Speech Communication Feedback,' *The Journal of Communication*, Vol, 22, pp. 7-35.

Gartside, L., 1981: *Model Business Letters*, London : Pitman.

Ghosh, R.N., Shastri, H.N.L. and Das, B.K., 1977 : *Introductions to English Language Teaching* Vol. 3, Methods at the College level. Hyderabal : Central Institute of English and Foreign Language.

Gladstone, J.R., 1969 : 'Language and Culture', In *English Teaching* XXIII — 1, pp 114-117.

Goud, L.M., & K.R. Dixit, 1976 : *Advanced Commercial Correspondence*, Kolhapur : Universal Publications, Kolhapur.

Gronlund, N.E., and R.L. Linn, 1990 : *Measurement and Evaluation in Teaching*, New York : Macmillan Publishing Co.

Groot P.J.M., 1975 : 'Validation of Language Tests'. In Leslie Palmer and Bernard Spolsky (Eds). *Papers on Language Testing 1967-1974.* Washington, D.C. TESOL.

Gulley, Halbert E., 1968 : *Discussion. Conference and Group Process*, New York : Holt, Rinehart and Winston, Inc.

Gumperz, J.J., 1964 : 'Linguistic and Social Interaction in Two Communities'. In J.J. Gumperz and Dell Hymes (Eds.) The Ethnology of Communication, *American Anthropologist*, Vol, 66, Part-2, 137-53. Menasha Wisc. American Anthropological Association.

— —, 1966 : 'On the Ethnology of Linguistic Change'. In William Bright (Ed.), *Sociolinguistics.* Hague : Mouton, 1966, 27-49.

— —, 1966 : 'On The Linguistic Markers of Bilingual Communication'. In John Macnamara (Ed.) Problems of Billingualism. *Journal of Social Issues*, 1967, 23, 8-28,11. Ghosh, R.N., Shastri, H.N.L. and B.K. Das, 1977: *Introductions to English Language Teaching*, Vol. 3

Methods at the college level. Hyderabal : Central Institute of English and Foreign Language.

Gupta, C.B., 1992 : *An Introduction to Statistical Methods* (18th Edition), New Delhi : Vikas Publication House Pvt. Ltd.

Gurky, Jean M., (Ed.) : *A Reader in Human Communication*, Random House, New York.

Habermas, J., 1970 : 'Towards a Theory of Communicative Competence', In Dreitzel, H. (ed.) *Recent Sociology*, No. 2 Collier, Macmillan.

Hall, Edward, 1959 : *The Silent Language*, New York : Doubleday.

Halliday, M.A.K., 1970 : 'Language Structure and Language Function', In Lyons, John (Ed.) *New Horizons in Linguistics*. Penguin

— —, 1971 : Towards a Sociological Semantics, In *Explorations in the Functions of Language*, Edward Arnold.

— —, 1971 : Towards a Social Perspecitve', In *Explorations in the Functions of Language*, Edward Arnold.

— —, 1972 : 'Towards a Sociological Semantics'. In *Explorations in the Functions of Language*, Edward Arnold.

— —, 1976 : 'The Form of Functional Grammar', In G.R. Kress (ed.) *Halliday : System and Function in Grammar*, pp 7-25, Oxford University Press, UK.

— —, 1978 : *Language as Social Semiotic*, London : Edward Arnold.

Hanania, E. & M. Shikhani, 1986 : 'Inter-relationship Among three Tests of Language Proficiency : Standardized ES Cloze and Writing' *TESOL Quarterly* 20, 97-109.

Harris, D.P., 1969 : *Testing English as a Second Language*, McGraw-Hill Inc.

Heaton, J.B., 1975 : *Writing English Language Tests*, London: Longman.

Heilenman, L., 1983 : The Use of a Cloze Procedure in Foreign Language Placement, *The Modern Language Journal*, 67, 121-126.

Hicks, H.G. and C.R. Gullet, 1974 : *Modern Business*

Management, New York : McGraw-Hill Book Company.

Hinofotis, F. 1987 : 'Cloze Testing : An Overview'. In M. Long & J Ichards (Eds) *Methodology in TESOL Rowley Mass*, Newburg House.

Hornberger, N.H. (1989); 'Tramites and transports : The acquisition of second language communicative competence for one speech event in Puneoo Peru'; *Applied Linguisties*, 10(2) 215-230

Howell, W.S. and E.G. Borman, 1971: *Presentational Speaking for Business and the Professions*, New York : Harper and Row.

Huebrier, T., 1983: 'Linguistic Systems and Linguistic Change in an Inter Language.' *Studies in Second Language Acquisition*, 6(1), 33, 53.

Hymes, Dell, 1971 : 'On Communicative competence', In Pride and Holmes, (eds.) *Sociolinuistics*, Penguin;

— —, 1972 : 'Models of the Interaction of Language and Social Life", In Gumperz and Hymes, (eds.) *Directions in Sociolinguisties*, Holt, Rinehart.

Isenberg, Nancy, 1990 : 'Literary competence and TEFL', In *ELT Journal*, Vol 44/3, July 1990.

Jacobovits, L.A., 1970. *Foreign Language Learning : A Psycholinguistic Analysis of the Issues*. Rowly, Mass : Newburg House.

Jacobovitz, L. A., Gordon, Barbara, 1974 : *The Context of Foreign Language Teaching*, Rowley, Mass. Newburg House.

Jayatilleke, C.L.V. ans S. Sivasegaram, 1979 : *Technical Report Writing*, New Delhi : Tata McGraw-Hill Publishing Co. Ltd.

Jeffrey, R.C. and Owen Peterson, 1983 : *Speech : A Basic Text*, New York : Harper & Row.

Johnson, K., 1976 : 'The Production of Functional Material', In ELT Documents, The British Council, 1976/1 pp 19-20.

Johnston, M., 1985 : *Syntactic and Morphological Progressions in Learner English*. Canberra, Australia : Department of Immigration and Ethnic Affairs, Canberra.

Johnstori, M. (1985). 'Syntactic and morphological

progressions in learner English'. Department of Immigration and Ethnic Affairs, Canberra Australia.

Katz, Daniel, 1947 : 'Psychological Barriers to Communication', From the *'Annals'*, Vol. 250.

Katz, D. and R.L. Kahn, 1966 : *The Social Psychology of the Organisations*, New York : John Wiley & Sons Inc.

Keltner, John W., 1970 : *Interpersonal Speech-Communication : Elements and Structures*, Belmont, Calif: Wadsworth Publishing Company, Inc.

Kementerian Pelajaran Malaysia [Malaysian Ministry of Education], 1975: English Language Syllabus in Malaysian Schools Tingatan [Level] IV-V Kementerian Pelajaran, Kuala Lumpur.

Klapper, Joseph T., 1960: *The Effects of Mass Communication*, New York : The Free Press.

Klein-Braley, C. 1983 : 'A Cloze Is a Question.' In J.Oller Jr. (Ed.) *Issues in Language Testing Research*, (pp. 281-328). Rowley Mass, Newburg House

Knapp, Mark L., 1972 : *Nonverbal Communication in Human Ineraction*, New York : Holt, Rinehart and Winston, Inc.

Koontz, Harold and Cyril O'Donnell, 1971 : *Essentials of Management*, New Delhi : Tata McGraw-Hill Pub. Co. Ltd.

— —, 1976 : *Management*, International Student's Edn. McGraw-Hill Koga-Kusha Ltd.

Labov, W., 1966 : *The Social Stratification of English In New York City*. Washington D.C. : Centre for Applied Linguistics.

Lado, R., 1961 : *Language Testing : The Construction And Use of Foreign Language Tests*. London : Longman.

Laech, K. & A. Van Kleeck, 1987 : 'The Cloze Test as an Alternative Measure of Language Proficiency of Children Considered for exit Bilingual Education Programs'. *Language Learning*, 37, 171-189.

Larsen, Freeman, D. & M. H. Long, 1991 : *An Introduction to Second Language Acquisition Research*. London : Longman.

Lee, Irving, J., 1952 : *How to Talk with People*, New York : Harper and Brothers.

Lesikar, R.V. and J.D. Pettit, Jr. 1989 : *Business*

Communication, Theory and Application, New Delhi : All India Traveller Bookseller.

Lindeman, R. Chand, *Educational Measurement*, Scott, Foresman and Company, Glenview, Illinois-60025, 1967.

Little, Peter, 1977 : 'Communication in Business'. In Doctor, R. and A. Doctor, 1977, *Principles and Practice of Business Communication*. Bombay : Sheth Publishers.

Logan, G.E., 1973 : *German Conversational Practice*. Rowley, Mass : Nerberg House.

Logan, G.E., Bals, Hilda, 1976 : *Spanish Conversational Practice*. Rowley, Mass. : Newburg House.

Long, Michael H. & Graham Crookes, 1992 : 'Three Approaches to Task-Based Syllabus Design" *TESOL Quarterly* Vol. 26, No.1 Spring 1992.11.

Luthans, Fred, 1973: *Organisational Behaviors*, New York : McGraw Hill Book Co.

Lyons, J., 1977 : *Semantics I & II*, London : CUP.

— —, 1981 : *Language, Meaning and Context*, London : Fontana.

Mackey, W.F.; *Language Teaching Analysis*, London : Longman Group Ltd. (1965).

Maclean, M. 1984: 'Using Rational Cloze for Diagnostic Testing In L1 and L2 Reading' *TESL Canada Journal* 2, 53-63.

Macnamara, J., 1973 : 'Nurseries, Streets and Classrooms: Some Comparisons and Deductions". *Modern Language Journal*, 57, 250-254.

Manning, W. 1986: 'Using Technology to Assess Secon Language Proficiency Through Cloze-Elide Tests'. In C. Stansfield (ed.) *Technology and Language Testing*. Washington D.C. TESOL.

Marting, *et al* (Ed.), 1977 : *Effective Communication on the Job*, Bombay : Taraporewala Publishing Ind. Pvt. Ltd.

Massie, Joseph, L. 1987 : *Essentials of Management*, New Delhi : Prentice-Hall of India Pvt. Ltd.

Mathews Margaret, 1990 : 'The Measurement of Productive Skills : Doubts Concerning the Assessment Criteria of Certain Public Examinations'. *ELT Journal*. Vol 44/2, Oxford University Press.

Mehrens, W.A. and I.J. Lehmann, *Using Standardized Tests*

in Education, 4th ed; Macmillan, New York, 1987

Meisel, H. Clahsen, H., & Pieneman, M. (1981). 'On determining developmental stages in second language acquisition.' *Studies in Second Language Acquisition*, 3(2), 109-135.

Mehrabian, Albert, 1981 : '*Silent Massages : Implicit Communication of Emotions and Attitudes*,' Belmost, Calif, Wadsworth.

Michael, V.P., 1992 : *Communication and Research for Management*, Bombay : Himalaya Publishing House.

Moller, A., 1975: 'Validity In Proficiency Testing". ELT Documents (75/3). London : English Teaching Information Centre. The British Council.

Mortenson, C.D. (Ed.), 1973 : *Basic Readings in Communication Theory*. New York : Harper and Brothers.

Mugali, V.N., 1975: *Business English*, Hubli : Book Centre.

Munter, Mary, 1987: *Business Communication, Strategy and Skill*, New Jersey : Prentic-Hall Inc.

Munby, J., 1978: *Communicative Competence and a Theoretical Framework*, In Communicative Syllaus Design. Cambridge University Press.

Myers, M.T. and G.E. Myers, 1982 : *Managing by Communication*, Tokyo : McGraw Hill Book Company.

Myers, G.E. and M.T. Myers, 1973 : *The Dynamics of Human Communication: A Laboratory Approach*, New York: McGraw Hill Book Co.

Newman, W. and C. Summer, 1977 : 'Process of Mangement' In Doctor, R. and A. Doctor, *Principles and Practice of Business Communication*, Bombay : Sheth Publishers.

Newmark, L., 1964: 'Grammatical Theory and the Teaching of English as a Foreign Language,' In D.P. Harris (Ed.), The 1963 conference papers of the English language section of the National Association for Foreign Student Affairs (pp. 5-8) New York

— —, 1966 : 'How not to Interfere with Language Learning'. *International Journal of American Linguistics* 32 (1), 77-83.

Newmark, L. and D.A. Reibel, 1968: 'Necessity and Sufficiency in Language Learning.' *International Review of Applied Linguistics*, 6, 145-164.

Oller, J. Jr., 1973: 'Pragmatic Language Testing'. *Language Sciences*. 28, 7-12.

— —, 1973 : 'Cloze Tests of Second Language Proficiency and what They Measure' *Language Learning* 23, 105-118.

— —, 1979: *Language Tests At School*. London: Longman.

— —, 1988: 'Pragmatic Language Teaching and Testing'. Lecture Presented at Temple University Japan Distinguished Lectures's Series, Tokyo, Japan.

Pal, R. and J.S. Korlahalli, 1979 : *Essentials of Business Communication*, New Delhi : Sultan Chand & Sons.

Paribakht, T., 1985 : 'Strategic competence and language Proficiency', In *Applied Linguistics*, 6, pp132-146

Patil, D.K., 1984 : 'The English Language Achievements of Shivaji University Arts Graduates', A Ph.D. Thesis, Kolhapur: Shivaji University.

Pauley, A. and F.H. Syder, 1983: 'Two Puzzles for Linguistic Theory: Nativelike Selection and Nativelike Fluency', In J.C. Richards and R.W. Schmidt (Eds.) *Language and Communication*, pp 191-226, New York: Longman.

Philios, G.M., 1973 : *Communication and the Small Group*, Indianapolis, Ind.: Bobbs-Merrill.

Prabhu, N.S., 1980: 'Reaction and Predictions' [Special Issue]. *Bulletin* 4(1). Regional Institute of English, Bangalore.

— —, 1984: 'Procedural Syllabus'. In T.E. Read (Ed.) *Trends in Language Syllabus Design* (pp. 272-280). Singapore: Singapore University Press.

— —, 1987 : *Second Language Pedagogy*. Oxford Cliffs, N.J.: Oxford University Press.

Rai, U.S., Rai, S.M., 1989: *Business Communication*, New Delhi: Himalaya Publishing House.

Ramesh, M.S. & C. Pattanshetti, 1986: *Effective Business English and Communication*, New Delhi: Published by G.S. Sharma, Prop. R. Chand & Co.

Rea, P.M., 1976: 'Linguistic Theory, Linguistic Description and Language Testing'. The Dissertation for M.A. The University of Lancaster.

Redfield, Charles E., 1954: *Communication in Management*, University of Chicago.

Reibel, D.A., 1969 : 'Language Learning Analysis'. *International Review of Applied Linguistics*, 7(4), 283-294.

Richards, I.A., 1928 : 'Definition of Communication' in *The New Encyclopaedia Britanica*, Vol-4, 1982: The Fifteenth Edition, University of Chicago.

Richards, J., Platt, J. and H. Weber, 1985: *Longman Dictionary of Applied Linguistics*, London : Longman.

Rivers, W., 1968: *Teaching Foreign Language Skills*. University of Chicago Press.

Roberts, Cheryl A., 1990: 'The Art of circumlocation: Teaching Strategic Competence', In *Forum*, Vol. XXVIII, No. 4, Oct. 1990.

Rodgers, T.S., 1984: 'Communicative Syllabus Design and Implementation,' Reflections on a decade of experience. In J.A.S. Read (ed.), *Trends in Syllabus Design* (pp.28-51), Singapore: Singapore University Press.

Rodman, George, 1981: *Public Speaking*, New York: Holt, Rinehart and Winston.

Rodriques, M.V., 1992 : *Effective Business Communication*, New Delhi: Concept Publishing Company.

Rubin, J., 1962: 'Bilingualism In Paraguay', *Anthropological Linguistics*, 1962, 4, 52-58.

Ruesch, Jurgen and Weldon Kees, 1956: *Nonverbal Communication*, Berkeley: University of California Press

Salvia, J. and Ysseldyke, 1988 : *Assessment in Special and Remedial Education*, 4th ed. Houghton Mifflin, Boston.

Samah, A.A., 1984: 'The English Language (Communicational) Curriculum for Upper Secondary Schools in Malaysia,' Rationale design and implementation. In J.A.S. Read (Ed.) *Trends in Language Syllabus Design* (pp. 193-214). Singapoe: Singapore University Press.

Sato, C.J., 1990 : *The Syntax of Conversation in Inter Language Development*, Gunter Narr, Tubingen, Germany.

Scheidel, T.M., 1972: *Speech Communication and Human Interaction*, Glenview, Illinois: Scott, Foresman and Co.

Scott, William, 1977; 'Organizational Theory' in Doctor, R. and A. Doctor, *Principles and Practice of Business*

Communication, Bombay: Sheth Publishers.

Searle, J.R., 1965: What is a speech Act? In M. Black (Ed.) *Philosophy in America*, London: Allen & Unwin.

— —. 1969: *Speech Acts*, Cambridge University Press. UK.

— —, 1981: *Speech Acts*, 2nd Edition, London; Cambrdge University Press.

Sekaran, U. Chicago, 1989: *Organizational Behaviour,* New Delhi: Tata McGraw-Hill Publishing Co. Ltd.

Sharma, R.C. & Krishna Mohan; 1986: *Business Correspondence and Report Writing*, New Delhi: Tata McGraw-Hill Publishing Company Limited.

Shastri, S.V. 1972: 'The Teaching of English as a Foreign Language in Bombay', Unpublished Ph.D. Thesis, Bombay: University of Bombay.

Shaw, P. 1992: 'Variation and Universality in Communicative Competence: Coseriu's Model', *TOSEL Quarterly*, Vol. 26, No.1.

Shohamy, E., T. Reves, and Y. Bejarano, 1986: 'Introducing A New Comprehensive Test of Proficiency'. *ELT Journal, Vol.* 40/3 1986. Oxford University Press.

Sinclair, J. M., I.J. Forsyth, R.M. Coulthard and M. Ashby, 1972: 'The English Used by Teachers and Pupils: Final Report to SSRC' Dept. of English Language and Literature, Birmingham University.

Smart, W.K. and D.R. Lang, 1979: *Smart's Handbook of Effective Writing*, New Delhi: Jaico Publishing House.

Steil, L.K., Barker, L.L. and K.W. Watson, 1983: *Effective Listening*, New York: Random House.

Stubbs, J. & G. Tucker, 1974: 'The Cloze Test as a Measure of English Proficiency'. *Modern Language Journal*, 58, 239-241.

Taylor, D.S. 1988; 'The meaning and use of the term "Competence" in Linguistics and applied linguistics;' *Applied Linguistics* 9(2), 148-168.

Taylor, W., 1983: 'Cloze Procedure: A New Tool for Measuring Readability'. *Journalism Quarterly*, 30, 414-438.

Tead, Ondway, 1959 : *Lecture at the School of Commerce, Accounts and Finance*, New York, delivered on 11th February, 1959.

Terry, G.R. and S.G. Franklin, 1984: *Principles of*

Management, Delhi: All India Traveller Bookseller.

Thomas, D.A. and M. Fryar, 1988; *Business Communication Today*, National Textbook Company, Lincolnwood Chicago, Illinois.

Underhill, N., 1987: *Testing Spoken Lenguage*, Cambridge; Cambridge University Press.

Upshur, J.A., 1983: 'Measurement of Individual Differences and Explanation in the Language Sciences' *Language Learning* 33(5), 99-140

Valdman, A., 1975: 'Learner Systems and Error Analysis' in Gillbert A. Jarvis, ed., Perspective : A New Freedom, *The ACTEL Review of Foreign Language Education*, Vol.-7, National Textbook Company.

Valette, R.M., 1977: *Modern Language Testing*. Harcourt, Brace, Jovanovich, Inc.

Vogel, R.A. an W.D. Brooks, 1977: *Business Communication*, Cummings Publishing Company, California.

Watzlawick, P., Janet Beavin and Don Jackson, 1967: *Pragmatics of Human Communication*, New York: W.W. Norton & Co.

White, R.V., 1988: *The Curriculum Design, Innovation and Management*. Oxford: Basil Blackwell.

Wickesberg, A.K., 1968: 'Communication Networks in The Business Structure', In *Academy of Managements Journal*, September, 1968.

Widdowson, H.G., 1971: 'The Teaching of Rhetoric to Learners of Science and Technology'. In *Science and Technology in a Second Language*. Centre for Information on Language Teaching and Rescarch.

— —, 1972: *The Teaching of English as communication.*

— —, 1975: *EST in Theory and Practice*. In English for academic study. British Council English Teaching Information Centre.

— —, (1989); 'Knowledge of Language and Ability for use'; *Applied Linguistics* 10(2), 128-137.

Wilkins, D.A., 1974; 'Notional Syllabuses and the Concept of a Minimum Adequate Grammar', In S.P. Corder & E. Roulet (Eds.), *Linguistic Insights in Applied Linguistics* (pp. 119-128) AIMAV, Brussels.

Wilkins, D.A., 1972: 'The Linguistic and Situational Content of The Common Core in a Unit/Credit System'. In *Systems Development in Adult Language Learning.* Strasbourg, Council of Europe, 1973.

— —, 1974: *Second Language and Teaching*, Arnold 1974, pp 1-4.

— —, 1976: *Notional Syllabuses*, Oxford: Oxford University Press.

Wofford, J. E., Gerloff and R. Cummins, 1977: *Organistaional Communication*, Tokyo, McGraw Hill Kogakusha, Ltd.

Wolf, M.P, D.F. Keyser, and R.A. Aurner, 1979, *Effective Communication in Business*, Cincinnati, Ohio, South-Western Publishing Company.

Wright, Charles R., 1974: *Mass Communication — A Sociological Prespective*, New York: Random House.

Zatter, Robert and W. George Gronch, 1961: *Successful Communication in Science and Industry*, McGraw-Hill Co. Inc.

Zelko, H.P., 1957: *Successful Conference and Discussion Techniques*, New York: McGraw-Hill Book Co..

INDEX